THE PRODIGAL THAT DIDN'T COME HOME

Navigating by faith through grief and disillusionment

By Christopher A Bell Sr

WestBow Press books may be ordered through booksellers or by contacting:

WestBow Press
A Division of Thomas Nelson & Zondervan
1663 Liberty Drive
Bloomington, IN 47403
www.westbowpress.com
1 (866) 928-1240

ISBN: 978-1-5127-6755-1 (sc)
ISBN: 978-1-5127-6756-8 (hc)
ISBN: 978-1-5127-6754-4 (e)

Library of Congress Control Number: 2016921465

Print information available on the last page.

WestBow Press rev. date: 02/28/2017

To every parent, guardian, or surrogate who has been able to weather the storm of losing a child to death, or for any reason for that matter—take heart. Your courage is an inspiration to all of us whether you know it or not. And to Conan, the prodigal who didn't come home.

Now that we know what we have—Jesus, this great High Priest with ready access to God—let's not let it slip through our fingers. We don't have a priest who is out of touch with our reality. He's been through weakness and testing, experienced it all—all but the sin. So let's walk right up to him and get what he is so ready to give. Take the mercy, accept the help. (Heb. 4:14–16 MSG)

Contents

Acknowledgments

My children have been an integral part of whom and what I have become. I would suspect that most parents would feel the same way. After all, what parent has not felt stretched to the limit as a result of some action carried out by his or her child? My wife, Renee, has a patient understanding that has served as a stabilizing force in my life. The ebb and flow of our marriage has proven to be a continuous stream of growth, joy, discovery, and excitement. I am the product of a combination of experiences, people, and circumstances.

There are three men who come to mind who played a major role in my spiritual development: Pastors Timothy Ruffin, Benjamin Tolbert, and Willie Richardson. I am eternally indebted to them for their wisdom, patience, and instruction. My parents, Robert and Laura Bell, created in me the foundation upon which others were allowed to build. The logical explanation is that I would not be who I am today if it were not for the problems I have incurred, the people I have known, and the challenges that I have overcome.

Last and certainly not least is my son, Christopher A. Bell Jr. (cbdesigns.me), the graphic designer who patiently worked with me in bringing to life my vision for the foundational thrust of this book, the aircraft flight control panel, chapter headings, as well as the cover.

Vision and Purpose for *The Prodigal That Didn't Come Home*

The Prodigal That Didn't Come Home is clearly biblical and clinically accurate with a commitment to practical solutions that will encourage, empower, and hold all readers accountable to live with spiritual integrity without regard for the outcome of one's life. The purpose of the book is to encourage people to pursue the development of Christ likeness through conforming to His image and thereby empowering them to live according to His standard not in spite of but because of personal loss, with the help provided by God's word, prayer, encouragement, comfort, and accountability coupled with personal experience.

You can expect this book to be the following:

- clearly biblical
- clinically accurate
- committed to practical solutions
- dedicated to conveying empowerment and accountability

Introduction

I have often heard testimonies about situations where the power of God intervened in the lives of those who were rebellious. These included everything from incarceration and drug addiction to suicide attempts gone badly as the Lord Himself stepped in just in the nick of time. It goes without saying that these stories were an encouragement to me as well as to countless others. After all, the Lord Himself said, "And they overcame him because of the blood of the Lamb and because of the word of their testimony" (Rev. 12:11 NASB).

But what about those who died in prison or never overcame their addiction and even to this day persist in it? Persons who attend religious services, on average, are generally believed to exhibit much lower rates of suicide. I'm saddened to report that even with this statistic, the suicide of believers does happen.

The title of this book automatically raises thoughts and feelings about one's immediate circumstances. I would suspect that the word *prodigal* caught your attention. The Bible no doubt has influenced your thinking. In the gospel of Luke, chapter 15, a story surrounding this word can be found with all of its dramatic possibilities and a conclusion that's fit for a Hollywood script. The thing that sets this book apart from that possibility is the author and his intention for writing it. I would invite you at some point in time during the reading of this book to explore that passage of scripture. You might find within the contents of this book some similarities to that story, but it is not a study of the gospel of Luke or chapter 15. It's based on the reality of my personal experience. And it's not parabolic in nature. What I intend to do through the pages of this book is to raise some issues that I have experienced in my life as a result of a prodigal that didn't come home and point out how I was able to navigate that process. Let me hasten to add at this point for the sake of you who may not fully understand the nature of a prodigal family member. In some cases, they don't have to leave home to become prodigal. I will explain that in detail in the pages that follow. In my case, the conclusion of this story will be completely different from that of the gospel of Luke, yet God's grace will be equally as clear and His love equally as sure. The route that we take to get to that conclusion will also be different. We'll be taking some turns down some unfamiliar streets yet arriving at some familiar locations.

I will be using the concept of the gauges on the instrument panel of an airplane to highlight various points of interests, as illustrated below. Our ultimate goal on this journey is to live by faith. Like the gauges on the instrument panel of a plane, when you are traveling off course, other gauges are affected by it in some way or another. Another thing to consider about this approach is the making of adjustments. When a pilot wants to make a 360 degree turn the adjustment on the turn and slip indicator is not realized until the turn is established. The complete turn takes two minutes. Depending upon the number of turns that need to be made during the course of a flight, each turn amounts to the pilot flying by faith for a portion of those two minutes. As that description indicates, change then comes slowly. As a matter of fact, the pilot doesn't want it to happen too quickly because the results would cause him or her to overshoot the target, creating a different kind of problem. This is what sets this book apart from others you may have read on the subject. The instrument panel is similar to that found in the cockpit of an airplane only in concept. My purposes are different. My goal is to use the control panel to illustrate and simplify the very complex issues of grief and bereavement and how to get through it when your way is not clear. You need help in navigating your way just as a pilot does in commandeering a plane safely to a specific destination. You will not know how to fly an airplane when you finish this book, but you will be able to glance at the gauges on the assimilated instrument panel and get a clear view as to where you are and what needs to happen in order to get to where you need to be. Therefore, it is incumbent upon the reader to pay close attention to the gauges and the various changes that occur based on a specific behavior or emotion that is being discussed. Take a moment to study the instrument panel (image 1). Make note of each gauge as we begin our journey. Faith, again, is our destination, and what you see is basically what life should look like when we are traveling true north, which for our purposes is walking by faith. As the prodigals' journey unfolds, you will notice various changes taking place on the individual gauges of the instrument panel. Each chapter will have a description of that activity illustrated by a gauge highlighting those changes and what area of life is affected by them. Again, pay close attention to the changes; though they are subtle, they can make a huge difference in your progress. For instance, the ground speed indicator represents your relationship with people. In times of loss, these relationships can be affected. And if not handled properly, other relationships can be affected by it, such as our relationship with God. That relationship is represented by the vertical speed indicator. When our relationship with God is out of proportion with that of people, we find ourselves isolated, which could prolong the grieving process and ultimately lead to other negative responses. The air speed coordinator represents our faith community, which is also neglected, driving us deeper into ourselves and farther away from the human element that is so desperately needed at this time. The turn coordinator represents our decision making, and when it is off, it will produce faulty decisions at best. Then there is the attitude indicator; the top half of the gauge represents a spiritual attitude and the lower a natural attitude. The indicator arrow will fluctuate based on the movement of the other gauges. Next is the throttle, which equals motivation, and fuel, which is the influence of the Holy Spirit. The emotion detector will reveal the stages that loss will take you through and the cure that lies at the opposite end of the spectrum. The indicator lights are self-explanatory and will light up when the appropriate response is required.

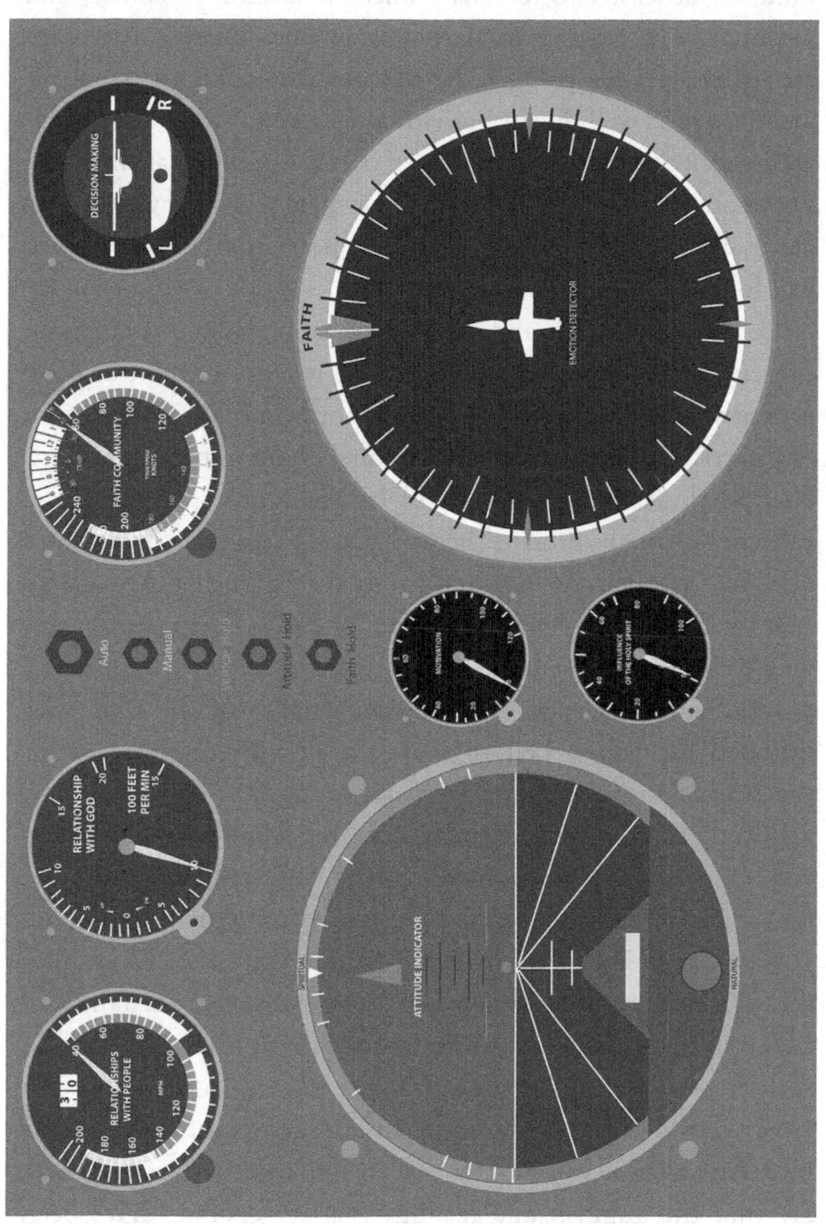
DECISION MAKING
L
R
FAITH COMMUNITY
FAITH
EMOTION DETECTOR
Auto
Manual
Attitude Hold
Faith Hold
MOTIVATION
INFLUENCE OF THE HOLY SPIRIT
RELATIONSHIP WITH GOD
100 FEET PER MIN
ATTITUDE INDICATOR
SPIRITUAL
NATURAL
RELATIONSHIPS WITH PEOPLE

This book is also going to be different from the gospel of Luke for at least two reasons—one, the author, of course, and second, and in this case more important, the outcome. Although the differences are going to be obvious, the similarities will be identifiable as well. Every individual life tells a story, and so it is with this writing; it will tell a story that is disjointed at times but systematically revealing. I intend to navigate this story with a clear destination in view, and undoubtedly hope and encouragement will follow us along the way.

I want to achieve and accomplish some things throughout this endeavor. I want you as a reader to recognize that this book is clearly biblical even though it will not be a biblical treatise on any particular doctrine of the scriptures. I am not a psychiatrist, but the clinical facts shared will be accurate with appropriate references to substantiate them. I am an assistant pastor of a large metropolitan church, and I have served in that capacity for over twenty years. I have been called of God to help people, and with that call, personal responsibility is coupled with experience, passion, integrity, and commitment worthy of the One who initiated the call. I believe that is a fitting combination for practical solutions to one of the major struggles of life and thereby appealing to all readers regardless of your religious affiliation. If you are a fellow participant on this journey called life and are navigating its various stages, then no matter your background, you have experienced the reality of pain in your life. "Resist him, standing firm in your faith, because you know that the family of believers throughout the world is undergoing the same kind of sufferings" (1 Peter 5:9 NIV).

I want to address a painful issue that many, many people face. And even if you have not faced this specific issue, chances are that the anguish and feelings that it generates have been experienced during some other occurrence in your life. Join me as we navigate the issues that surround the experience of *The Prodigal That Didn't Come Home,* and see if we can't glean from it the ability to face life with a new resolve to take advantage of the opportunities that this kind of experience presents and become whole people as a result. God has ordained that each one of us should be where we are, and it becomes our responsibility to see to it that we do not miss the opportunity to not only grow but to also benefit from our various experiences. Keep in mind that no experience will ever prevent you from carrying out the will of God, death included. Another thing I would like to make you aware of is my commitment to the memory of my son, which will also be discussed later in the book. I intend to do this by what I call Conan Citings. These are an inside glimpse into the heart of Conan. As you observe the various readings of the instrument panel gauges, you will see numbers and notations to point to an aspect of Conan's life. Read carefully and see if you can identify the experience that coordinates with the gauges, and in doing so you will keep the memory of Conan alive. Let's begin.

Chapter 1

The Beginning of the End

It was a clear Tuesday morning on October 2, 2007. I was traveling my usual route to work; I had just left home with a confident feeling that my instructions would be carried out by my youngest son, David. My cell phone rang at approximately 9:15 a.m. The voice on the other end of the phone was frantic—it was David. I anticipated a need for additional information to carry out an assignment that had been given thirty minutes earlier, but what I heard instead was a cry of desperation, despair, and hopelessness. His response to my "What's the matter?" would forever change my life. He said he had received a call from the city morgue, and they had informed him that Conan, his brother, was dead and that his body needed to be identified. Conan is the third of our four sons. He was thirty years old. The natural questions followed with no satisfying answers. All I knew for sure was that things would never be the same. Instantly, I lost the ability to be happy or hopeful. I never thought three words could have such a devastating effect on my life. That day is forever etched in my mind. I have had many experiences in life that I classified as difficult, but none could compete with the loss of a child, regardless of age. I suspect that none ever will. But through it all, I have come to understand life from a perspective that can only be acquired through a loss such as this. The body and mind do some very unusual things when they are severely tested. They become flooded with survival tendencies. Everything from bereavement to misplacing a set of keys is designed for this purpose. There develops in your thinking a desire to do whatever it takes to get through the pain of loss.

The beginnings of most things are difficult due to the adjustments required for change to take place. I find that when I look at things from a perspective that's never been considered, not only does the body prepare itself, the mind literally makes involuntary decisions on the basis of what the body says. The communication between the two becomes acute. This is what I call spiritual body language. I automatically went into autopilot, and the security of routine overpowered despair. This is why it's important to maintain a sense of normalcy in circumstances such as this. Each landmark that I passed on that first drive became a vivid reminder of where the end started. Even ends have a beginning and a life expectancy. Little did I know that what I was experiencing would help me navigate through the emotions that lay ahead. It was up to me to get the most out of the beginning of this end because it surely would have a conclusion. A life had ended prematurely, but I didn't want the end to end prematurely. I wanted it to run its course. It was an attempt on my part to keep the memory of my son alive. The issue was not remembering him but rather never forgetting him.

Here again we have the body communicating with the mind.

Life doesn't give in to death easily; even after the pronouncement, it fights to remain alive. Memories that take the place of life are better than no life at all. Faith has a significant place in the conclusion of a life. Expectations play a major role in one's ability to navigate through the maze of the unknown. Some things will never be clearly understood, and they must be accepted by faith. That journey can be just as mysterious as the outcome of one's life. Love not only makes for healthy relationships; it is stronger than death in that it enables us to get the most out of a relationship and at the same time gives us the ability to deal with the conflicts and disappointments that may develop within that relationship. All too often people believe that avoiding deep and meaningful relationships will prevent them from experiencing heartache and pain due to the disruption of those relationships. In love's army, only the wounded can join. I have heard some say that they would rather not have children than to risk the possibility of the hardships that a child may cause and, of course, the unbearable possibility of losing one. I beg to differ with that kind of logic. I believe the opposite is true in that the deeper you love, the more fulfilled you are, which in turn enables you to deal with whatever negatives may result, no matter how great the loss—keeping in mind that love is stronger than death. The father–son relationship is special in that it engulfs the transference of leadership, headship, and authority. When this transition is thwarted by death or any other obstacle, the impact is much greater than what is visibly imaginable. Posterity is tied into it. Future possibilities are tied into it. The very continuation of life and legacy are tied into it. None of us enjoys losing anything no matter how small. The feelings of loss are the same no matter what the object. It may be hard to fathom at this time, but when a wallet or a purse is lost, the feeling that's generated is the same as that of losing a loved one, only the latter is magnified to the tenth power. All of the smaller losses in life are preparation for the greater ones that may be experienced later in life. The more frequently the losses occur, the greater the preparation. You can and will get through this namely because all of life has prepared you to do so. God has prepared you for it.

Nothing in life is wasted, no experience is unnecessary, and all of life is good no matter how evasive the benefits may appear to be. We see this clearly in the animal world. As violent as things appear, balance is maintained and life continues. Young eaglets are known to peck their siblings to death to assure the survival of the species. The strong survive for a reason. There is always a bigger picture that is just outside of your view. Of course, in the wild kingdom, animals are protected from emotional trauma that comes from loss and have no way of experiencing pain associated with losing one or more of their offspring. Instinct is the driving force behind their behavior. What allowances has God made for us to offset the intense emotions that death leaves us with? What then has God provided for us when all we see is negativity and pain? We should look for opportunities. Opportunities always come to the surface when the foundation of our current experience is shaken. When life as you know it changes radically, what can be expected? You can rest assured that new possibilities will emerge.

These possibilities, however, are not without problems. They are hidden behind all of the challenges that come from emotional trauma, namely grief and bereavement. In the book *Caring for People God's Way,* contributing author Sharon H. May describes the stages of grief as denial, anger, bargaining, depression, and acceptance.[1] I've found that these stages, plus others, must not only be handled strategically but also consistently. The stages are involuntary responses to a loss. In order to handle them

---

1 Tim Clinton, *Caring for God's People God's Way* (Nashville, TN: Nelson Publishers, 2005), p. 365.

effectively, one must act deliberately and decisively. For instance, in order to offset denial, you have to force yourself to be open. If anger is going to be handled correctly, you are going to have to be honest with God in regard to how you feel and ask Him the questions that naturally come to mind without fear of retaliation or judgment from Him. When it comes to bargaining with God, you have to meet Him on His terms, remembering that He is in charge and knows exactly what He is doing.

Depression comes with the reality of a void that appears to be impossible to fill. To those of you who may not understand that kind of language, these and all other negative emotions must be viewed through the lens of Isaiah 63:1–3. There we find the Lord declaring what his mission to humankind is all about. I liken these three verses to God's replacement therapy program, where we find comfort and gladness replacing mourning, beauty replacing ashes, and praise replacing despair. I believe that the process that God uses to bring this to pass is simple with profound implications. The negative feelings that you may be experiencing can only be replaced as they are brought to the surface. Then they are to be viewed as positives simply because they are the means God has chosen to remove them. Their very existence becomes a clear sign of hope. Once they have been exposed, they can be removed by being replaced. Early detection as in the case of most terminal diseases is critical for survival. When issues are discovered early, it not only prolongs life but also improves the quality of life. You no longer have to be driven by a flood of negative emotions.

Acceptance will then follow shortly thereafter. As you can imagine, this requires time, effort, and discipline, the likes of which you may not feel that you have. Even though this is not a clinical study on the steps of bereavement, it will serve as a reminder of a dynamic that is always at work regardless of the stage in which you may find yourself. This appears to be a subconscious cleansing process. Emotions that linger must be brought to the surface and ultimately eliminated. This occurs as subtle reminders take you by surprise. These are not indicators that you have not overcome; rather, they indicate that your experiences have taken on new identities. They show themselves in ways that are completely unexpected. They peek through TV commercials, emerge during holiday celebrations, and even show up at bus stops. Subtle reminders will attack you when least expected.

Nevertheless, even the new identities are eventually replaced with more positive reminders, so be encouraged. This is a sign of the beginning's end. Prepare yourself for new perspectives that will emerge in replacement, and the cycle of life will continue as it takes on new meaning. Seeds that fall to the ground and die reproduce themselves. The seed itself, though dead, is responsible for the type of new life that emerges. It may resemble the old in appearance but will be completely new. And the life of pain will give way to a life of purpose and meaning. The feelings of remorse are once again stored in their proper place to await life's next experience to summon them when needed in the future. It's similar to cancer cells that are in remission. Extenuating circumstances can trigger an outbreak.

As I waited in a state of shock, the responses of family and friends who were willing to share in my pain and ultimate recovery taught me the genuine meaning of compassion. I shudder to think what could have happened if it had not been for the overwhelming response of love, care, and concern from them. Shock has a strange way of sensitizing you to everything that is going on around you. I cannot actually recall every person from whom I received an expression of kindness, but I do remember vividly those who I felt should have come or called but did not. But even they were mentally put into a category of expressing their concern silently. Sometimes the fear of saying the wrong thing can prevent people from saying anything, and that kind of paralysis must be identified as a form of care, albeit distant. I began to appreciate shock because it was through it that I discovered that I had the ability to withstand enormous amounts of insensitivity and personal discomfort. Shock is one of the greatest protective devices known to man. Of course, there are negative sides to shock when it is the result of physical deprivation or an insect bite such as that of a black widow or brown recluse. Nevertheless, the anesthesia that shock provides is second to none.

My concern is primarily with shock that is caused by the loss of a child and other traumatic experiences. The body temporarily shuts down in an attempt to centralize all of its efforts on the situation at hand. Shock enabled me to give myself permission to grieve and to determine how long I would do so. As a man, my tendency was to maintain a certain image at all times and not to show any signs of weakness. Shock rejected that approach and forced me to be open and honest with what I was feeling. As I stated earlier, my belief system was important to my overall response to all that was happening to me. So I was able to begin my journey toward healing on the basis of what I had been prepared for through the many experiences of life and the support of those who were concerned about my welfare.

Having gotten those clinical things out of the way, let's begin our story. Conan was born on April 5, 1977. He was an extremely emotional child from his birth. From the time he was able to lift his arms, he would grab my wife and me around the neck and squeeze us real tight as if to say, *I need all of your love.* Not only was he affectionate, but also he was soft-spoken and intelligent. He picked things up quite easily and was very compliant in whatever he was told to do. As I think about those years, I cannot help but become emotional as I reflect upon what could have been the anticipation of a bright future for Conan. It didn't take long for that dream to become unraveled. Problems developed between my first wife and me. The end result was separation leading to divorce. There was no animosity between us, though, and it was agreed that I should take the children. Even though it did not appear to be so at the time, I came to realize that, as always, the children felt the brunt of the breakup.

I had three sons at the time—Chris, Corey and Conan—and a fourth, David, came later. I was a new Christian and was given the responsibility of raising three sons alone. I had no frame of reference concerning the degree of difficulty involved in doing so. My personal upbringing had not prepared me for the job. I just did it. The oldest, Chris, was five; Corey was twenty-three months; and Conan was eleven months old when the end began. Life was filled with excitement, to say the least. We progressed from the daycare mother's system to day care and ultimately to school. We spent time at camping sites, fishing holes, and baseball fields. It was not going to be said that I did not do the best I could for my children, even with my limited resources.

As difficult as things were, I was never resentful or bitter. My life was being stretched to proportions that were unimaginable. I learned about the challenges of parenthood from the perspective of both a mother and father. I was introduced to love on a level that could not be experienced otherwise. I was a grateful dad who loved his children. We went to church every Sunday, and I attended all of the extracurricular activities the boys participated in. This lasted for eight years. My life had become quite a testimony. I was the talk of the neighborhood.

In September 1984, a new end began. I met my current wife, Renee, and my relationship with my children had to be adjusted. We were married in March of 1986. Even though life was difficult during those single-parenting years, I had a sense of control in the whole thing because I did not have to answer to anyone and all decisions were made without collaboration or discussion. Life took on new meaning after remarriage; the possibility of having a wife was not only exciting but having a mother for my children brought great relief. I knew that they would be as excited as I was. March 1986 would no doubt be an early Christmas for them.

Unfortunately, it did not turn out that way. Rebellion began to creep in, and resistance became a constant struggle. Each child was affected in a different way, but all were affected. It became obvious that of the three, the one who took the separation, divorce, and remarriage the hardest was Conan. His general attitude was one that said, *I will not comply with any of this.* Since he had a need for control, he began to take it by creating his own environment regardless of how negative it was. He was eight at the time. His intelligence became devious. His sensitivity became cold and calculating, and his relationship with the family was severely strained. There came a point in his life when his anger became obvious, and it never let up. He was determined to cause disruption no matter what the cost. If we went on fishing trips, he would eat others' share of the food that had been prepared equally for all. He would find ways to break things, tangle his line, or break sunglasses and the like. Of course, I didn't realize it at that point that Conan was trying to overcome his pain by creating greater pain in another area, pain that he could control. I believe he did all of this to gain some control over what he was feeling. Conan's rebellion was a response to his pain.

Being in control is important to men in particular. Some men would much rather create a problem that can be controlled than to have one assigned to them by someone or something else. Control meant a lot to Conan. I have often wondered what makes being in control as important to us as people and in particular to us as men. I came to realize that, for one, being in control gives us the option of exercising our freedom of choice. The operative word here is *freedom*. Whether it is responsibility or entertainment, we want to reserve the right to go where we want, do what we want, and answer to no one in particular while we are doing it. I suspect this kind of free thinking was driving Conan's behavior. Circumstances that are created for the purpose of control never allow the person to stay in them for very long before they realize that they have lost control once again. The cycle then repeats itself and continues to repeat itself for so long and consistently that it becomes literally impossible to determine where this newly adopted lifestyle originated.

The age of innocence was rapidly ending, and a new beginning was replacing it. Conan was moving headlong into the maze of confusion and mass deception. Like any other behavior pattern, it strengthens itself and gains momentum as it is repeated. His name and *trouble* became synonyms. He walked in rebellion, and with each step he was moving further and further away from the family. As a parent, nothing is more difficult than watching your child spin out of your control, ignoring sound advice and direction. Control really isn't lost; it has been replaced. The form that took its place in the case of Conan was that of manipulation, which gave him a purpose for living. That purpose, simply stated, can be defined as the ability to determine not only what happens to oneself but also what happens to others. Making things happen in the lives of others as a result of what you do lies at the heart of control. This power in the hands of the rebellious gives them some control of their future. A broken family makes life unpredictable; manipulation, on the other hand, brings with it some stability. Conan lived his life according to the way he wanted to.

Control also gives you a sense of being in charge. You become somebody when you do what you want to do regardless of the consequences. You become your own authority, the likes of which does not have to answer to anyone. Society doesn't matter, friends do not matter, relationships in general do not matter, and of course family does not matter. You are the sovereign ruler of your life. Since you know what is good for you, you determine what acceptable behavior is and conduct yourself accordingly. You live by your own rules. The feelings of others are no longer a consideration outside of how they can assist in achieving your personal desires and reaching the ends that you are striving for. The basic essentials of life are to be supplied by others. Your influence over the lives of other people brings you satisfaction. Everybody exists for your benefit. Nothing is more important than your agenda. And when that isn't satisfied, destructive behavior becomes the alternative.

And then, of course, there is the impact that trauma has on one's need to maintain control. There are different causes for what the clinical world calls post-traumatic stress disorder (PTSD). Listed within the categories of risk factors is something called omission. John Briere describes abuse by omission as "the great unrecognized trauma." This occurs when a child does not receive normal social stimulation, soothing, or support from a parent and lacks the opportunity to learn how to regulate emotions, which decreases the child's ability to cope with the pressures of life.[2] Instead of adjusting to unpleasant circumstances and making the best of them, the lack of proper nurturing causes one to resort to controlling one's environment, which often results in severe behavioral problems. Omission prevents one from seeing the good in other people and from developing a healthy view of oneself. All of this gives a person a sense of security in life.

From these descriptions, you can clearly see that love and nurturance are important aspects of one's development. These are the needs that a child has that cannot be expressed in words.

---

2 John Briere, *The APSAC Handbook on Child Maltreatment* (2nd ed.), (Thousand Oaks, CA: Sage Publications, 2011).

Yet when the needs are not met, the impact of their absence can be clearly seen in a child's behavior. Without his natural mother to provide Conan with the nurturing that he so desperately needed during those formative years, the trauma of it all went into hiding and was replaced by a desire to find that nurturing elsewhere, namely through self-perpetuating control. His hunt took him from one false attachment to another, none of which were successful in helping him to cope with the interpersonal struggles of life that he constantly grappled with. It is easier to see some of the things that were taking place and how they played a part in my son's life in hindsight. But whether in the midst of a calamity or reflecting on it, there was always a stabilizing factor that ran deep in the heart of every recurrence of trauma that I experienced. What I often discovered was an overriding element that enabled me to gain an understanding of the unknown and push toward a power that surpassed not only my understanding but also my personal conclusions of what it took to maintain the ability to cope. Though things may seem to be out of control in your life, if you look hard enough you'll find the same stability deep within.

It doesn't take long to realize that, no matter how much you know, it is not enough to deal with and be prepared for the uncontrollable or the unpredictable. Whether it's omission or something else, you need a source of power. So what becomes important is your perspective of not only God's existence but also his involvement in the everyday lives of people. The natural response to the loss of a child is to call out to God for help, regardless of how you identify Him. I dare say that even atheists make this call when the pain of ended dreams and dashed hopes fall upon them in the form of a lost child. In times like these, any help is readily accepted and even welcomed. The human experience is common to us all. Whether you are from the Middle

East, South America, or the distant shores of Zimbabwe, the pain of a lost child is the same. My concern is not to advocate a specific way of thinking but to become an advocate of the specific way you may be thinking and adjust it if it is not meeting your need. My concern is assisting in the healing process as well as gaining insight into the circumstances you and I may be experiencing. The loss already appears to be a complete waste, so capitalize on it and don't waste it. As you pick through the debris that this loss has left in your life, you'll discover reasons to be grateful, and of course, as by-products, hope and purpose will rise from the ashes.

I suspect that some of you who are reading this book do not believe or accept this whole concept of a personal relationship with God, nor do you feel comfortable talking about God, let alone considering his involvement in the lives of people. So the question you have to ask yourself is this: in whom am I placing my faith? When the unknown is upon you, there is something built into you that reaches outside of yourself to gain assistance in the midst of whatever you may be experiencing. That place in your heart is reserved for God. It's been called a God-shaped vacuum that can only be filled by Him. Even though God gives us the freedom to allow someone or something to occupy it, the ideal is to relinquish that space to the rightful owner and allow Him to do what you cannot do. If you choose otherwise, you then become responsible for the outcome. This area of control is God's way of offering you help. This decision will determine the impact that your end will have on your future. This decision will also provide for you the footing necessary to maintain your balance in the future. It is important to choose wisely as you face these most challenging issues and those things that you will be contending with in the future. If what you have placed there is not sufficient to handle the challenge, I strongly urge you to make some adjustments as soon as possible before the end that you may be facing gets swallowed up in the unrecognizable abyss of misunderstood emotions. Please feel free to contact me by e-mail (otnt3927@comcast.net), Twitter @Bellotnt3927, Facebook, or LinkedIn for assistance in making that decision or answering questions. (A website will also be made available in the near future. The goal for this site is to provide an interactive device designed to give the reader a hands-on experience in navigating the emotional phases that one goes through after losing a loved one.)

One thing that's often overlooked in the midst of traumatic experiences is opportunity. I personally believe that no circumstances are to be wasted; they all have meaning and all come with possibilities. As a family, we agreed to spend time together every two years to commemorate the life of Conan and reflect upon the experiences we have each had over the previous year adjusting to his absence. One of the questions that we discuss is, What positive things have you experienced this year as a result of Conan's death? Discussing that question gives an opportunity to express what is by nature overlooked when death occurs. Be prepared for negative responses, such as, "I don't see anything positive about it, nor do I want to consider the possibility." However, more often than not, positive responses will emerge, including gaining a deeper appreciation for life and coming to the realization that tomorrow is not promised. Life is short, and therefore a sense of urgency should develop as a result of a death. And then there will also be the spiritual responses that may include the realization that your loved one will be seen again. Personally, I have come to appreciate every moment that I have with those I love, and I have developed a deeper sensitivity to those I am called upon to help. At the time of this writing, seven years have passed and we have had three outings, which proved to be all that was needed for the family to adjust to Conan's absence. The goal of this event has been fulfilled in that the need to gather has diminished and we have developed a general attitude of acceptance and appreciation for what Conan represented to each one of us. Though positive, this is by far not the end of the story. The vision that I have for the book is to stimulate others to engage in a process similar to this family exercise. It will expedite the healing process. This reaction should be a part of the initial preparation process following the death of a loved one. It will build memories and strengthen relationships.

Learning is the key to navigating through the next year or two, whether it is acquiring a greater understanding of your personal feelings or a better idea about how to go about getting outside support from those who understand and are equipped to assist. "My people are destroyed because they have no knowledge" (Hosea 4:6 NCV). You then have to learn more about yourself and what can be expected of you. You have to learn more about some of the normal reactions that you may experience. For instance, growth is a requirement as a result of your experience. Nowhere in the universe will you find growth taking place without its being accompanied by some discomfort. Once you have accepted things as they are, you will emerge a stronger and healthier person. This strength comes only as a result of your understanding of the nature of the process. It is as predictable as snow in the winter. Consider this: even though snow falls on the East Coast, which is the area in which I live, I am still amazed the first time it happens. I often respond to it by saying, "I can't believe that it is snowing," especially if there is an inordinate amount of it. It is not because I wasn't aware of its possibility—it happens every year to some degree or another—it's just that I had relaxed my awareness of what I knew to be true. Some learning is simply being reminded of what you already know to be true, but intentionally activating that knowledge must be done. Remember, your emotions will become your enemy, and you will find yourself continually fighting against them until you have learned to make them your friend. Anticipating their arrival will help in the process.

There are four categories in life that tend to dominate our focus when we are faced with the loss of a child. The manner in which we respond to them can either increase or decrease our progress and our ability to cope with what they bring with them. The first category is that of *pain.* There is no amount of warning that can prepare you for this level of pain. The natural inclination is to seek relief, and the manner in which that is sought is largely dependent upon how you have managed other painful experiences. Your current response will be affected by the thoughts you have entertained, the places you have gone, and the people you have been talking to. If there has been any success in these areas, you will return the methods you used. It is my hope that the results that you experienced were positive. Insight should have been gathered through these encounters. The most important factor in this exchange is how your need was met. As members of God's creation, we respond like most other creatures when it comes to having a need satisfied—we return to the place of satisfaction.

Another category is *prosperity.* Just as pain drives us to get relief, prosperity drives us to get more. Keep in mind that these responses are heavily influenced by the nature of your circumstances. We need to have our attention diverted from the reality of what's going on, so we become top-heavy in our desire to prove that we can still be successful in spite of the loss. There is nothing wrong with success, but any extreme can detract from the beginning of a new understanding that naturally wants to express itself through the rearrangement of your emotions and the sorting out of your feelings.

The reason this is necessary is that the tendency is to resort to what has brought you relief in the past. This becomes a coping device and not a means of genuine growth. You must remain open if you are going to enter a dimension that you have never experienced before. It is on this level that the end is exposed to a new beginning.

Then there is *pleasure*. It is a proven fact that the best way to ward off the discomfort of the unknown and the devastation of the unpredictable is to do something, anything, that makes you feel good. This is an attempt to turn an intense training session into a leisurely stroll through the annals of remorse, grief, and extreme disappointment, trying to enjoy the beauty of the scenery. These two paths just do not go together. They are as contradictory as trying to celebrate a person's years of faithful service in a particular work environment while serving that person a pink slip due to the need to downsize. Pleasure has its place in the overall scheme of things, but if handled incorrectly, it will contribute to the acceleration of one's downfall and generate confusion in one's thinking. Feeling good comes as a result of doing well, and doing well comes as a result of putting forth effort in light of discomfort. You have to learn how to be friends with discomfort. Remember, the issue is not discomfort but the manner in which you respond to it.

And finally, let's consider *poverty*. This is the response that says, *I cannot do anything and don't intend to. I am bankrupt and incapable of handling the smallest responsibility.* This is where depression does its deadliest work. Poverty is a mind-set that affects the way people view life in general, not only how they make financial decisions or the amount of income that they earn in a year. If you adopt this mind-set, you will find yourself on an emotional roller coaster most of the time. The obvious becomes hard to fathom, and common sense is very elusive. Impoverished people have a tendency to overcompensate for their lack of visible purpose and positive involvement in life. How they feel becomes more important than prosperity and pleasure combined. How they feel becomes more important than pain, even though that pain is designed to alert them to a need for change. Change is not what this mind-set dwells on; rather, it desires to hold on to whatever it can in the way of memories, good and bad—but primarily bad. After all, they cannot afford to waste one experience.

Let me hasten to say that this is a normal reaction to the loss of a child. You do want to maintain memories. You do long to remember them in as positive a light as you possibly can, even if the cause of death was unnatural (murder, drug overdose, car accident, and the like) or if the child was rebellious and disobedient. Life, as I shared earlier, does not give up easily. It fights to stay alive even if that life can exist only in one's thinking. It is only experienced in the mind. It not only hinders where you are now but can affect your ability to anticipate anything positive in the future. As devastating as that may sound, if handled properly, a person can emerge enriched. In order for this to take place, the following must be carried out:

- One, you must regulate your emotional responses by allowing your thoughts and actions to determine how long any given emotion will be allowed to persist.
- Two, when the time has expired for an emotion to continue, you then want to trade in all negative emotions and substitute them with ones that are positive and pleasurable. I am convinced that the best way to change behavior is to focus on and exercise another behavior, thereby rendering that which has been exchanged inoperable and useless.
- Three, yield your personal desires to that of the desired behavior. This, of course, may sound easier than its execution would be. Depending on the nature of your

> immediate circumstances, extensive time may be required. This process will serve as a constant reminder of what your responsibility is in overcoming the very things that have immobilized you. You need help to overcome and do the thing you want to do (reflect upon your loss), but from a positive perspective, it will serve as a means of healing and hope. As you persist in carrying out these steps, you'll find that the memories that once brought tears will now bring feelings of appreciation, thanksgiving, and pride. You have been entrusted with the responsibility of not only having a child but being able to accept the outcome of that child's life, even though it differs from what you feel is best. New beginnings are subject to adjustments and new ways of thinking. One of the things that you have become accustomed to is waiting. According to Isaiah 40:31a, "Those that wait upon the Lord will renew their strength." The natural question arises, How does waiting make one strong?

I believe there are several situations in which waiting on God results in becoming strong enough to handle whatever the circumstances may call for, in particular the loss of a child. Waiting makes you strong because it requires you to depend upon the trustworthiness of God. Being true to His word every time it is spoken is a character trait that exclusively belongs to God. We have all at some point in time made promises that we could not keep for various reasons; this is not the case with God. He is absolutely trustworthy, and you can put your full confidence in him. Proverbs 25:19 puts it this way: "Confidence in an unfaithful man in time of trouble is like a broken tooth and a foot out of joint" (KJV). In essence, it can be a painful experience to depend upon an unreliable person when you need him or her. Waiting brings strength because it sensitizes you to the anticipated arrival of what you are expecting. This is why Christmas was much more exciting when you were younger, in part because of the anticipation of what you were expecting. As a matter of fact, depending upon how things turned out, the anticipation was often better than the actual gift. There is a line in the poem "Ode on a Grecian Urn," written by John Keats in 1819, that goes, "Heard melodies are sweet, but those unheard are sweeter." Sometimes, the expectation can be more satisfying than the fulfillment thereof. Have you ever experienced the joy and excitement of preparing for an event only to have the results of the event not live up to your expectations?

Waiting brings strength by providing you with wisdom and experience that could not otherwise be acquired. The entire process is designed to equip you for future opportunities. Whether they are for personal use or for that of others, you will be prepared, and that should promote a sense of well-being, which always translates into strength.

Something often overlooked while waiting is the increase in the value of your expectations. The longer you wait, the stronger you become and the greater your desire to experience fulfillment becomes. What was once a fleeting emotion of sorrow now becomes a deep longing for expression. You are a person of value, and all that you will become is valuable. Waiting only increases your value. Some things increase in value only through time, while some things improve only through experience. Some things can be developed to their fullness only through the anticipation of an outcome that in some cases may be even greater than the actual results. Even sorrow can be viewed with a positive light as you wait on the Lord. Limitation increases value in that it creates a greater sense of appreciation upon fulfillment.

David Wiersbe, in his book *Gone But Not Lost* says, "In some ways those in sorrow are the healthiest people in town. They know they hurt. They express their feelings. They cry. They ask tough questions they know no one can fully answer. They get mad and say angry words. For those in grief, this is normal. It shows their minds and feelings and bodies are functioning in healthy ways."[3] All of this, of course, is new, and anything new requires an adjustment period. Waiting assists in the process. One of the greatest allies that postponement offers is time. It has a tendency to put distance between you and displeasure, between you and success, between you and the difficulty involved in facing the beginning of this end. It is not stagnant but very much alive.

Even though we want to be honest in our expression of feelings, we have to keep in mind that "We are to God the aroma of Christ among those who are being saved and those who are perishing" (2 Cor. 2:15 NIV). The example that the author uses here is based on a Roman triumphal procession, the victory parade awarded a conquering general in which enemy prisoners were forced to march.[4] This is extremely important at a time such as this. I believe the fragrance was an important aspect of this parade. During these times, people could not stay home and observe the victory parade on TV as we do today, whether it be for Thanksgiving or New Year's Day. They were dependent upon their sense of smell. If they couldn't be there and observe the triumphant procession in person, they could rejoice where they were because of the aroma. The battle we are fighting is more intense than that of a military campaign.

We are being led by the victory that we have in Christ, and the onlookers need to understand that the victory has been won.

---

3 David W. Wiersbe, *Gone but Not Lost* (Grand Rapids, MI: Baker Book House, 2011).

4 John F. Walvoord and Roy B. Zuck (Eds.), *The Bible Knowledge Commentary : An Exposition of the Scriptures.* (Wheaton, IL : Victor Books, 1983-c1985), S. 2:559.

What assures them of our victory is the fragrance of our aroma. What does a fragrance represent? It represents freshness. When we enter into a situation, we should bring with us fresh ideas and concepts about old issues. It is impossible to go through this kind of thing and not be changed, which is inclusive of the way we think as well as the way we process things. The loss of a child, though devastating, unfortunately is often viewed as a common occurrence that normally triggers the predictable grief responses, albeit intensified. This is true to some extent, but it does not tell the whole story. Even though an end has come, it brings with it some fresh possibilities. This is what should emanate from us, a fragrant understanding of the influence we can have on others, and fragrance represents restoration. When the atmosphere is putrid and the smell is unpleasant, something fragrant can restore it to normal and even enhance it into something more pleasurable. Of course, in most cases, depending on what is applied, the atmosphere becomes better than it was before the fragrance was applied.

So it is with the possibility of those of us who are in such a position. We are not only called to restore things to normal; we are required to make them better than they were before the loss occurred. Fragrance represents confidence. Once the atmosphere has been restored to normal, one can now function with confidence. When the triumphant procession came through town, all of the inhabitants were filled with confidence. Their side had won; they were the victors. They celebrated with confidence because the threat was over and the enemy had been defeated.

Once you have influenced others through your response to Christ, the fragrance of that response and your presence precedes you, and others are blessed as a result. The aroma that you generate stimulates the senses of others, and they long to have what you have. I'm certain you have come home to a delightful aroma of something cooking in the kitchen. After a few whiffs, your response is, "When is it time to eat?" The natural desire is to taste what you have smelled. Psalm 34:8 instructs us to "taste and see that the Lord is good"(NIV). It's not enough to smell what's desired; you have to taste it. The ability of God is verified once you taste Him for yourself. Job came to a similar conclusion in Job 42:5, where he says, "My ears had heard of you but now my eyes have seen you" (NIV). In other words, I have tasted you for myself. The reality of what God was capable of doing was verified by Job's personal interaction with Him. What was anticipated has now become experience.

Consider the story of the woman at the well in John 4. After her encounter with Jesus, she went home to her townspeople and began to share the news of what she had discovered, and she invited all to come see a man who had told everything about her. They responded by believing in the person of Christ. But then the scriptures go on to say, "And because of his words many more became believers. They said to the woman, 'We no longer believe just because of what you said; now we have heard for ourselves and we know that this man really is the Savior of the world'" (John 4:41–42 NIV).

The attitude or fragrance that we project will either attract or push those away who stand in need of what they are sensing to be true. May you develop an aroma that prompts others to want to taste what it is their senses are longing for—peace.

My father used to tell me that I should always shine the backs of my shoes because it was the last thing a person would see and that's what they would remember about me. The impressions that we leave are very important. In your thinking, life may have taken a wrong turn simply because your surroundings are no longer familiar. The unfamiliar is not bad in God's economy because we are not dependent upon what we see. We are pilgrims and strangers passing through unfamiliar territory. Ours is a reality that transcends the immediate. We have to become more attentive to what is not seen and more conscious of what will be. Consciousness of the unknown should translate into a heightened awareness of future possibilities. So then, how is one to be an example for others after one's whole world has just come crumbling down? I believe the answer to that question lies within our understanding of pain.

It doesn't take long in life to recognize the value of pain even though you may disagree with the vehicle in which it comes. You may feel that you have been victimized and everything about you has been violated. But in reality, what's happening in your life is being validated so that it will have the right to assist others who may not like the mode in which their pain is traveling either. We are all on the same journey even though we are traveling in different vehicles. Your destination is the same as mine; it's a place called peace. You want to be able to articulate not only where you are going but where you are as well.

Conan knew where he was going, but he did not know how to get there. He wanted his life to be his regardless of the needs of others. He wanted his life to be his regardless of the hazards that his position posed. It was his way of responding to pain. He made allowances for himself so that any unacceptable behavior could be justified. The remarkable thing about pain is its ability to compensate for whatever is missing in your life. It dominates your thinking and in most cases your behavior. It becomes very instructive. It is one of the best tools to modify one's behavior. The demands that it places on you could easily put you in the category of a workaholic. There are some benefits in its demands, but they are short lived and have very negative results. Even though the benefits are temporary, the consequences can be permanent.

Retaliation makes you feel better but only for a little while and is usually followed by remorse or disdain.

When pain is approached incorrectly, it almost always results in a compounded problem with multiple layers of deception. It takes on a personality all its own. It becomes very elusive, as we have seen in the case of other traumatic experiences. The positive aspects of pain are protective in nature. Growth, of course, takes place, but so much more is going on all of the time. You gain access to a part of you that has been imprisoned for as long as you have been alive. These resources can only be unlocked through pain. The reason I believe this takes place is that the painful experiences of life have been nurtured by different responses to them. Some of those responses are acceptable, while others are not. The ones that are contributing to continual growth are embraced the ones that are not must be flushed out to either remove them or qualify them for growth. Remember, nothing in God's economy is wasted, but in some cases the true benefit cannot be experienced through conventional means. Assistance is needed; hence the need for pain. This is the response of those who respond to pain in a normal way. You fit into this category if you make the adjustment to pain in a manner in which all of the above can take place. This was not the case with Conan. His was a maladjusted response in that he was determined to beat pain in his own way.

Whenever this kind of thinking is present, it is often accompanied by outside stimuli such as drugs, sex, violence, and procrastination. Any one of these can dominate a person's life, with destructive results. The drug world can lead you down a path of crime and physical breakdown. It is all too often the primary cause of incarceration, leading to career criminal status and ongoing brushes with the law. This kind of behavior shows itself very early in life. Sometimes seemingly small criminal acts are incorrectly interpreted as childhood irresponsibility and immaturity. But if examined closely, you may find signs of mishandled anger irritated by the presence of pain that is kept so far below the surface that it cannot be detected by the natural eye.

Sex, of course, can bring about disease and unwanted pregnancy. But when pain is the underlying culprit, the pregnancies are not unwanted but desirable for the purpose of creating alternate responses to the pain that seems to be out of reach by the sufferer. One of the clear signs of the presence of this hidden pain is a total disregard for all that comes with bringing a child into the world due to, I believe, the person's desire to anesthetize his or her own pain by creating pain in the lives of others. Those who are closest to the person are normally the targets. The pain only intensifies through this approach to handling it. But, unfortunately, the victims can only identify the behavior as totally irresponsible and beyond understanding. Naturally, the children cannot escape this kind of upbringing and are severely affected by it. That subject alone would require an entire book to adequately explain.

Pain that goes unaddressed can lead to rage, which is another attempt to compensate for the discomfort that the person is feeling. Anger is a more acceptable behavior than expressions of pain. It is easier for the person to say, "I am angry" than it is to say, "I am in pain." This, as I said earlier, compounds the problem because it causes the person to lose confidence due to his or her lack of control of the situation, which results in not only feeling inadequate but even stupid. This is a totally unacceptable way for an intelligent person to feel, so something has to replace it as quickly as possible, and the most accessible emotion is anger. The deposit of stupidity now has accumulated interest, and the true problem continues its descent with an additional layer of camouflage.

As devastating as these responses can be, I believe the

granddaddy of them all is procrastination. Nothing is more heinous than intelligent people with oodles of potential who refuse to apply themselves to the extent of their capacity. All too often I hear of total derelicts being referred to as great even though their current lifestyle is everything but that. I believe the underlying cause in some cases could be the misappropriation of pain management. Calvin Coolidge summed it up nicely.

> Nothing in this world can take the place of persistence. Talent will not; nothing is more common than unsuccessful people with talent. Genius will not; unrewarded genius is almost a proverb. Education will not; the world is full of educated derelicts. Persistence and determination alone are omnipotent. The slogan "press on" has solved and always will solve the problems of the human race.[5]

The unwillingness of people to reach their potential is a problem to say the least, but I believe it is a problem that, once planted, grows at the same rate as dandelions when its soil has been fertilized by pain. Undoubtedly, you can recount numerous times when you may have experienced some disappointment in someone who has failed and you knew within your heart of hearts that he or she could have done better. Parents, I'm certain you can attest to at least one occasion when the expectations you had for your children were disappointed by the buds of procrastination pushing through the soil of their good intentions and rendering their progress all but null and void. Realizing the work of

---

5 GoodReads.com, "Calvin Coolidge," Retrieved from http://www.goodreads.com/quotes/2749-nothing-in-this-world-can-take-the-place-of-persistence. Accessed 10/10/2013

procrastination (pun intended), one must take drastic steps to not only recognize it but classify it as a very viable enemy that must be contended with. Admitting that the problem exists is still one of the greatest foundations from which to facilitate positive change.

In order for this to happen, a foundation for change must be established. In doing so, circumstances will not only dictate the potential for overcoming but will serve as a motivator to encourage the necessary adjustments, which often result in permanent improvement. Habits, believe it or not, are just as easy to break as they are to start if you use the same approach to ending them that was used to start them. Consider for a moment a time when you began a behavior. Can you remember how difficult it was at the beginning of that practice? The steps no doubt were unintentional but continual. For example, in order for a room to fill up with dirty clothes, there had to be a starting point and repetition. The end result, of course, was a mountain of responsibility that would be gotten around to later. But "later" stays in that location, therefore making it a permanent recourse of action whenever the need calls for it. If repeated, the stage has been set for the next steps to take place. The mountain has to be overcome—not for achievement but as a stepping stone to get to the next developmental project of avoidance. Since the mountain has now become painful to look at and impossible to overcome, at least in your thinking, a new one is developed in some other area to numb the pain caused by the first mountain. The process continues until there is nowhere left to go. As you can see, this kind of thinking can permeate one's entire life. It is no wonder that it becomes almost impossible to determine what the real problem was without some concentrated effort.

Beginning with the last numbing approach created to cover the procrastination, let's begin to dismantle it piece by piece. The important thing to remember here is that it took time and effort to avoid doing what needed to be done. What's often overlooked is the amount of work required to procrastinate. The mental energy required is phenomenal. Everything that is being avoided has to be thought through in order to continue to be avoided. So the dismantling must begin in the mind. I am convinced that the first thing that must be addressed is apathy, that thing that convinces you of the futility of attempting to do anything. The pattern of this kind of thinking can be summed up as an upward climb to the bottom. There is no loneliness like the loneliness of a vital element that is unwilling to engage in the progress of the human existence. I use this term with the utmost respect for the sanctity of life and firmly believe that it takes all of us to assure its continuance. That element is the person who has disengaged his or her connection from the link that holds the living together and in doing so has expedited his or her descent to the bottom. Of course, when this is added to the other possibilities of a life that is driven by camouflaged pain, you have a combination suited for the destruction of anything that gets in its path. There is not a wildfire that can compare to it, there is no tsunami that can compete with it, and it dwarfs the category EF-5 tornado.

Then there is the stubbornness that is developed in this turbulent environment, which makes for a volatile mixture with toxic implications that are highly contagious. You cannot come in contact with a person infected by this attitude and not be affected by it. Apathy indeed breeds apathy. Keep in mind that underlying this behavior is pain, and this approach renders the victim immobile because he or she feels that any movement could result in additional pain. It is no different from the person who may be experiencing back pain and trying to find a position that promotes relief, causing the person to remain in that position as long as possible to avoid the pain associated with movement. The thing that tends to motivate those trapped in this cycle to stay there is the lack of pain in their immobile position. Until they become uncomfortable with where they are, the chances of change are remote. Some recommendations to help you and possibly them are to create some discomfort by considering the following.

- Make them aware of how much time has been wasted in their current state.
- Point out what progress could have been made if effort had been put forth.
- Measure the effort in small, manageable segments. Make comparisons with those you know who have done so in the allotted time, with accompanying rewards.
- Give no assistance when and if called upon to do so. Be aware of how much help you inadvertently give without giving it any thought.
- Avoid any encouragement and or support when no progress is being made.

Since life is hard for those who have become comfortable in doing nothing and doing it continually, stirring up a different way of thinking is the answer. Seldom will you find a person in this state who is not willing to talk about what they need to do. But unfortunately, that is usually the extent of the willingness to become involved in a proactive way. They need help. There is a desperate need for success in one way or another. In the case of the procrastinator, that may not be easy to do.

Conan was not a procrastinator from birth. He learned to operate as such through one bad experience after another. His attitude took on the shape of the circumstances he was exposed to. So then instead of relying on success to achieve his objectives, he allowed his objectives to determine his success. What I mean by that is that instead of attempting to accomplish predetermined goals such as graduating from high school, going on to college, and getting a job, he decided to write his own rules for goal setting, namely by following the whims of his personal desires without restraining himself whatsoever. This kind of thinking most always leads to failure and not only violates the rules for success but also hinders the innate desire that we all have to continue to progress in life. The capability to do so was there, but the "how to" was clouded by unwillingness and irresponsibility.

Truly this is a difficult position to be in because of the potential and ability that is possessed and readily available to the person. Today in the world of sports, we see this all too often, where star athletes with unimaginable salaries cannot carry out basic responsibilities such as staying of out trouble with the law or following basic instructions like coming to practice, being on time for games, and avoiding staying out until late hours. Many an athlete has thrown away a lucrative career because of an unwillingness to maintain the basics. Of course, I believe there are other dynamics at work in such cases, but the bottom line is universal; potential and ability alone are not enough to ensure success. Obedience to the requirements of your particular craft must be not only established but also maintained.

What does this have to do with procrastination? you might ask. Well, the answer to that question is found in the true nature of the beast. Procrastination swallows up the agony of resistance by replacing it with a more acceptable behavior, namely, arrogant independence. Remember that the procrastinator is really a person who has chosen a course of behavior that, in his or her mind, is more acceptable than the actual problem being experienced. It goes back to trauma. As you recall, when something has been upset in the thinking and the response that is given is a more palatable one for the person initiating it, that form of behavior is what I call phantom behavior, which means "not real but fabricated to give the appearance of reality." That behavior could be anything from extreme anger to drug addiction and of course the very thing we are discussing, procrastination.

Included also in this kind of thinking is a deep desire to have one's needs met. It goes without saying that procrastinators are looking to have their needs met. As a matter a fact, they are not willing to do anything until that actually happens. It doesn't take long to see the futility in that kind of thinking. Something must be done if what they want done is ever going to take place. Added to the already existing problems that accompany this type of thinking, you have all that is needed to witness a full-grown problem that is just waiting to express itself. If these things are prevalent, you can rest assured that it is just a matter of time before their full expression will begin to take you down an ever-winding road of turmoil and grief. As you can imagine, the longer you travel on this road, the more difficult it becomes to interpret the behavior of those who have chosen this route. The reason is obvious—each experience adds another layer to the already camouflaged behavior. There was clarity at the beginning, and as long as you can recall where you came from, there is hope for the future.

One thing that you must keep in mind is the influence that you can have on any given encounter with those trapped in the whirlwind of anger triggered by trauma but now covered with procrastination. Each individual encounter must be viewed as a potentially explosive situation that can be further aggravated by the devil. I have come to find out that there is not much that can be done to prevent his involvement, but you can minimize his effectiveness. In James 4:7, we are told, "Resist the devil and he will flee from you" (NIV). Resistance is key for developing a plan to nullify his effectiveness. All too often you can find yourself in the midst of a skirmish and not know how you got there; prodigal children don't handle confrontation well. In most cases, there was a series of events that led up to the encounter. Let's consider for a moment what could have happened if the following took place instead.

Number one, do not retaliate. There is a big difference between resisting and retaliating. To retaliate is to get even or to strike back, and to do so only makes things worst. The viciousness of the devil is heightened, and with his experience, it's impossible for you to win. It only gives him momentum and increases his strength. One of the mistakes that we make is to try to avoid conflict by running from it or attempting to ignore it. According to 1 Peter 5:8, "Your enemy the Devil prowls around like a roaring lion looking for someone to devour" (NIV). If you know anything about the animal kingdom, you know that the worst thing you can do when confronted with a possible attack is to run. Running triggers an automatic chase response in the lion. Second, you have to strive to be silent. I use the term *strive* because it is going to require effort to maintain quiet. Silence in this case is indeed golden. You can make very little progress in a one-sided argument. Proverbs 17:14 says it best: "Starting a quarrel is like opening a floodgate, so stop before a dispute breaks out" (NLT). We have all seen in one way or another the impact that compromised levees had during Hurricane Katrina. The same is true in opening the floodgate of uncontrolled words; the levees of self-control will only hold as long as they are actively applied. And then there is the need to examine oneself. There are always some conclusions being drawn on the inside. Those, of course, are usually the culprits when it comes to communication breakdowns. Once you learn to control those thoughts, you will find that they will serve you in a more positive way if allowed to run their course in silence. Honesty is an absolute must in this process because oftentimes you will find that some of your conclusions were unfounded and even wrong in some cases.

There is also an added benefit that occurs when you consider this internal activity—you gain insight. Insight sensitizes you to things that were previously hidden. Your perception becomes sharpened, and what was initially viewed as a problem now becomes an opportunity to learn. You begin to realize that you are not in this alone. One of the most effective weapons in the devil's arsenal is that of isolation. When you begin to think that you are all alone, your life becomes stifled and unproductive with very little enthusiasm at all. The nature of the circumstances creates this kind of thinking. Oftentimes, what you desire is to isolate yourself due to the weight of burden that you are carrying. Resisting isolation can now be viewed as a training session, preparing you for the next encounter. Our response should always be to resist the temptation to give the confusion any momentum by submitting to isolation, which so desperately needs to be avoided. Remember, no matter how difficult, no matter how devastating, and no matter how painful, you are not alone.

Your job is to resist retaliation, strive to be silent, and examine what's going on inside of you. Be on the lookout for insight and turn the circumstances into a training session where new ways of dealing with issues will emerge. All arrogance and pride must be done away with and submission to the will of God must be maintained. In so doing you can expect God to intervene.

The human experience is challenging to say the least, but for the benefit of those negatively affected by those experiences, God has orchestrated each challenge for the spiritual development of the believer. Even the loss of a child can be placed in this category. In 2 Corinthians 12:7–9, God verifies this kind of reasoning. The passage points out the strategy behind circumstances that are persistently difficult. First, it reminds us of our weakness in a particular area. Countless explanations concerning the nature of Paul's thorn in the flesh have been offered. They range from incessant temptation, dogged opponents, chronic maladies (such as ophthalmic problems, malaria, migraine headaches, and epilepsy), to a disability in speech. No one can say for sure what his was, but it probably was a physical affliction (for the work of Satan in this, cf. 1 Corinthians 5:5; 10:10). It is understandable that Paul would consider this thorn a hindrance to wider or more effective ministry (cf. Galatians 4:14–16) and that he would repeatedly petition God for its removal (cf. 2 Corinthians 12:8). But he learned from this experience the lesson that pervades this letter and one that I believe we all have to learn; that is that divine power is best displayed against the backdrop of human *weaknesses* (cf. 2 Corinthians 4:7) so that God alone is praised (cf. 2 Corinthians 10:17). Rather than removing the problem, God gave him grace in it. This grace is sufficient (*arkei,* i.e., adequate in the sense of providing contentment).

In 2 Corinthians 12:10, we see how God's grace transformed Paul's perspective. Experiences in his ministry that he would naturally abhor are ones he would welcome supernaturally because the evidence of Christ's power in the midst of them brought glory to Him, not Paul. "When Paul came to the end of himself, Christ alone was seen. When he was weak, then Christ, by His strength, could make Paul spiritually strong. ('Power,' *dynamis,* in v. 9, is the word 'strength,' thus matching 'strong,' *dynatos,* in v. 10)." [6] The issue that we are facing has to go through the same scrutiny as those listed above. Everything that we are experiencing has come by way of permission. The Lord Himself signed off on it; it has met the approval of God and has qualified to serve Him in

---

cf. *confer*, compare

i.e. *id est,* that is

6 Walvoord and Zuck, *The Bible Knowledge Commentary* (2:583).

His ultimate objectives for each one of us. They are instruments to be used for the improvement of the human experience. They have been handcrafted to fit perfectly those who are designated to appropriate their effectiveness. Take heart, those of you who have been chosen as such—God knows and cares not only about you but also yours. If you submit to the plan that God is interweaving into your life, the end result will be a thing of beauty.

Prayer

Father in heaven, as I embark upon this journey into uncharted waters, my experience of losing a child is extremely difficult to navigate. The terrain is splattered with constant reminders of the relationship, which can be unbearable at times. But I am determined to stay the course until this ending exposes evidence of a meaningful beginning. With your help, I know that this is not only possible but also desirable and welcomed. I am certain that my steadfastness in the midst of the unknown will be transformed into clear evidence of Christ's power in my life, which in turn will bring glory to you.

Memory Verses
2 Corinthians 12:8–10

When you are off by one degree, it can change your destination by several miles. Shock freezes your location momentarily; however, when you recover, you can be so far off course that it feels impossible to get back on track. Keep in mind that the feeling of disorientation need not affect your progress.

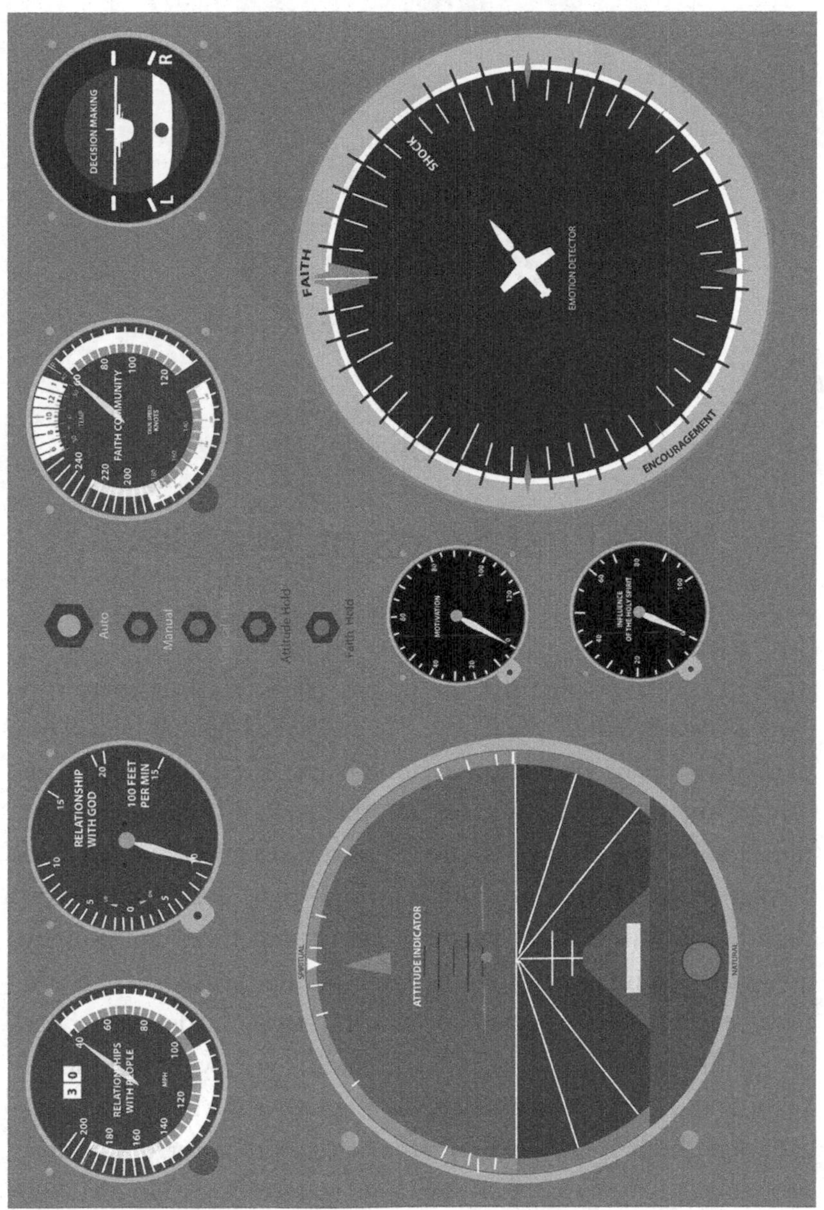
DECISION MAKING
L
R
FAITH COMMUNITY
RELATIONSHIP WITH GOD
100 FEET PER MIN
RELATIONSHIPS WITH PEOPLE
Auto
Manual
Attitude Hold
Faith Hold
FAITH
SHOCK
ENCOURAGEMENT
EMOTION DETECTOR
MOTIVATION
INFLUENCE OF THE HOLY SPIRIT
ATTITUDE INDICATOR
SPIRITUAL
NATURAL

Chapter 2

The First Signs of Trouble

Conan was a delightful child. He was very affectionate and people oriented. He enjoyed being picked up and held. One of the first things he would do upon being lifted off of the floor was to hug us very tightly around the neck. This was the first indication to me that he not only wanted affection but also had a great need for it, as all children do at that age. His was one that did not diminish as he grew. He wanted to be emotionally attached to someone. Of course, in a natural sense, that should have been his mother, coupled with the strong leadership of the father. Since there was a shortage in this very vital emotional element in his daily experience, he sought it elsewhere. At a very early age, he began to exhibit unusual control over discomfort and pain. He didn't even cry when he was teething. He was very compliant with bedtimes, nap times, and the like. For all intents and purposes, he was an ideal single parent's child.

Life was hectic as a single parent. My weeks consisted of preparing three small children for day care, church services, and school. We rose early each day at approximately four thirty in the morning. Let me hasten to add that we went to bed very early. They were washed, dressed, and fed. Their clothes would be laid out the night before to minimize some of the complications the following morning. Fortunately, I was able to take them to a nearby Day Care Mother, as they were called at that time. Two were under the age of two, and one was soon to start preschool. This routine went on for several years. The locations for child care changed and the distance to these new locations grew greater and greater. By the time I arrived at work, which began at 7:00 a.m., I was glad to get a break from the demanding schedule of a single parent. Work became a place of refuge for a few hours. Now the job itself was not that exciting; it just gave me the freedom to be concerned about myself for a few hours.

This mind-set was one that I came to understand as a means of survival. I was not equipped to handle this kind of responsibility. My prior training had been insufficient. Both of my parents did a good job, but their training was limited. Life in general was good, and I didn't have any complaints. My father worked hard, was very independent, and set a pretty good example for me in regard to handling one's responsibilities. All of the bills were paid on time, and we always had a roof over our heads. To this day, I mimic that same behavior. Unfortunately, that wasn't the only behavior that I mimicked. I also inherited some of his bad traits, such as becoming too independent and not relying on others for help. His way of finding relief from the stressors of life was not to glean support from the family but to drink socially on weekends. This habit estranged him from the family and often resulted in bouts with drunkenness, which further desensitized him from the emotional needs of the family. My mother was a very affectionate person, and by her general demeanor, she stabilized me emotionally Even though this provided me with security, it did not prepare me for what I would ultimately encounter. Basic skills were overlooked—not intentionally but out of a lack of training on her part. This kind of thing did not come with a manual, as they say. My family life, of course, affected the way I chose to operate in life. Even though I made a lot of bad decisions earlier on in life, I was able through a personal relationship with the Lord Jesus to overcome most of the emotional dysfunction that my family life may have imposed upon me. Through Him, I was able to override the lasting effects of neglect and emotional depravity and generate the ability to maintain a responsible way of living. As a matter of fact, I determined as years progressed not to fall into the same trap that had consumed my parents. Even though I was not properly equipped to deal with the issues that I faced, I was indirectly qualified to learn what needed to be done. I was always faced with two options: become a victim of my circumstances or master my own fate. I'm proud to say that I chose the latter. Undoubtedly, my story is no different than those of millions of others, but since it belongs to me I have the liberty to share it.

Initially, my concentration was more on survival than on nurturing. Even so, the children were not totally neglected in that area because I am by nature a nurturer. The problem is that the nurturing was not intentional and was therefore insufficient, keeping in mind that the primary nurturer, their mother, was not providing them with what I could not provide. Conan complied in order to receive what recognition he could for as long as he could, and when it no longer met his needs, he turned to other ways of satisfying that need. When he couldn't acquire it through affection, then he turned to attention-getting techniques instead.

Anger became one of the first obvious signs of his new approach to satisfying his longing to be loved. At first, it was the normal temper tantrum kind of thing that is prevalent in children his age, but when it escalated to the point of sabotaging others and circumstances to provoke others into heated exchanges, I knew it had moved beyond the norm. There is a thin line between normal developmental anger and that of premeditated provocation of conflict inducement for the sheer pleasure of doing it. In other words, when you start making others angry for the sake of expressing your anger, you have entered into the realm of what I call premeditated provocation. When this kind of approach is prevalent in one's behavior, taunting, aggravating, and annoyance characterize most relationships. It takes a keen eye to notice this in the light of normal childhood development.

Feelings are not easy to deal with when you don't understand them and they are uncomfortable to you. Feelings are deigned to be expressed but within the proper context. When the art of give and take is not properly developed, the expression of feelings becomes totally selfish in nature. When you cannot have your way, you pursue satisfaction in other ways. Remember, the feelings now become the issue, as does how to process them in the light of not having your way. What tends to happen at this point is an internal search in pursuit of a feeling that is more desirable than the one that is being experienced. Anger is more comfortable than defeat.

A disappointed expectation always leaves you with a negative feeling. Those of us who have learned to anticipate that make the necessary adjustments and move on. When adjustments cannot be made, the disappointed expectation must be viewed as a potentially life-threatening problem, meaning it will influence you for the rest of your life and will make a lasting impression on all those you come in contact with in the future. In order for this to be minimized, concentrated effort must be placed on the need to get feelings out into the open. On the part of the parent or guardian, this requires great patience, concentrated effort, and an unselfish approach to putting your child's needs above your personal feelings and desires. I believe one thing has been lost in the parenting process with catastrophic results, and that is sacrifice. It not only takes a village to raise a child; it also takes the total commitment of parents to give their children everything that they will need to equip them with the ability to do likewise for their children. Parenting is a generational process that requires repetitive behavior if it's going to be successful.

Pride must also be sacrificed. Your reputation must be set aside, and your focus must be on a well-adjusted child with a clear understanding of what life is all about and what that child can expect to face in this life. It is within this environment that feelings can be expressed and explored. Early childhood is not a time when deep, meaningful conversation is going to take place, but it is a time when foundations can be established through an open forum of discussion that promotes future conversations. It is a time when habits can be forged and knee-jerk responses can be introduced and cultivated. It is a time when children find out that the world does not revolve around them.

This is the time when they learn how to have fun. This is a learned behavior. I think some have gone to the extreme of isolating their children from the outside world and providing them with everything that they feel is needed within their own home settings. I have heard both good stories and bad surrounding this approach to developing a child's positive traits and offsetting the negatives. That is a decision that is left up to each parent. One thing that is common in whatever approach you decide to use is the need to understand the necessity of fun and how it is communicated.

Conan was fun loving as a young child and played with intelligence. He was exceptionally bright and appeared to love life.

Little did I know what was brewing on the inside and what it would ultimately require to overcome. As a part of God's creation, we are endowed with the resources necessary to handle the obstacles that will come into our lives. It begins with learning how to protect ourselves from the external issues of life such as the basic elements of nature, extreme weather, dangerous animals, and maladjusted people. Of course, this is known as self-preservation. Some of these responses are learned, and others are innate. The same is true with the internal enemies that we face. There has to be a strategy in place to defend ourselves against emotions' becoming free radicals roaming about in our psyche, influencing our behavior in negative ways, and attaching themselves to anything they can get their tentacles around.

In the world of chemistry, free radicals are molecular structures that are highly reactive. This means that in order for them to gain stability, they have to react to their surroundings. So they attack the nearest stable molecule, "stealing" its electron. When that happens, the formerly stable molecule becomes unstable and turns into a free radical itself, beginning a chain reaction. As you may remember from high school, atoms consist of a nucleus, neutrons, protons, and electrons. Cells split when two electrons are formed within the atom. In some cases, the split is not clean and the remaining molecule is left with an odd-shaped, unpaired electron. Environmental factors can also cause this impairment, such as radiation, pollution, cigarette smoke, and insecticides. Vitamin E and others have been found to minimize free radical damage and in some cases repair it.[7]

So it is with the emotions, I believe. When certain emotions

---

7 "Antioxidants and Free Radicals," Retrieved from http://www.rice.edu/~jenky/sports/antiox.html; HealthCheck Systems, "Understanding Free Radicals and Antioxidants," Retrieved from http://www.healthchecksystems.com/antioxid.htm Accessed 10/20/2014.

go unexpressed and are not dealt with in a proper manner, they become highly reactive and attach themselves to the closest emotion they can identify with that resembles the one someone is actually feeling. One of the healthiest antioxidants to repair and prevent a chain reaction of these emotions is play. In this environment, emotions are allowed to run their course safely and intentionally. If you have noticed, most animals engage in some form of play, which we have come to understand as preparation for the survival of their species. In the case of the human species, the same is true. The ability to relate to others socially is directly connected to the idea of play. For instance, consider the game hide and seek. Do you remember how you felt when you were attempting to hide? There no doubt was excitement, anticipation, and a sense of superiority. And of course, if and when you were discovered, anger, frustration, and even disappointment could occur. None of these emotions stayed long enough to cause any degree of difficulty because, in due time, it would be your turn to seek. When you imposed the same kind of thing on others as you became the seeker, the exchange of roles became a powerful antioxidant, nullifying emotional free radicalism.

In order for you to appreciate this kind of thinking, you have to realize that a child's response to the major issues of life is going to be determined by how that child plays. We have come to understand this to some degree, I'm certain, but I do not believe we have associated the child's emotional well-being and healthy development to the child's ability to play. This is the place where trouble surfaces and can be handled most effectively if incorporated into the game itself. Their reactions have to be taken seriously and observed carefully, not just corrected for the sake of peace.

Several books have been published concerning play as therapy, but my concern is play viewed as a device to detect problems before there becomes a need for therapy. Outward behavior does have an impact on what's going on inside of you. Proverbs 17:22 declares, "A cheerful heart is good medicine" (NIV). The attitude that you take does influence you internally. Situations must be developed in order to provide an outlet for emotions that may be deformed or odd shaped. Something has to be done before they begin to look for an outlet that is inappropriate in its expression. Once an emotion is stolen, it has a tendency to function improperly even when it is expressed at the proper time. This can be seen in such cases as joy being expressed for acquiring success but at someone else's expense. Enthusiasm can be exhibited but with ulterior motives, or remorse can be shown for the tragedy of someone else with no concern to help but for the soothing of your conscious because of a similar experience.

Play offers an opportunity to categorize those feelings and express them in a controlled environment. This is how play, as an antioxidant, works. When the game is being played, whether it is formal or self-made, the main focus of the parent is to observe the child's activity and their responses to different scenarios. Have you ever played the game Claim the Car in which the participants claimed a passing car to become "the owner"? It sounded like this: "I got that Bentley," "That's my Cadillac," and so on. I believe a child's value system is being forged as a result of such play. Notes must be taken for future discussions or research into the choices that are made. As a parent, you can initiate this game whenever you and your children are driving in your car or in anyone's car, for that matter. Just play close attention to the choices and discuss them later under the appropriate circumstances. The kinds of things that you are looking for are as follows:

1. What happens when your child wins?
2. How does he or she respond to losing?

3. How long do they rejoice, and what accompanies their rejoicing?
4. Is there any concern for the opponent's feelings, either good or bad?
5. How is the relationship after the game is over?
6. What were their choices (cars or trucks)?

These and other responses will become key to future discussions surrounding behavior that will emerge in relationships outside of play. I have heard some say that winning isn't everything; it is the only thing. This sounds good, but if it reaches the psyche of a troubled child, it will serve as a catalyst to many other types of negative behavioral patterns. In the case at hand, "it's not whether you win or lose but how you play the game" is a better way of approaching this type of play. Remember, we are looking for deformed and depraved atomic tendencies (Adamic nature). All of us fit into this category, including our children, regardless of how well-adjusted we may be. The chances of a clean split are far better within the context of a whole atom or family in this case. The thing that we are trying to address is the operating system of a person, which is developed in childhood. The way you respond to circumstances in play will be similar to the way you respond to them in adulthood. Your way of responding to problems or decision-making responsibilities becomes your operating system. Jordan Ayan, in his book *Ignite Your Creative Spark*, says,

> Fun is a great creativity enhancer. Sometimes the best thing you can do to get your mind thinking creatively is to relax, laugh, and enjoy yourself. Adding fun to any situation can be as easy as sharing a joke, playing a game or going to an amusement park. The key is to figure out what is fun for you, and then make it a point to do it

> more often. What counts is finding a way to let your "child" out.[8]

Let me add, "and let your child in." Each time a problem develops, you have a tendency to respond to it in the same way you did before. Through constructive play, the proper way of responding can be encouraged. It is the equivalent of upgrading the operating system in a computer. In doing so in the life of troubled children, their developmental systems must be upgraded, training their responses in such a way that a new habit is formed that becomes the automatic response to new circumstances, which can be overridden only by a new set of stimuli. Default behavior is automatic, but the behavior must be chosen and practiced in order to be accessed and appreciated. Troubled children need to know what they like and be encouraged to participate in those areas often through play. In so doing, a default response is being created and reinforced. When they reach adulthood, they may resort to that default response, enabling them to engage in wholesome pressure-releasing activities versus destructive ones.

Jesus has the answer to the overriding new stimuli mentioned above. He told his disciples that he had chosen them to bear fruit (John 15:16). The first thing we see in this statement is that Jesus himself initiated the relationship. That meant that the process began with a selection, but it didn't stop there; it brought with it responsibility—the requirement to bear fruit. In this context, fruit could be anything from more love, joy, or peace and even winning the lost to Christ. But then there is also the practical side of bearing fruit, and that I believe is where you will find the need for a new mind-set. Something is needed to override the existing system that is in place and to do so quickly before the

---

8 Jordan Ayan, *Ignite Your Creative Spark: 20 Ways to Fire Up Your Imagination* (Successories Library, 1999).

person responds in a former way of doing things. We are what we are by nature, and to become something different, we need a new operating system. Our point of view must no longer be the dominant factor in our decision making, replaced by dependence upon God.

That is what is meant by, "...Whatever you ask the Father in My name He may give you," in John 15:16. NIV It indicates the need for input from another source, namely God Himself. Since He is responsible for the blueprint of the original operating system, He knows what is required for an upgrade to take place. From the perspective of Christianity, all of us have an internal virus that affects the way our systems operate. It's called the sin virus, and it's deadlier than Ebola. Children do not have the ability to offset the negatives that are associated with sin. There must be another system installed to override the effects of the existing program. That is the only cure.

As you can well see, our operating system can become complicated, but it can be upgraded not to improve our way of thinking but to replace it with a more effective way of doing things. This of course is all realized through faith. The language that I have been using can be better understood if faith is applied. The circumstances we are experiencing are those of despair, to say the least, but they need not lead us to hopelessness. An upgraded operating system runs best with the supporting program called "faith." Faith is a key element in handling the first signs of trouble. Faith is a powerful alternative to despair. The first thing that needs to be understood about faith is that it is challenging. Acts 14:8–10 points to a man whose operating system had been severely damaged for reasons unknown. He was born crippled and had never walked in his life. Therefore, he did not understand what it meant to stand on his own two feet, which of course is the same plague that affects our immature children. His feet were serving another purpose but not what they were intended to do. This was all that he knew. He had to be told that there was more to life than what he was experiencing. He brought to the table curiosity and wonderment. The apostle Paul observed him intently—that is, he paid attention to what he was doing—and in so doing, he saw something that he otherwise would not have observed. He saw that the man had faith. Faith cannot be recognized with the natural eye; it takes supernatural ability to see it. This was not something that was initiated by Paul. It resulted from paying attention to the behavior of another. An answer that was not present initially was revealed, and an operating system was upgraded. The challenge in all of this was in looking for insight when there was none, looking for answers where there were none, and being patient and considerate enough to give someone else a chance to stand on his own feet and not to allow him to continue in the troubled state he was in. In many ways, the same is true in child development. Children only know what comes naturally. All other behavior has to be learned. As parents, we have the opportunity to look for things that they cannot see on their own and call on them to meet the challenge of responding differently than the way that they feel.

Of course, this kind of thinking comes with conditions, the first of which is to look for something good in the midst of all the negative that may be occurring. The apostle Paul saw something because he ignored the immediate condition and recognized that, in the midst of it, something positive was brewing. It's not easy to find good things in death with the natural eye, but opportunities can and do open up when faith is activated. Most negatives have a positive side to them if examined carefully. Troubled children—all children, for that matter—need to know that there are ways to express themselves without bringing harm to others or themselves. Drastic measures in some cases may be necessary, but it can be done. When the eye of faith is engaged, rage can be converted into enthusiasm, impatience can evolve into creativity, and anger can become the energy source necessary to handle the need for control in the future.

Investigation plays a major role in assisting those who need to understand how life and feelings work regardless of the way things may be. Most pursuits in life have rules that have to be adhered to for success to be experienced. When these are violated, problems occur and life becomes unusually difficult. As we have seen to some degree, feelings also have rules that have to be followed; they were designed to be expressed, and when they aren't expressed at the proper time and in the proper manner, they become harmful. In other words, a rule has been broken and a price must be paid in order for restoration to take place. Once this is known, it becomes the obligation of those who are familiar with the rules to respond accordingly. It is within this context that trust is established and real progress can take place. Even those who disagree with them will applaud anybody who is willing to take the time to find the positive side of negative behavior.

It takes courage to interfere with a person's predetermined way of doing things. It takes confidence to address issues that may prove to be harmful when there is no evidence whatsoever that harm will be done. It takes faith to see things in this manner when there may not be any accompanying feelings to support your actions. The phrase "Things will be all right" has a shelf life, and when its expiration date has passed, those kinds of remarks are not helpful at all. Faith, as was the case with the apostle Paul, has to be seen in others, even when you may be lacking it yourself. Communicating this truth is not an easy thing to do, but the benefits far outweigh the degree of difficulty that may be involved. This all has to do with expectations. Enough has been said about the need for recognition, but much more needs

to be said about the power of expectations. These tie directly into maintaining hope, which is a key element in the overall scheme of things. When hope is lost, one stops trying; when hope is lost, all horizons become shorter. A shortened horizon exposes the end prematurely, and when the end is always in view, the possibility of the future is clouded. It also causes too much emphasis to be placed on what is visible rather than on what is unseen. Here, potential has no limits and the possibilities are endless.

Remember, unheard melodies are sometimes sweeter than those that we hear. Approaching your relationship with your child with this in mind will enable you to see things that you would normally miss, vital things that at some point in time will prove to be life changing and attitude altering. There were times when my son exhibited behavior that was troubling but not severe enough to cause me any concern. As I consider those things in hindsight, I can get glimpses of a pattern that was in progress all along. Once a behavior becomes a habit, it operates on autopilot. The only way to offset this kind of thing is to create options for your child to choose from. Then the child will have more than that one automatic option to choose from. With the proper motivation of concern, parents who have taken the time to steer activities through play will reap a harvest of positive decision-making and an abundance of responsible character traits. Keep in mind that all of what we do and say is dependent upon the power of God and His intervention.

Human nature has a built-in response system that, if left alone, will tend to lean toward inappropriate behavior. This is due to that virus that is lying dormant, waiting to be aroused by the right type of circumstances. It can begin with a dysfunctional family structure or a disappointed outcome. It does not take much to stir up activity in the disease-ridden terrain of a sinful nature. It all started in the Garden of Eden and has affected all that we

do ever since. Those of you who may not subscribe to this kind of thinking can substitute your own name for it. Undoubtedly you will find that the outcome will be the same—inappropriate behavior. As Christians, we live believing not by seeing, and seeing what we believe normally comes after any action is taken. The heart is helpless in trying to conform itself to new ideas and offsetting the wickedness that lurks within. This is why we are prone to do things that go against our moral standards. Decision making is going to be warped even in the best of circumstances; how much more in the heart of a disappointed child. This is a hard lesson for a parent to learn and is clearly identifiable by statements such as, "My child would not do that." At the risk of sounding too morbid, this kind of thinking, if left unaddressed, can lead to a faulty belief system that makes it possible to believe that your child is not capable of doing anything wrong. Such thinking is an indication that correcting your child is no longer a priority; instead, finding an excuse that is suitable to address any immediate concern is. There is an innate desire on the part of children to please those who have authority over them. When you cover the truth or refuse to face it, you run the risk of allowing some other authority figure to take your place.

One of the greatest difficulties that we have as parents is that of penetrating the minds of our children. It is a known fact that independence is a sought-after commodity by us all, but its conception took place early on in life and was developed to a greater or lesser degree depending upon the conditions under which it was born. When you face a need in life, the natural tendency is to satisfy that need yourself. When you cannot achieve that satisfaction personally, another means—that may not have the capability of satisfying that need—could be resorted to. When it does meet the need and the manner of satisfaction is repeatable, a dependence upon having that need met in like manner in the

future is established. If and when the satisfier receives a return on meeting the need, he or she too becomes eager to satisfy future needs. As complicated as this may sound, it simply means that an enabling relationship has been established.

When this happens, a greater difficulty than was in the initial problem emerges, and an ongoing cycle of failure and defeat continues until someone breaks the cycle. This type of relationship is forged over an extended period of time, and the longer it goes on, the stronger it becomes. It gains strength and momentum that ultimately becomes a contributing factor to future problems. If this has been your experience, take heart and be encouraged; most of us are guilty of looking back and feeling guilty about what we didn't do. But keep this in mind—as long as your intentions were good, God honors that.

It's all about intention, not outcome. That is left up to the Lord. When codependency has reached its maturity, no sacrifice is too great to ensure that the relationship will continue. I believe this can be curtailed in the arena of play if it is conducted deliberately and intentionally. It doesn't take much to create scenarios from different types of games, most of which will enable you to interject a principle here and there naturally based on the flow of the game. This will offer the opportunity to develop this mind-set and come up with creative ways to deal with it. Try games such as Scrabble, Monopoly, and Pokeno, for starters. For example, let's say you are playing Pokeno. The rules are as follows: each player except the dealer is given a board and some chips. The dealer shuffles an ordinary deck of fifty-two playing cards and turns the top card over, calling it out—for example, "Jack of spades." Each player who has the Jack of spades on his or her board covers it with a chip. The dealer continues turning over cards in succession, and the players continue covering cards on their boards until someone has covered a complete row of five, either horizontally or vertically. The player calls, "Out." The player who wins becomes the next dealer.

Becoming the dealer indicates that you have won, and your role changes. The person who was dependent upon the dealer now becomes the one upon whom others are dependent. Words to this affect can be shared with the winner to reinforce the process of disrupting the enabling syndrome. What begins to emerge is a clear balance of dependence and being dependent upon. In time, the child unconsciously begins to operate accordingly in other, more significant relationships. The manner in which the game is played and the intensity that is shown in any given area reveals the general make-up of the person responding. If the player becomes frustrated, upset, and aggressive in an attempt to win by circumventing the rules of the game, trouble is on the horizon, and an opportunity to address the issue needs to be taken.

Frustration is a very real deterrent to responding to life if handled inappropriately. Those who are successful in coping with it productively are those who tend to succeed in life. A close eye must be kept on those who respond negatively. Creating situations where it can be monitored will prove to be much more effective than attempting to curtail it in the midst of real-life situations. Games offer the former possibilities for doing so.. It may not be practical for you to implement this kind of practice in your busy schedule, so I propose that you incorporate it into your daily routine. Paying attention to what's going on around you and then taking advantage of every opportunity can do that. The influences of the world and its systematic way of dismantling wholesome structure can also be overcome. But like any other challenge that you may face, it requires determination, patience, and discipline. Wisdom does not come easily or hastily; it comes from revelation that is provided by God to those who have learned the art of combining spiritual thoughts with spiritual activities.

Never forget that you have an internal teacher who is always in the classroom with additional information and insight to provide for those who ask for it, who look for it, and are willing to wait for it. Patience will prove to be an asset if you allow things to unfold naturally. Keep in mind that patience is an attitude, not a pace.

Some of these ideas may be resisted and conflict could develop, but if you keep in mind your overall objective, the very resistance that comes can be used as a tool to further not only your understanding of yourself but also the response of your child. This should not be viewed as failure or even negative for that matter because resistance can serve as a support to propel you into a deeper understanding of what needs to be done in the future. Jetliners can take off safely only with the proper resistance from the wind. It lifts the plane and causes flight. Resistance in your case is similar in that it can lift you above the immediate circumstances and provide you with a viewpoint that is normally invisible from ground level. So whenever resistance arises, remember your flight plan, which requires you to operate according to the instrument panel and not by what you see. Your faith must rest in the power of God and not in your experience or your position. Stability comes not from depending upon yourself but from dependence upon God and adherence to His flight plan. This requires adjustments to the faith factor, which is an instrument that gives readings that appear to be contradictory to what is actually going on but always results in a positive outcome. Sometimes you may feel like you are flying upside down, but you must trust God's instrument panel to realize that you are still on course. It also assures you of a safe landing when the weather becomes extremely turbulent. It's not unusual to become frightened in the midst of a devastating loss. As a matter of fact, it should be understood that fear is part of the instrument panel that is designed to give guidance in the midst of the storm. Storms do that to you. They provide a heightened sense of urgency caused by the activity going on around you. This in turn makes you aware of available resources that were previously unknown while enabling you to rely upon the stability of God.

Included on that instrument panel is a gauge that I call honesty. Being in a frightening situation only gets worse when you attempt to cover up the reality of what you are feeling. This approach creates confusion and doubt and in some causes a sense of hopelessness. Thinking becomes clouded, and personal growth stops or at best becomes severely stunted. I have found that one of the best ways to avoid this natural tendency when times get troubled is to give yourself permission and time to experience whatever it is that you may be going through. When you face the issues head on in this manner, it defuses the anxiety of the unknown and fleshes out the true nature of what you may be experiencing. Facing life's issues this way is necessary for continual progress. Listening to what's going on inside of you becomes a very real platform for further understanding. Denying the things that you may be experiencing only prolongs the process.

The challenge of personal awareness is to prevent the information being disclosed from overwhelming you with negative feelings, regardless of how negative things may appear. Control becomes the key issue to handling it properly. Once a period of time has been designated to face the challenge, it must be adhered to tenaciously. Openness not only ushers information in but also flushes out unwanted information as well. The designated time parameters will provide adequate space for this transition to take place. You cannot just forget; you have to remove and replace. This takes systematic planning, and that requires time. Periodically there can be some traffic tie-ups due to the amount and nature of the information passing through the highway of your memory. Emotions are one of the biggest causes of this internal traffic jam. They seem to have a mind of their own. But what really matters is the flow of positive traffic, which always occurs when you put a time limit on negatives. Keep in mind that honesty serves as a police officer that directs traffic from the standpoint of knowledge the likes of which you do not have access to. In most cases, it is for your protection.

Emotions are your friend as long as they are kept under control. We have no trouble with that statement as long as the emotions are positive and pleasurable. But when they become uncomfortable to us, the problems begin. I like to view emotions that occur in the midst of a loss as reminders of inside work being done on my behalf. It fits into the category of what I call replacement therapy. In other words, whenever a negative emotion arises, I automatically consider it. In order for me to fully appreciate a positive emotion, the opposite and negative emotion must be made obvious so that it can be removed, which then clears the way for the positive to take over. A good example of this can be found in Isaiah 61:1 and 3, where the prophet declares that the lord will "Bind up the broken hearted, comfort those who mourn, and provide for those who grieve in Zion." He goes on to say that God will "Give a crown of beauty instead of ashes, the oil of gladness instead of mourning, and a garment of praise instead of a spirit of despair" (NIV). The point is that these positives can only be experienced after you have come to recognize the existence and need for the removal of their counterparts, which are negatives. Honesty helps to speed this process along. Occasionally you may find yourself leaning toward the negative side of this transaction, which is often the case when loss is experienced. This need not discourage you, but rather it should be used as a signal to prompt you to thank God for his replacement therapy, recognizing the source of these constant reminders and what they are designed to do. The devil does not want you to thank God for anything, so he discourages it whenever and wherever he can. And so is the case with thanks being offered for what may be negative at the moment. If it brings honor and praise to God, it will be discouraged even if it means removing the very thing that was designed to bring you difficulty. He refuses to participate in anything that promotes the Lord in a positive manner. You will find circumstances changing when this approach is applied.

Every so often, your life may feel like it will never return to normal—this is normal. There is always going to be some mystery attached to your personal understanding of what God may be doing at any given time. This is not designed to confuse but to build confidence and assurance in the capability of God. Death still has some mystery attached to it even though it has been around for a long time and is known and acknowledged by most, if not all. But when it strikes in a disproportionate manner not fitting into the statistical norm, such as children dying before their parents, then it can bring with it a heightened sense of disillusionment. The devastation increases on the basis of the relationship that you had with the deceased. Remember that no matter how much information you have, you still do not have all of the facts. No matter how well you knew your child, there are still some things that you were not privy to. Consider your own upbringing—did your parents know it all? This automatically places most situations into the category of mysterious. But keep in mind that God knows the end from the beginning. He knows the past that did not happen, He knows the future that will not happen, and He knows what's best for what we are currently experiencing. He makes His decisions on the basis of what He knows, not on what we may know.

We are driven by what we can see, hear, touch, taste, and smell, so when we are required to operate on the basis of something outside of normal parameters, we are lost as to what to do. Normal is not as simple as it initially appears. It's defined on the basis of each individual situation as it appears within the general rule of thumb. I'm certain that you have heard the term "new normal." It fits situations in which a large number of people find themselves or can easily relate to those who have lost a child. Trial and error will prove to be the best way of handling what cannot be seen and adjusting to this new normal. Once you determine what direction honesty is leading, you can follow that direction with full assurance that the instrument gauge is correct regardless of how you may feel, what you do not know, or the way things may appear. God enjoys revealing mysteries to those who are mature enough to handle the outcome—that is, if you search for it with your whole heart (Prov. 2:4 NIV). Peace is by far the greatest determining factor of a safe landing. It is the thing that will keep you balanced in the midst of turbulence, no matter what the wind velocity. We have to keep in mind that the Lord is always dealing with us on at least three levels of our lives. The first level is that of the heart, our central control system, the thing that motivates us, our purpose for living. That would include your attitude. The attitude that you take at the beginning of most of what you do will determine the results of that activity more than your performance. That includes intelligence, training, skill, money, and prestige, to name few. It is your attitude that will make the difference. This is what the heart generates. What the Lord expects of us in terms of our attitude is that we would "Be joyful always" (1 Thess. 5:16 NIV). It's not easy for us to do anything consistently, so to be told to rejoice in that manner is indeed a challenge. Furthermore, the emotional stress that death leaves makes matters even worse. A definition of the biblical idea of the word joyful" as it is found in the original language may be of some help here. It actually means "an attitude of calm happiness." That definition brings with it enough insight to level the playing field. A calm attitude of happiness can be defined as a steady acceptance of the way things are regardless of the degree of difficulty involved in doing so. Calm happiness exudes with confidence in a future that may not have all of the details concerning its outcome. Calm happiness expresses itself in a manner that is attractive to others because of the stability it provides.

You cannot separate peace from prayer; they go hand in hand. The Bible commands us to participate in prayer in the same manner in which we are encouraged to rejoice, without stopping, or in the terms of 1 Thessalonians 5:17 (NIV), without ceasing. That word *without ceasing*, when attached to prayer, brings with it the meaning of "constant" or "frequently that is never ending." Anything that's done ceaselessly will automatically become associated with the person who is carrying it out. In this case, prayer and the one praying become inseparable. During biblical days, the word without ceasing was used to describe a nagging cough, which enables us to understand the association of the word with that of prayer. A cough is not continual, as it occurs in intervals over a period of time. If that time should extend beyond a twenty-four-hour period, it could be said that a person was coughing all day long. This is the metaphor surrounding the act of ceaseless praying.

Peace, then, can be continuous in the sense that it comes in intervals during the course of any given day. As we are maintaining a calm sense of happiness, we experience the ongoing confidence that spurs us on to do all that is necessary in the face of insurmountable odds. Because we have focused our attention on the instrument panel and not on our abilities or the things surrounding us to remain afloat, we will soon find ourselves not only flying comfortably, but in due time we may even come to appreciate and enjoy the flight.

Progress is what we are all looking to accomplish, and with the right attitude it can be achieved. Attitude regulates character.

It's important to know what that progress looks like so that it can be appreciated when it arrives. When trouble no longer frightens you, you are making progress. When you refuse to run from your responsibility in any direction or to anything as a means of relief other than the Lord Himself, you are making progress. Keep in mind that you do not have to be in motion to run. You can be running right where you sit. When you are open and honest about your feelings, you are making progress. When you are able to give encouragement to someone else, you are making progress. The joy in this journey is in the trip, in addition to arriving at your destination.

We must always keep in mind that the instrument panel is not only there to give direction, but also included in its design is the distance we have traveled and the distance we still have to go. These will help us plan for the journey and make adjustments where necessary. In order to reach your destination, you have to stay on course. One degree may not appear to be damaging initially, but in the long run it can throw you off by hundreds of miles. One bad decision can set you back by years. The evidence of what's being experienced on the inside will clearly be seen on the outside when the gauges are operating properly. These instrument readings will help us keep in touch with what we can call vital signs of good mental, emotional, and spiritual health. A mind at peace is a mind that is open to explore opportunities outside of immediate circumstances. It does not get bogged down with the surrounding negative stimuli as we have described elsewhere. Every time you decide to violate what you know to be right, you impede your progress. When that happens, you distort your perspective, push yourself further into despair, and short-circuit your thought process. When thoughts become distorted in this regard, they often lead to selfishness and self-centeredness. This state of mind can only lead to regret and the rehearsing of the original pain that was experienced when trouble began.

Not all but some of these things can be avoided if your responses to the first signs of trouble are well thought through. This insight will help steer your child in a direction that will give him or her a better alternative. The very course of your child's life could be altered as a result. Let me emphasize, though, that as much as I would like to say that you could avoid all trouble if you pay attention to your child's behavior, I cannot in good faith say that. But I can say that looking for early warning signs can prove to be an effective tool in handling potential problems.

The course of Conan's life was altered. He made choices on the basis of internal promptings that I do not believe he understood. The complications that surrounded his life intensified internally, causing him to respond to life with a clouded picture of what things actually were. His responses to challenges and responsibilities in general were never handled as effectively as they could have been because of some valuable lessons that were never fully understood or ultimately internalized. I have some regrets in life, but one thing I do not regret is the desire that I have always had to see my children succeed and to do whatever necessary to ensure that their success would be lasting. What I long to do at this point in life is to now capitalize on what the results were. In the case of Conan, it was a tragic ending, and it has left me with several possibilities. I can continue with life, as I understand it to be. Or I can now improve upon life by taking advantage of every opportunity to encourage those who have not yet arrived at their destinations. In life, we are always faced with two options: 1) Become victims of our circumstances, or 2) Become masters of our own fate. The ups and downs of life must be interpreted differently if we are going to benefit from those areas that we do not understand and even dislike. But you are always faced with a choice. When life began with Conan, it was filled with expectation and excitement, from the nursery to the home to school and to college. There was always a hint of disappointment attached to each one of these transitions. At the time, the reason was not clear to me since each instance resembled normal childhood resistance or rebellion. Trouble in these areas was just so common. What separated him from others was consistency. No matter what the accomplishment was, it was always accompanied with intentional sabotage. This kind of thing occurred time and time again, so much so that it got to the point that I expected it. Whenever there was a positive result from any given area, I would brace myself for the negative repercussions. He just did not like success.

Whenever there is consistent resistance to positive performance, it should be viewed as a sign of a much deeper problem. This can be a difficult sign to identify simply because of the innate desire you may have for the problem to be a part of a phase that will soon pass. But it must not be viewed as such for the sake of eliminating the problem before it becomes even further entrenched in the psyche of your child. One thing that has been proven to help in this area is to talk about the negative side of success and how it is arrived at, such as the motive that accompanies it. We often think that success is to be achieved because it is the right thing to do, but there are other reasons that some pursue success, and those may or may not be positive. When you pursue success to please someone else, that is a negative reason for pursuing success. If you pursue success to prove that you are better than your competitors, it is for the wrong reason. Failure with genuine motivation is far better than success for the wrong reason.

Failure then becomes the objective that must be clearly understood if you have an overachieving child who continues to respond negatively to his or her success. You must always keep in mind that the effect of all actions is cumulative, not immediate.

So the issues that one experiences must be viewed from this perspective.

- The things that can be undone should be handled accordingly.
- Remove any distractions that may prevent your children from facing the reality of their behavior.
- Love your children unconditionally.
- Accept them as they are, keeping in mind that part of them is actually you.
- Take time to talk to them when things are going well and when things are not.
- Invite the support of those who are in like circumstances; their input can be priceless.
- Place a high value on the success of your children and go the extra mile to make sure your communications to them are clear and that their success is clearly understood.
- Maintain high expectations for your children, knowing that they are always under the protection of God.

Let me say this because I feel you may be experiencing some degree of fear depending upon where you are in your circumstances. General Stonewall Jackson said, "My religious belief teaches me to feel as safe in battle as in bed. God has fixed the time for my death. I do not concern myself about that, but to always be ready, no matter when it may overtake me."[9] Taking that thought a step further, Hebrews 9:27 (NIV) tells us that death is a divine appointment, which brings with it the promise of judgment. God holds the power of life and death in His hands,

---

9 GoodReads, "Stonewall Jackson," Retrieved from https://www.goodreads.com/author/quotes/546888.Stonewall_Jackson. Accessed 11/21/2013

and He determines the time when it is to take place. I always marvel at those who feel that people can die prematurely. If that is the case, then you have to believe that some people live longer than they should. Everybody dies on time. All you need to do is look at nature and you'll find that some animals do not make it to adulthood. Predators attack and kill whatever is available. Birds fall out of nests; as a matter of fact, some are pushed out of nests by siblings, and lions have a reputation for eating young male lions. We are a part of God's creation, and life ends for us at different intervals. Psalm 139:16 (NASB) says it best: "Your eyes have seen my unformed substance; and in Your book were all written the days that were ordained for me, when as yet there was not one of them." So it makes no difference how the death occurred, how it will occur, or when it occurred; the author of that experience, who is God and God alone, had to approve of it. Our responsibility is to follow this admonition: "Teach us to number our days and recognize how few they are; help us to spend them as we should" (Psalm 90:12 The Living Bible, or TLB). All deaths come across His desk for final approval. Of course, there will be some who disagree with this way of thinking, and that is understandable. But let me caution you to remember that there is a mystery associated with God, and some things will never be completely understood. Those things that God has revealed to us are to be handled in a way that our response helps others, not hinders them, and I believe the scriptures are clear on this issue.

God expects us to experience His peace as we journey through this life. He wants you to do what's required of you, and He will do what is required of Him. The depth of the Lord's concern about that peace being a part of our existence can be seen by one of the names He identifies Himself with: Jehovah Shalom. It means "The Lord is Peace," and it is a description of the deepest desire and need of the human heart. It brings with it the greatest measure of contentment. When it is fully understood, it frees you from the fear of the future. One of our greatest concerns as parents is whether or not our children are going to avoid some of the many pitfalls that lie ahead of them as they progress through the maze of life. God's peace will bring you stability and balance as you observe them on this journey. Of course, peace is an easy thing to talk about but something altogether different to experience. As a matter of fact, it is elusive for many because it has requirements attached to it. You must establish a relationship with God and be obedient to a life that honors Him. Like any other discipline, there are rules that must be followed, and obedience is one of them. "Oh, that you had listened to my commands! Then you would have had peace flowing like a gentle river and righteousness rolling over you like waves in the sea" (Is. 48:18 NLT).

Another is that of faith. We have talked about that briefly elsewhere, but faith is absolutely essential to sustain the peace of God. It is an ongoing battle to maintain a positive attitude toward life when you lose a child. The peace of God is the only thing that can sustain you throughout. As a matter of fact, this peace can be as consistent as a river. "This is what the Lord says: 'I will give Jerusalem a river of peace and prosperity. The wealth of the nations will flow to her. Her children will be nursed at her breasts, carried in her arms, and held on her lap. I will comfort you there in Jerusalem as a mother comforts her child'" (Is. 66:12 NLT). Peace is related to a flowing river, which sometimes rises and falls with the surrounding conditions. Drought can cause a river to subside, while excessive rain can cause a river to flood. But in both cases, the river continues to exist. Peace can be affected by those moments when the memories of your loved one floods your soul with constant reminders of what it was like or could have been like, reminders that bring an overwhelming sense of grief resulting in weakness and despair. These reminders are to be viewed as debris floating with the current of an ever-flowing river of peace. From time to time, this will occur due to pollution that is self-induced or by those who have contaminated it with insensitivity and, in some cases, inconsiderate recklessness. What needs to happen at this point is for you to, first of all, recognize that the objects in the river will pass as long as the river continues to flow. The focus then should not be on the debris but on the ebb and flow of the water level of peace.

I would like to identify that ebb and flow as the fluctuating presence of God moving away from surrounding circumstances and back into your heart, just as the water returns to the sea during low tide. When the tide rises, it brings with it the good and the unwanted. In the sense of God's peace, the unwanted, even though it may be visible, has been brought to the surface only to be flushed from your heart and back into the sea of your memory banks to give you a fresh view of God's presence. This ebbing and flowing of memories are actually going through a filtering process. The removal of debris from the heart keeps the heart from becoming bitter. What was once viewed as an obstacle now becomes a reminder of the power of God. It is absolutely essential that we always be on the lookout for God's presence in the midst of all of our thoughts because sometimes the flow of the river can become so violent that our visibility can be affected by it. In such cases, you will learn the value of yielding to God. To yield to God is to remain in fellowship with him. He then serves as the life raft that keeps you afloat amid the most turbulent of waters. Yielding to God is to say yes to His will and to view reminders as signals of the cleansing process that's taking place in your heart. Out of the heart flows the issues of life, and it needs to be kept clean. Out of the heart flows the direction of your future, and it must be kept open. Out of the heart flows the desire to do God's will and it must be kept active. When the waters of the heart are not allowed to flow, they become stagnant and ultimately diseased. This is the penalty of resisting the will of God and not yielding to Him. Isaiah 57:20–21 (NLT) puts it this way: "But those who still reject me are like the restless sea, which is never still but continually churns up mud and dirt. 'There is no peace for the wicked,' says my God." As you can see, there is nothing but restlessness for those who lose sight of what God is doing, who trust in their own judgments, and who prefer to do things their way apart from God. The passengers on ocean liners that are in trouble do not put their hopes in the attitude of the captain but in the captains ability to navigate the ship through the turbulence based on his or her knowledge of the sea and command of the ship. God, my friend, not only has the right attitude and knowledge and understanding of the sea, He created it. And He knows what you are capable of doing. Let him control the helm as he navigates you through these troubling experiences, no matter how frightening these signs of trouble may be. Unfortunately, we have reduced God's peace to a feeling when in reality, it is much, much more. It's God's peace that enabled the church fathers of history to endure extreme suffering in the face of undeniable mistreatment with poise and resolve.

Thomas Cranmer was Archbishop of Canterbury in the days of Henry VIII, and he defended the position that Henry's marriage to Katharine of Aragon (Spain) was null and void. When Edward came to the throne, Cranmer was foremost in translating the worship of the Church into English (his friends and enemies agree that he was an extraordinarily gifted translator) and securing the use of the new forms of worship. When Mary came to the throne, Cranmer was in a quandary. He had believed, with a fervor that many people today will find hard to understand, that it is the duty of every Christian to obey the monarch and that "the powers that be are ordained of God" (Rom. 13 NIV). As long as the monarch was ordering things that Cranmer thought well, it was easy for Cranmer to believe that the king was sent by God's providence to guide the people in the path of true religion and that disobedience to the king was disobedience to God. Now Mary was queen and commanding him to return to the Roman obedience. Cranmer five times wrote a letter of submission to the Pope and to Roman Catholic doctrines, and four times he tore it up. In the end, he submitted. However, Mary was unwilling to believe that the submission was sincere, and he was ordered to be burned at Oxford on March 21, 1556. At the very end, he repudiated his final letter of submission and announced that he died a Protestant. He said, "I have sinned, in that I signed with my hand what I did not believe with my heart. When the flames are lit, this hand shall be the first to burn." And when the fire was lit around his feet, he leaned forward and held his right hand in the fire until it was charred to a stump. Aside from this, he did not speak or move, except that once he raised his left hand to wipe the sweat from his forehead.

In 1555 Nicholas Ridley was burned at the stake because of his witness for Christ. On the night before his execution, his brother offered to remain with him in the prison chamber to be of assistance and comfort. Nicholas declined the offer and replied that he meant to go to bed and sleep as quietly as ever he had in his life. Because he knew the peace of God and had the peace of God, he could rest in the strength of the everlasting arms of his Lord to meet his need.

Hugh Latimer was famous as a preacher. He was Bishop of Worcester (pronounced WOOS-ter) in the time of King Henry but resigned in protest against the king's refusal to allow the Protestant reforms that Latimer desired. Latimer's sermons speak little of doctrine; he preferred to urge men to upright living and devoutness in prayer. But when Mary came to the throne, he was arrested, tried for heresy, and burned together with his friend Nicholas Ridley. His last words at the stake are well known: "Be of good cheer, Master Ridley, and play the man, for we shall this day light such a candle in England as I trust by God's grace shall never be put out."[10]

Jesus himself has perfected our peace and has promised the assurance of its continuation based on our obedience in believing that he is peace and has freely made it available to those who believe in Him. He is the author, auditor, and the authority behind the peace of those who believe (Heb. 13:20 NIV). His peace cannot be shaken; it is beyond disturbance, it surpasses the intentions of the heart, and once in motion it has a natural progression beginning with the peace with God (Rom. 5:1 NIV) and then moving to experiencing the peace of God (Phil. 4:9 NIV) followed by peace with others and circumstances, no matter how troublesome they may be (Heb. 12:14 NIV), all of which will enable us to endure any and all extremes. Our resolve has to be to maintain our focus on the God of peace, not the flames of discord or disappointment, and we must be willing to subject ourselves to the pain associated with our loss knowing that if we allow Him to burn off the dross of our lives, we will emerge powerful witnesses who will far outlive the difficulty associated with our immediate circumstances.

Prayer

Keep us, O Lord, constant in faith and zealous in witness, in spite of what may be troubling us at this time. We have the examples of others to encourage us; help us to utilize this privilege. As we reflect upon those who have gone on before us, may it

---

10 *Wikipedia,* "Nicholas Ridley (martyr)," Retrieved from en.wikipedia.org/wiki/Nicholas_Ridley_(martyr). Accessed 12/12/2013

challenge us to a deeper commitment to you and a determination to not be afraid of anything but to live in your fear alone in everything and rest in your peace for the sake of our Lord and Savior Jesus Christ, your Son, who is the forerunner of all that we will ever experience, including death.

Memory Verses
Hebrews 13:20–21

As the journey of loss unfolds, it brings with it possibilities and problems. Noticeable inconsistencies, if not handled properly, can result in major complications along the way. When this happens, normal feelings can turn into anger. When you view it as normal, it can be transformed into positive energy for adjustment and change.

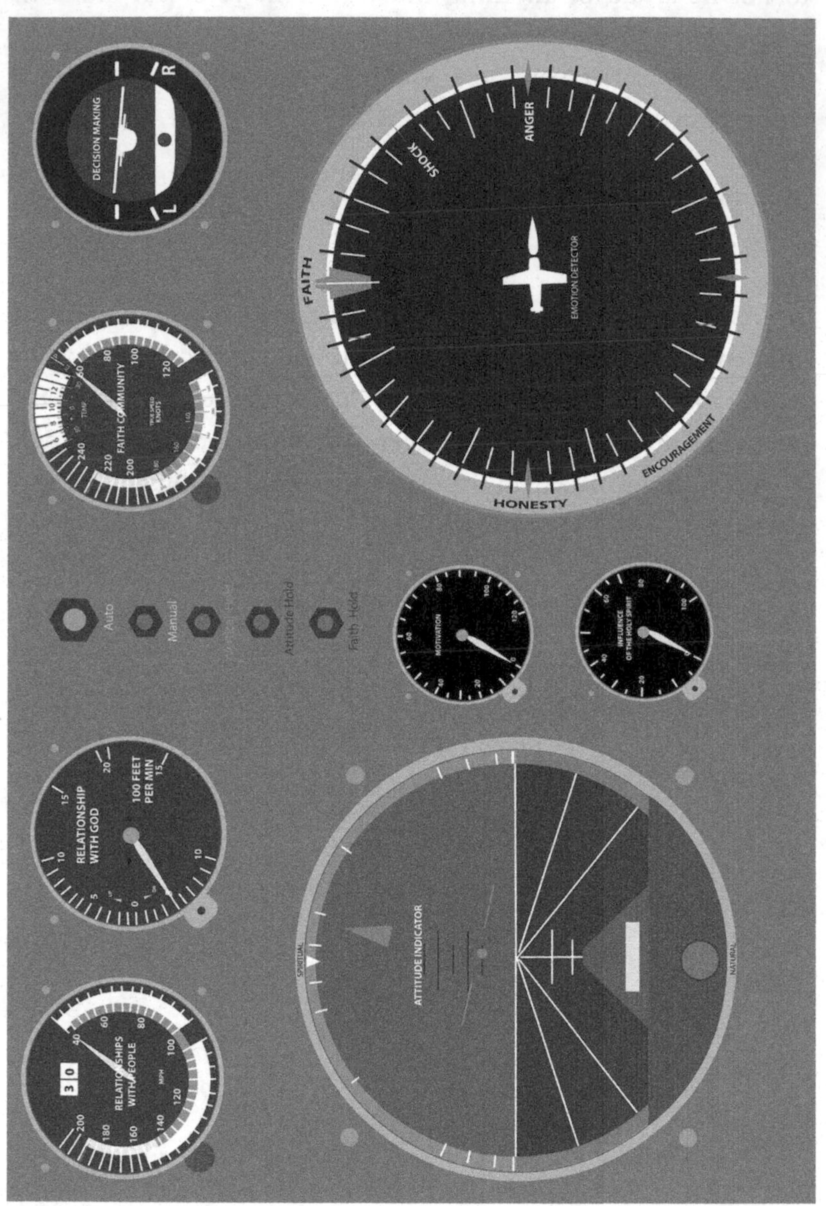
DECISION MAKING
L
R
FAITH COMMUNITY
TRUE SPEED KNOTS
EMOTION DETECTOR
FAITH
SHOCK
ANGER
HONESTY
ENCOURAGEMENT
Auto
Manual
Attitude Hold
Faith Hold
MOTIVATION
INFLUENCE OF THE HOLY SPIRIT
RELATIONSHIP WITH GOD
100 FEET PER MIN
RELATIONSHIPS WITH PEOPLE
MPH
ATTITUDE INDICATOR
SPIRITUAL
NATURAL

Chapter 3

The Prison Call

From a layman's perspective, the penal system is structured and designed on multiple levels. It begins with juvenile offenses on level one and moves all the way through to maximum security in adulthood. I have drawn this conclusion on the basis of my personal observations of how the system treated Conan. I must say this very candidly: as confusing as this system may appear to be to those who have ever encountered it, there has been a lot of thought put into it, and it is designed to help those who find themselves in it. Of course, it has developed a reputation for not being concerned with certain classes of people, filled with corrupt personnel, and the like. Granted, this may be true in some cases, if not many, under certain circumstances; however, it was not designed to be that way. I was brought to this realization as I watched my son get a sampling of the process. He was not a career criminal, nor did he spend a lot of time in jail, but his experience was frequent enough to paint a clear picture of what the system actually looked like and what it was designed to do. Let me say first of all that the system was fair to him, and at each level of involvement, opportunities were made available to him to avoid further involvement. I am not a prison advocate, nor am I an expert by any stretch of the imagination, but I have been given the privilege to see it work from an inside perspective without being on the inside.

Conan was exceptionally intelligent in his capabilities to handle whatever school assignments he was given. It was obvious early on that he did not have any trouble with the academic side of learning. His trouble began to surface when his assignments were complete, and later before they were completed, and eventually without being completed at all. Recognizing this at an early age, I felt he needed closer supervision than the specific school that he was enrolled in could provide. There was a magnet program in progress at the time, and through it I had him and his two brothers bussed to a school in another section of the city and placed in what I felt was a better environment for him to learn. Though better, it was not adequate to meet all of his educational needs. Things did improve, but I felt that there was still an area in his life that needed more attention than the public school could provide. As a Christian, it was important to me to expose my children to an ongoing diet of what God's Word, the Bible, taught in addition to all of the other sources of information that they were being exposed to. As a single parent, I did my part at home, but with the demands of parenthood, there was very little time left for any solid devotional time with my children, so I sought help from the Christian school system.

I believe his exposure to the church, the Christian school, and his Christian family was instrumental in helping Conan to solidify his understanding of what was available to him in Jesus Christ.

One of the things that I was not prepared for was the racism that surfaced in one school in particular that Conan attended, and for the sake of the furtherance of the cause of Christ it will remain unnamed. I believe they did more harm than good with their mixture of Christian doctrine and racial discrimination, the likes of which should not be found in the same location. His reaction to it was rebellion, and that rebellion continued throughout the remainder of his life. His acts of rebellion in the school resulted in his being removed from the school. He was then transferred back to the very system I had attempted to avoid, and fortunately there was not enough time for him to be overly exposed to this environment, which I felt would surely swallow him whole. He graduated without major incident. He was awarded an academic scholarship to Mansfield University, located in Mansfield, Pennsylvania. This was great cause for rejoicing for me, and I felt we had weathered the storm and Conan was going to be all right. He completed his first year without a hitch, and the peace that floods your soul when you know your child is going to be all right had replaced my fears for his survival and well-being. That excitement was short lived, however, as I received a call from the legal authorities in Mansfield informing me that Conan had been arrested for shoplifting.

Mansfield was a five-hour drive from my home, and a stressful drive it was. As I think about it, I believe that I aged at least a year or two during that drive. The impact that it had on my body was phenomenal. It was during that drive that I began to realize the depth of my concern for my children and the overwhelming desire I had for them to avoid heartache at any cost, compounded by the rocky start that their journeys in life had. This, of course, was not the first time my concern surfaced, but the intensity had never been so great. I must be honest with you at this point by giving you this revelation—I thought God would do something special for me because of my commitment to my children and my willingness to hang in there with them when so many others were abandoning their families. After all, I had made great sacrifices as a single parent to weather all of the odds to not only keep my children together but to provide for them more than they needed. So each time I was brought to the realization that this was not the case and I was not going to be treated any differently than any other parent, either single or married, it sunk deep within my heart and generated an array of emotions, some good and some bad. Even today the thought still surfaces from time to time when things take a turn for the worse where my children are concerned. This drive, however, was taking its toll on me in that it had surpassed any disappointment that I had experienced in the past. Since Conan was still under my guardianship as a minor, I could not hide behind the idea of allowing the system to pick up the training process while I kept my distance and awaited the outcome from home. When I arrived at the school, I was glad to see Conan, yet at the same time I didn't want to see him. I went through all of the proper parental jargon about what would happen to him if he continued on this path and how he was showing no appreciation for all that God had done and all that I had done for him as we made our way to the county court of Mansfield.

The courtroom polity was one of the most depressing experiences I have ever encountered in my life. The wait for his number to be called, the lack of concern for those who spent most of their time there, and the movement of defendants in and out of the courtroom was sheer torture. It was so difficult for me that I determined in my heart that I would never undergo the experience again. The outcome did not match up to my apprehensions, but the damage had already been done. The judge pronounced a series of legal comments that amounted to nothing more than a stern warning and a recommendation that Conan leave the town of Mansfield. As difficult as that experience was for me, I recognized even then that the system was not out to hurt Conan but to keep him out of it. It reminded me of the rattlesnake that shakes its tale not as a precursor to biting someone but rather to warn those who are nearby to stay away lest they encounter the effects of its deadly venom. The legal system has a deadly venom that is designed to uphold and protect, and it prefers to frighten more than it does to strike. The slamming of prison doors and the striking of the gavel in a courtroom setting are nothing short of venomous warning signs for all in the vicinity to stay away. It rattles its verdicts to ward off potential offenders. Just as the venom of a snake affects the entire body, overexposure to and involvement with the legal system will have an impact on one's entire life. Conan had been warned, and now only time would tell if it would be sufficient to keep him out of the system. It wasn't long before problems began to surface in other areas of Conan's life. Rebellion does not dwell in isolation; it influences one's entire life.

School was no longer a priority in Conan's life, but it served as a location to get involved in things that suited his fancy. One way in particular that rebellion began to show itself was that Conan began to find ways to do things that totally disregarded authority. He was privileged to have a car—a well-used and barely running one, but a car nonetheless. Those of you who are familiar with college campuses know that in order to have driving privileges, students must follow some basics rules and guidelines. Certain locations were designated as student parking and so on. If these were violated, a citation was issued, and a fine or loss of driving privileges would result. Needless to say, the number of infractions became so numerous that not only was he banned from parking on campus, he was not allowed to drive the car period. He allowed his registration to expire, therefore making it illegal to drive the car at all. This became a feeding ground for him. Since rebellion strives on opportunity, these circumstances required no effort whatsoever; they were built in. He eventually completed his third semester and decided to follow the recommendations of the judicial arm of the legal system to leave Mansfield, and he left.

It doesn't take much to recognize the end result of a behavioral pattern such as the one that Conan was constructing. In his defense, I must add that Mansfield is not your fast-paced inner city, nor does it offer exciting activities to participate in during your off times. There are at least two things needed to succeed in any university environment. A genuine commitment to education and the discipline to adjust to the requirements needed to achieve well-designed goals without wavering. The very thing that this combination could not tolerate was rebellion. Child-development specialists are quick to say that rebellion is normal in children and is an indication of growth and one's desire to expand beyond parental authority. John White, in his book *Parents in Pain,* describes it this way: "In adolescent years our children vacillate between an innate drive to become independent from us and the habit of childhood to cling to us dependently. The nearer they get to adulthood, the greater becomes the drive for independence. And independence implies learning to trust one's own judgment."[11] I might add that the direction they choose will undoubtedly be influenced in part by the manner in which rebellion was handled throughout the process. Independence becomes defiance, and dependence turns into entitlement. These two working together make for a volatile mixture of heartache and sorrow.

Conan returned home in the winter of 1991. It would indeed be a cold winter. As I consider the events of that winter, it was not long before I recognized that he was on a mission and nothing in

---

11 John White, *Parents in Pain* (Downers Grove, IL: InterVarsity Press, 1979), p. 219.

his path would stop him. Smoking became a part of his lifestyle; drinking and drug use followed shortly thereafter. With the exception of the smoking, these were invisible to the natural eye, but I could tell the difference; it was a difference that would affect his life and our ability to communicate from then on. Life indeed had taken a radical turn for him, and things got worse. I remember a cartoon illustration that hung in a neighborhood restaurant that I had frequented while growing up. It read, "I sat musing sad and without a friend, a voice came down to me from the gloom saying, 'Cheer up, things could be worse,' and so I cheered up, and sure enough, things got worse." I chuckle about that caption even now, but there is some truth in its contents. It's at times like these that we need a perspective check. As believers, we have been given the mandate to keep our focus on the Lord Jesus Himself and no other. He fully understands the obstacles that often come to disrupt our focus. We then have to become well acquainted with the ongoing challenge of being deterred by distractions.

This requires what I call faith thinking—that is, seeing what things can become as opposed to what they are. There is always an opportunity for improvement or growth. Seeing things from the vantage point of growth or improvement broadens the playing field and enables us to capitalize on possibilities that were not previously available to us. The inclusion of the Lord in any equation always increases the denominator to the highest power. The bottom line will always be positive as a result. Being able to recognize a positive end from the beginning is indeed a gift. It is one that surpasses positive thinking because it is derived from the very attitude and example of Christ. Instructions are an important aspect of looking beyond where you are and benefiting from what is expected to come. What needs to be learned is that life at its finest will never compare with the reality of what is to come.

There is always more that should be expected. I believe that this kind of thinking is what propels us to continue to strive to achieve as well as improve. In light of what you may be facing, a glimpse of the future possibilities is a breath of fresh air.

Then there is the need to be excited about the process. It's no marvel why the Word of God exhorts us to "Rejoice in the Lord always," and as if we may have misunderstood what was said, it goes on to add, "and again I say Rejoice." (Philippians 4:4 NIV) Being excited about life is an absolute must if you are going to capitalize on faith thinking. I have a little procedure that I follow when I am faced with most anything that proves to be a bit uncomfortable. I ask the Lord to show me what I can view as pleasurable in the midst of whatever it is that I may be experiencing. How else can rejoicing be a perpetual experience when in fact all things at first glance may not be pleasing at all? In the light of difficulty, there is always the option of handling things your way. Unfortunately, this often includes doing things that go against God's Word and His standards. When that does not happen, whatever success you may have had will be negated because God will not honor disobedience, nor can He. Let's be realistic about the nature of these circumstances. This kind of behavior can be painful simply because it goes against the very fiber of your being. The anticipation of future possibilities actually becomes the antidote for pain. That's not to say that pain is anything to laugh at, but the excitement that one can experience as a result of anticipation can produce an unusual amount of joy and excitement. Needless to say, the reality still remains, yet the impact of it has been minimized. As rebellion picks up momentum, an array of things begins to happen to the one in rebellion and to those who may be required to deal with it in one way or another. One of the first things that I began to notice was how there was very little regard for responsibility and how Conan's behavior affected others. A textbook titled *Psychopathology* described this kind of thinking as antisocial personality disorder, which is indicated by "a lifestyle that is marked by the immediate gratification of impulses and desires without regard or concern for the feelings and welfare of others."[12] This summary identifies those who fit into this category as having no sense of loyalty or responsibility; other people are to be used and exploited. The true sociopath does not experience genuine anxiety, guilt, or remorse for the anguish and suffering he or she may cause others.

Noyes's *Modern Clinical Psychiatry* cites this personality type as often irritable, arrogant, and unyielding and rarely genuinely remorseful. Frequently, people who fit this type show a rebellious attitude toward society and authority.[13] Conan was never clinically diagnosed as having this disorder, but he certainly fit the MO. He exhibited these tendencies as he continued to lose job after job. He appeared to be unable to set goals and work toward them. His was an attitude that sought to avoid all discomfort at all costs, even the discomfort of waiting. Every desire had to be fulfilled immediately, and when it wasn't, frustration would set in, shortly followed by anger. I believe that gratification is something you earn; in no other way can it be fully appreciated. When it is expected for any other reason, the outcome is normally disastrous. When a person is driven by results, it only leaves room for almost any means to get you there. What disturbs me most about instant gratification is the idea that one is never satisfied when the results come; it is such a heinous taskmaster. Satisfaction comes only through the fulfillment of other obligations that are necessary ingredients in the process. You cannot call in sick on Monday,

---

12 James D. Page, *Psychopathology: The Science of Understanding Deviance* (Chicago: Aldine-Atherton, 1979), p. 317.

13 L. C. Kolb, Noyes' Modern Clinical Psychiatry (Philadelphia: W.B. Saunders, 1968), p. 505.

come to work late on Tuesday, leave work early on Friday, and expect to enjoy the weekend. One is totally dependent upon the other. The same is true for those who are trying to satisfy themselves at the expense of those who are normally closest to them by placing them and any and all others on the altar of their own desires. As the flames of their own egos are lit, they set ablaze any and everything that they come in contact with. The tension in the home is constantly above normal. The conversation in the home centers around them, and other family members are at odds with one another because of them. This was indeed the case in the Bell home during the winter of 1991. It was an inauguration of sorts. Conan was a self-appointed candidate, and he was being nominated as the center of attention. Most of what would take place from then until now would somehow become a roller coaster ride that he personally conducted. After his departure from Mansfield, the requirement of the home was to get a job and begin to take on the responsibilities of an adult. After all, he was making some very real adult decisions. Even though they were unwise and filled with immature motives, the consequences were adult size. Of course, he did not comply and responded by leaving the home. He moved across the street. The proprietor was just a few years older than Conan, and so she was a peer. There was a deep sense of disdain and disappointment in my heart as a result. I often thought about what I could do to coax him to not only return home but to comply with what coming home meant. I was even willing to lower my standard to make it happen, but one area I could not compromise was my relationship with my wife, his stepmom. There had been many discussions concerning Conan and the impact he was having on our relationship. The conflict that developed was tremendous in that I was always forced to choose between him and my wife. Of course, the deck was stacked in that I knew my obligations as a husband superseded my parental role. The Bible made it clear that all was to be forsaken for the sake of one's spouse. I had all of the answers intellectually, but emotionally I was torn. Somehow I understood the depth of Conan's pain but was powerless to do anything about it if he did not cooperate with alleviating the problem.

When a parent leaves a child, the impact is immeasurable, as was the case with Conan's birth mother. It makes no difference if the absence is due to marital discord or death; the pain is the same. I believe one's ability to cope with it is determined in part by the nature of the relationship prior to the departure. Now, if there was no relationship, one has to be created. Unfortunately, the design that one creates is overwhelmingly negative if there is no justification for the absence. If it wasn't death that caused the separation, then the child concludes, "It must be me." The child may ask internally, *What is it about me that caused them to leave?* The normal operation of the parent–child relationship then changes, and the child becomes disoriented and confused about how he or she should respond to the circumstances that everyone else appears to be adjusting to without major difficulty. I believe that one of the ways this period of adjustment can be handled is by positive discussion concerning the missing parent. If the parent is willing to participate, that's a plus, but if not the situation may become a bit complicated. The discussion is designed to eliminate the false mental images that one has a tendency to create. This can be positive or negative, but if not handled correctly, it can become a problem. Of course, the child may have no knowledge of this whatsoever depending upon the age, but his or her behavior will be a clear indication of which position has subconsciously been taken.

The mother is the parent in question in our discussion, so it's no wonder that the dynamic took a turn in the direction of the way women would be treated. When the proper nurturing is not being received, a replacement will be sought. Rebellion is the most convenient reaction to begin with, which in turn leads to greater opportunities of expression as resources are increased and experience is acquired. Of course, parents' leaving children these days is almost common practice; we frequently hear of one parent or another vying to gain custody of their children. But during the time of Conan's upbringing, it was uncommon, and when made public, it was viewed very cautiously. There wasn't any positive talk being communicated about it. Ministries in churches were not geared toward men. It was a matter of drawing your own conclusions and functioning accordingly. To further complicate matters, there was a growing anger in Conan's heart that would surface from time to time without warning, which resulted in his fathering three children by three different women. The cycle was gaining momentum rapidly, and the stage was set for a future generation of angry and disillusioned children who would have to function at best with a father who probably would not be there to give them adequate support. The mothers of those children and one phenomenal aunt have done an incredible job in filling the void that Conan left during his life and after his death. Rebellion has a life all its own and a course that can only be determined by the passage of time. It renders all attempts to correct it ineffective and unproductive. The Bible associates it with demonic influence. In 1 Samuel 15, King Saul was given some specific instructions to punish a group of people who had mistreated the Israelites during their exodus from the land of Egypt. The instructions were clear: "Now go and completely destroy the entire Amalekite nation—men, women, children, babies, cattle, sheep, goats, camels, and donkeys" (1 Sam. 15:3 NLT). Saul decided that it would be better to hold on to the best of the livestock and the king himself. What's interesting about his response is that he chose the animals over the children. It doesn't take long to see the damaging effect that rebellion has on people's thinking and their ability to discern right from wrong. The moment you decide to do anything that is contrary to the will of God, distortion sets in and your decision making becomes warped.

When you do things your way, it points out the fallacy of attempting to reason with those who find themselves in a state of rebellion. When oxen and sheep become more important than children, the next step is normally continued rebellion—but hidden with efforts to cover up and engage in passive disobedience. The amazing thing about this encounter is that God associates this kind of thinking with witchcraft or divination. Once momentum is in motion, forces come into play that surpass even the knowledge of the person who is rebelling. This is the reason that supernatural intervention is needed. Parent, your help is in knowing that the Lord is ultimately in control. This is not a motivational appeal but a statement of fact. All of life is being orchestrated by His divine plan and cannot be aborted by the likes of a person's rebellion. Take for instance the control that the Lord has over the various aspects of life such as animals, angels, and even the entire galaxy. Throughout scripture, we find the Lord revealing His control over the animal world. The mouths of lions were shut by Him in response to a need that His servant Daniel had. The sun was commanded to stand still as a result of a need that Joshua had. The Red Sea was parted by the power of God in response to a need that the Israelites had to exit Egypt. He has power over the spiritual world in that the devil himself has to get permission before he can do anything against God's people. He elevates and He brings down; He exalts and He abases. This is the kind of reflection that is necessary if you are going to survive the next few years. It is not until we find ourselves powerless that we resort to the assistance that God offers. Nothing will be done until we realize that we can do nothing. It is at these points that God then intervenes. He dispatches angels if necessary. The work of angels on your behalf may be invisible, but you can rest assured that they are on the job. Psalm 34:7 (NIV) says that they have a permanent responsibility to provide protection for us even to the extent of surrounding us. This is strong language that may be misunderstood by some, I know, but it is necessary in order to combat the forces that are activated when one chooses to rebel against authority beginning in the home.

Rebellion is devastating, leaving a trail of broken promises, disappointed expectations, and heartache in its wake. What I believe makes this so difficult is the fact that there are often glimmers of hope in the midst of any given ordeal. For instance, when Conan returned from Mansfield after a few minor incidents, he decided to enlist in the US Army. In light of the way things were going at the time, I thought it was a good idea. The military would take over the responsibility of instilling in him some things that he continued to resist coming directly from me. I felt that he would begin to see the very things I had been trying to caution him about and in some way begin to respond in obedience to them. The first few months were typical of a new recruit in the military. We exchanged letters, and he appeared to be taking on the shape of a young man who was working his way out of the rebellious stage of life. He made a few comments that supported the idea that the requirements that had been placed on him in his formative years were now paying off. After his basic training, there was a marked difference in his language as we continued to communicate with one another. I could detect a low-level yet constant disapproval of what the military was doing where he was concerned. I could almost sense that the honeymoon was over and complications would soon resurface. The day came when I received a call from Conan informing me that he was going to be discharged from the Army. Of course, I inquired as to the reasons why, and to this day I have never really gotten the true story.

Within the next few weeks, Conan was back with a new determination to resist any and all attempts to steer him in a positive direction. My wife and I agreed that he would not be able to continue to live in the home because of the tension he was causing between the two of us. The blended family life is a difficult one to navigate, and when it is accompanied with rebellion, the degree of difficulty is greatly increased. Needless to say, I was emotionally torn between my son and my wife. I knew that my main obligation at this point was to provide my wife with what she needed and give Conan some kind of support in spite of his rebellion, keeping in mind that he was still my son. There were times when we attempted to allow him to live in the home. Without exception, there was always conflict, strife, tension, and a deliberate approach on his part to make things difficult for all other family members involved. His behavior defied logic. In hindsight, I realize that self-destructive behavior has its own rules and follows its own logic. As difficult as things were, when they resulted in his departure from the home, it was always voluntary. There would come a point when he would declare that he could not live under these conditions any longer and leave. I purposed in my heart never to sever the communication between us because I knew one day he might need me and in desperation call out for help, and I wanted to be there to help. Fast-forwarding for just a moment, let's go to the day Conan died. He had collapsed on the sidewalk, and a passerby called 9-1-1. The paramedics were able to revive him on the way to the hospital. During that ride, he was able to give them his name, date of birth, and my phone number. All of these were clear enough to him no doubt because of the constant communication that we continued to have. Only the Lord Himself will ever know the value of that basic information.

Let me add here with as much emotion as I can that it's important that the lines of communication remain open at all times no matter how bad things may get. It could be the difference between life and death. If I had not received the information that I did, I would have been forced to rehearse the possibility of Conan's death again and again for the rest of my life. The old adage "no news is good news" would not have applied in this case.

I recall the time I was in the process of leaving the house for work when the phone rang. It was an insurance investigator who inquired about Conan's whereabouts. At the time, I did not know because he had moved out of the house. The investigator was friendly enough, as they often are when trying to gather information concerning a suspect. Later that day, I came in contact with Conan and asked about the situation, and he downplayed the whole thing, stating that it had to do with an incident that took place in a parking lot where he was struck by a vehicle and was filing suit against the person. It was during this time that insurance advertisements were springing up all over the place with the popular caption, "Commit insurance fraud and meet new friends." Of course, this was a subtle way of saying that insurance fraud would result in jail time. Needless to say, this was the end result where Conan was concerned. I received the call on a dreary weekday afternoon even though the sun was shining because there is no such thing as a good day to receive a call indicating that your son had been arrested.

Bail was set at ten thousand dollars, of which 10 percent was required for his release. I had the money available, but I became frantic when I attempted to post it. The system that I reported earlier had been fair with Conan instantly turned into a nightmare. It was then that I did not see the reason for the initial scare tactics because it was a system that you did not want to be a part of, nor did you want to experience the pain and discomfort that it could cause. I figured since parental discipline couldn't do it, college couldn't do it, and the military couldn't do it, surely this system would provide the cure necessary to break Conan out of his rebelliousness. I posted bail, and he was released. It was a day of celebration for us both, and it came with promises of never allowing it to happen again. This kind of offense is classified as a felony, and it wouldn't take long for me to realize the significance of having such a thing on one's record. It is synonymous to a meat-eating animal being sprayed by a skunk. What appears to be a little aggravating turns into a death sentence. That animal will not be able to get within miles of a potential meal, resulting in starvation. The same is true with those who have been sprayed with the reality of a felony on their record. They cannot come within miles of a potential job without the employer's recognizing the scent and rejecting the resume even before it is read. This did nothing more than add insult to injury where Conan was concerned. It pushed him further and further away from responsible thinking because even with a clean record he had difficulty keeping a job. In spite of the nature of his circumstances, he was able to get jobs from time to time. He was an ambulance driver for a while but received several driving violations and was ultimately released because of driving under the influence and other infractions. Telemarketing was another popular position that was made available to him, but the pay was so poor and the working conditions were just not conducive to the underlying resistance that ruled in his heart. Of course, discouragement began to set in, and I could see the temptation for him to give up on responsible thinking altogether.

Then there was what I called a golden opportunity. Through the influence of a friend, an organization provided for him not only employment but also good benefits and a promising future. This was the first time that he made it clear that part of his problem was a fear of success. He expressed to me that he was afraid of not being able to make it on this job primarily due to his past history and things that he alone understood. His admission of fear generated some very meaningful discussions between us, and even today I remember them with a sense of tenderness. Well, it wasn't long before I got word that Conan had been let go, and that would prove to be his last viable means of employment. The insurance fraud trial finally came up and Conan ignored the court date, so a warrant was issued for his arrest. He stayed on the run for several months; however, with my constant hounding, he surrendered to the police. He stayed in jail for approximately one year. It was during these times that he came to understand the benefits of a personal relationship with Jesus Christ. Conan had made a commitment to the Lord some years earlier as all of my other children were led to do through a constant barrage of Bible stories, Sunday school classes, and regular church attendance. He said all of the right things during those times, but of course from his behavior, it was clear that he did not have a genuine understanding of what the Lord had made available to him. But now, in those confined circumstances, he was able to listen with very little distraction. As a matter of fact, these conversations were almost daily.

We covered the plan of salvation in minute detail. We looked at some of the great doctrines of the Bible, as well as some basic understanding of the sovereignty of God and how He did what He wanted to do when He wanted to and no one could thwart His plan. When we got around to discussions about Conan's location, it was understood that even there, God was actively at work in his life. Join me as we read one of the letters written by Conan during this time.

Mom & Dad,

Greetings. I received the package you sent. Thanx. The bible is beautiful and should afford me many hours of detailed instruction. I really enjoy the story of Joseph's life. I pray for insight, as Joseph had, to see things from a different perspective. I also spend time in Exodus marveling at how God continued to work with Moses and compromise with him to make things comfortable as possible. In general, I am discovering principles and truths that don't seem all that abstract anymore. It's now real to me. I can't thank you enough for all the support you're giving me as I grow and mature in Christ. I see God's fingerprints on everything around me. I know he's not only working in my life but also in the lives of the "students" around me to make my stay here as spiritually and educationally fulfilling as possible. I'm hungry. I'm hungry for knowledge. I want more and more. That's a sign for me that I am moving in the right direction. Sometimes I get scared when I see what's going on around me. I find comfort in Psalm 34:4 where the Psalmist says, "I sought the Lord and he answered me and delivered me from all my fears." I realize that if I fear the Lord I don't have to fear anything else. I know that God is speaking directly to me because the words seem to jump out at me. As soon as I start to doubt the next line or verse urges me to, "Doubt not." I love you, mom and dad, please continue to pray for me. Mountains are moving in my life.

Love Conan

These were reassuring times that would prove to be extremely important in the days that lay ahead. I also sent materials to him on a consistent basis. He enjoyed reading and had a very sharp mind. As a matter of fact, he introduced me to John Grisham, and I have been reading his books ever since. In some ways, his jail experiences were the most significant times that we spent together in that they gave us a sense of pure connection that surpassed even those times of fishing, camping, and amusement park attendance. Rebellion is indeed an unmerciful taskmaster. Life offers all types of experiences with no warning about the significance that those experiences may have on the future. It is so important to capitalize on each moment while it is being experienced so that the occurrences of the moment will not be able to successfully confuse their future impact and replace them with fuel for rebellion and heartache. We live in a fast-paced society, and everything is geared toward preparing for something else. It is as if we don't have time for anything because we are taking the time to prepare for what we are yet to have. We look for faster computers, quicker automobiles, and a shorter workweek so we can find time to think of more things that we need to do.

I'm reminded of the Lord Jesus and how that will find it difficult to find any evidence of Him being in a hurry. As I explored the scriptures, I found it very difficult to find Him even using words such as *hurry up, immediately, right away, right now,* and so on unless it applied to offering help or meeting a need. As a matter of fact, I haven't found any as of yet. I'm still on the lookout. What I do find Him saying is things like, "Take no thought for tomorrow for tomorrow will take care of itself, (Matthew 6:34 NIV) and "Cast your cares upon me for I care about you." (1 Peter 5:7 NIV) He promises "to give perfect peace to those whose minds are focused on him."(Isaiah 26:3 NIV) In essence, I find Jesus exhorting us to slow down, not speed up.

You may recall the story of Lazarus and how he became ill, and his sisters contacted the Lord in hopes that he might help their brother (John 11 NIV). Their concern was legitimate, for in verse 5 it is declared that Jesus loved Martha, Mary, and Lazarus. Then we also find in verse 35 these words: "Jesus wept." Having become overwhelmed with emotion, He broke down and cried. I have heard several different reasons as to why this may have happened, and the list is too extensive to mention here. This one thing I do know—that the nature of the event was an emotional one and the natural response in such a situation was to cry. The admonition to "Weep with those who weep" Romans 12:15 should suffice. My point is not to determine the reason for the tears of Jesus but for the words that are found in John 11:6: "So when he heard that he was sick, He then stayed two days longer in the place where he was." Jesus was not in a hurry, nor was he filled with anxiety and fear. If there was ever a reason to hurry, this would have been one. But Jesus chose to take his time and to follow his own counsel. A large majority of the mistakes that I have made in life were made in a hurry.

Jesus takes it a step further and indicates that He not only thinks this way but that He gets excited when others feel and act the same way. The story of the centurion's servant serves as a vivid illustration of this. In Luke 6:1–9, we find the story. By way of summary, the centurion had a servant that he cared about deeply, and he was ill. He then sent word to Jesus to see if Jesus would save his servant. The men came to Jesus with a great sense of urgency, and Jesus accompanied them to the location of the sick servant and was willing to help him. The centurion sent his servant to meet Jesus before He could get to the house and beckoned Him not to trouble Himself by coming into his house, saying rather to just speak the word and the servant would be healed because he was not worthy to allow the Lord into his home. In response,

Jesus said that He had never seen such faith in all of Israel. Jesus was excited about this man's confidence in His ability to heal. The lesson is clear—trust in Jesus is sufficient to handle whatever our concerns may be with a minimal amount of involvement from each one of us. We have to relish the moments that we have with our loved ones and not be too caught up in what we don't have. Jail is not a pleasant place to be, but if viewed properly in the light of rebellion, it can prove to be an ally.

Then there was the time when I was on my way to work, and a call came in from an attorney informing me that Conan had been arrested and bail had to be posted immediately if he was to avoid being sent to Jail. Once in that location, trying to post bail can get very aggravating. The system becomes unfriendly in those settings. They appear to not have an ounce of compassion in anything that they do, and that attitude is transferable. I had gained a little experience, so I was not pressured to respond immediately and decided to let Conan go through the process. The bail was set at the customary ten thousand dollars, requiring the 10 percent cash payment. He was clearly on the career track, but I was determined to do everything that I could to change his direction. Other incidents had occurred, but they hadn't amounted to the higher level of involvement that I anticipated would be his experience. I believe something happens to a person on the inside when jail life becomes an active part of one's experience. I don't know how to define it, but it is as tangible as any other reality that you can put your hands on. I struggled through these years as I watched my son refuse to surrender to the will of God and to persist in doing what I knew he did not like but preferred over doing the right thing. Once rebellion builds momentum, it continues to grow throughout one's lifetime. The private war to overcome has been lost, and there is no longer any desire to do things any differently than they are being done.

I remember vividly the time when I got a call from an amusement park, and the police officer on the other end asked if I had a son by the name of Conan. I said yes. He went on to ask some other questions to verify Conan's identity. He had been arrested for shoplifting and gave an alias, but midstream he had decided to come clean and the officers did not believe him. By the way, Conan was notorious for not carrying identification. I assured the officer that he was who he said he was, and he was released under his own recognizance. Before any wrong conclusions are drawn, let me say this—in some ways, I have been able to understand and accept Conan's behavior primarily because of his rough start. His mother and I were separated. This undoubtedly left a permanent scar that surfaced and resurfaced in different ways at different times in his life. I don't know that any two people respond alike in such circumstances, and of my four children, Conan took it the hardest and had the hardest time adjusting to it. Just a word of caution to anyone who may be entertaining the idea of leaving his or her children: it is devastating. The end result will far outweigh any pain you may feel you can no longer bear at this time. Children for the most part have some built-in resilience and can overcome most anything. But that fact applies to each individual child and is not a guarantee that your child will be one of those who are successful in overcoming. To put it as plainly as I possibly can, it's not worth it. Whatever your discomfort, it is temporary and will surely pass. I am totally amazed at how little we can take when it comes to our children and losing sight of what's really important. If you are a believer, remember that you carry a legacy that is under constant spiritual attack. There are forces at work that are not satisfied with disrupting your life, but they have in view generations to come. Ideally they prefer death, but in some cases destroying the effectiveness of a new generation is even better. When that happens, many new people are now subject to the same devastation of generations past. The results are more heartache, more pain, more disappointment, more disillusionment, and more rebellion, resulting in more calls from the legal system.

I don't feel that I could have done things differently and caused the results to be any different than they were where my son is concerned. His was a life that had to be lived his way, and that could not be changed. I believe certain people are bent on doing things their own way regardless of circumstances and opportunities. A solid family background can keep those things in check and could even minimize the consequences, but without submission to the will of God, the end result will be the same. Whether it's in a jail cell or a palace courtyard, the final decision is left up to the individual. They have to choose eternal life and begin living it now or accept the consequences that surely will follow. The aftermath of a prison call compares to none. An entire life is brought under scrutiny within the few brief moments that it takes for you to be informed. Don't put yourself in that position. Answer the question now—is my need greater than the need of my children? Invariably that answer should be no. Assuming that it is, make the sacrifice necessary to give your children a fighting chance before you end up having to fight the system in an attempt to get that chance back.

A brief word to the rebellious: stop now before it is too late. I understand the depth of your pain and your need to transfer that pain to someone else—anyone initially, but ultimately those who are closest to you. I realize that it may be difficult for you to adjust to the circumstances that you find yourself in, but it is not impossible. The awful thing about this is the fact that it makes no difference how old you are; a change must be made. I've seen parents with fifty-year-old children grieving their rebellion and unwillingness to live in spite of those things that cannot be changed. That's not to say that you are not justified in how you feel, but when your feelings affect your behavior in a negative sense, a change must be made. I guarantee you that your life will improve if you begin to obey the will of God and submit to His purpose for your life. In so doing, you will discover that what you had been viewing as a problem is actually a resource. All things do work together for the good of them that are deeply committed to the things of God and are sold out for His kingdom. (Romans 8:28 paraphrase mine) This is going to be challenging to say the least, but the benefits will far outweigh the degree of difficulty needed to overcome. There are a lot of things in life that we will never understand, but some things are crystal clear. That would include the issue that we are currently discussing. The reason I have taken the time to address the issue of the victim is so that you, as the victim, do not become a victimizer. Habits are easy to form when repetition is an ongoing part of your lifestyle. Whether it's the repeated use of positive encouragement or the daily practice of finding reasons to cause people discomfort and grief, the decision is left up to you. But let me warn you that even though you are free to make a decision such as this, you lose total control in terms of how the consequences will impact others. As I stated earlier, it's just not worth the risk. Let me give you an example of how this works from a positive and a negative perspective as we explore a couple of biblical examples. In Acts 23, we find the story depicting Paul the apostle as he is brought before the Sanhedrin for proof of his guilt or innocence. The court appearance turns into a major ordeal as he raises the issue of his Pharisaic background. The encounter had to do with the differences between the Pharisees and the Sadducees. One believed in the resurrection of the dead and the existence of spirits as well as angels, the group of which Paul was a part, and the other group believed in neither. When Paul declared his position, the opposing group reacted by separating themselves from those in favor of Paul, and division resulted.

Paul was then placed under the protection of the commander in charge in an attempt to protect him from bodily harm. The conflict did not end there in that a group of those who opposed Paul made a vow not to eat until the apostle was dead; included in the plot were forty people. The plan was to use the spiritual leaders as a ploy to get Paul in a specific location and then end his life. But in the process of discussing this plan, Paul's nephew overheard the details, and he requested a meeting with him. When he disclosed the information to Paul, he was instructed to tell his story to the commander in charge. In so doing, the plot was thwarted, and Paul made it safely to his destination. The unknown nephew of the apostle was used by God to ensure the protection of Paul. He became indirectly responsible for Paul's writing more books in the Bible than any other author. The apostle Paul is responsible for twelve books in the Bible, and some even feel that he may have written thirteen. A small amount of information from an almost anonymous bystander has played a major role in the overall design of God's Word, as well as the very advancement of the gospel itself. There was no way that this young man could have known the impact that his decision would have on the future of not only his people but also the entire world for countless generations to come, up to and including you and me.

Then there is the drama surrounding Joshua in chapter seven. There we find a military campaign in progress. The nation of Israel was doing well, and all those who approached were dealt with handily. Under the leadership of Joshua, the name of the Lord was being glorified, and his personal fame spread throughout the entire land. The campaign was going so well that they entered the battle at Ai with enough confidence to minimize the number of troops they would need and thought it a great opportunity to give the majority of the troops some well-deserved rest. Instead of a resounding victory, the nation was devastated by a staggering defeat. A total of thirty-six men were killed, and the army was routed. Through a series of checks and balances, it was discovered that one soldier had violated the instructions that the Lord had given to the Israelites about not taking any of the spoils or, as they were called, the devoted things. When the dust settled, the guilty party, by the name of Achan, would be responsible for not only his own death but also the deaths of thirty-six soldiers and every one of his living relatives due to his single act of rebellion. Can you imagine that distant uncle who lived in another part of the country being given the message that the family was meeting in the Valley of Achor, and "On your way, please make it a point to stop by and pick up all of the men, women, and children. In addition don't forget the livestock, which is all of the oxen, donkeys and sheep." I am certain that if Achan had known the devastation he was going to cause as a result of wanting to do things his way, he would have reconsidered his actions. The impact that his rebellion had on everyone—the army, the civilians, and his immediate family—was phenomenal and would result in the loss of an entire generation of people. Only the Lord knows the potential that was lost. As I stated earlier, the devil is not satisfied with one person or even one family for that matter. He is bent on destroying generations—that is, generation after generation after generation. It began with the death of Abel and has been continuing ever since. Consider very carefully what you may be doing to those who love you and, deep down inside, those you love before a generation is lost. And when that happens, a failure pattern is established that will not easily be broken, if ever.

Prayer

Lord, it is so easy to get caught up in wanting things my way and overlooking the needs of others. My pain sometimes becomes so great that I am unable to see beyond what's going on in my life and the impact I may be having on the lives of others. My desire is to become a complete person capable of facing not only myself but also the reality of my need to take full responsibility for my actions and to stop acting on the things that may be missing in my life and to focus on those things that are really important—the care for others, the posterity of future generations, and the well-being of my fellow believers.

Memory Verses

Matthew 25:34–36

The further away you move from faith, the greater the level of doubt you will have, which minimizes your chances of remaining focused. When you are bombarded with one issue after another, when your life appears to be spinning out of control, and when you are filled with disillusion, remember that God has a plan for your life and what you are experiencing is part of it.

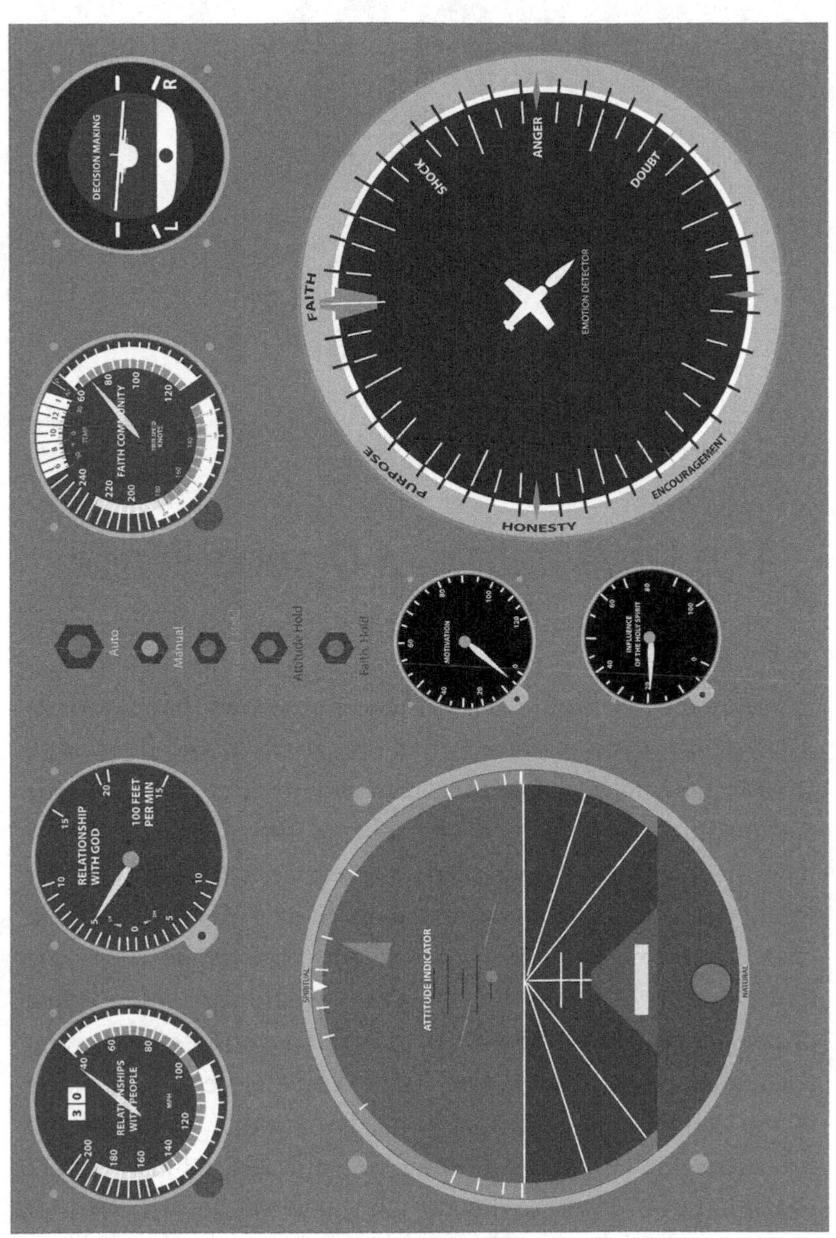
DECISION MAKING
L
R
FAITH COMMUNITY
TRUE SPEED KNOTS
EMOTION DETECTOR
FAITH
SHOCK
ANGER
DOUBT
ENCOURAGEMENT
HONESTY
PURPOSE
Auto
Manual
Attitude Hold
Faith Hold
MOTIVATION
INFLUENCE OF THE HOLY SPIRIT
RELATIONSHIP WITH GOD
100 FEET PER MIN
RELATIONSHIPS WITH PEOPLE
MPH
ATTITUDE INDICATOR
SPIRITUAL
NATURAL

Chapter 4

The Devastation of Disobedience

In the Bible, we find in several places a pattern that continues to emerge. For a period of time, the people would be blessed, at ease, without war, but then they would turn to other gods and begin to worship them. Because of this, God would give them over into the hands of their enemies, and their enemies would treat them harshly. Being oppressed by their enemies would cause them to cry out to God, and the Lord would raise up a leader to serve as a deliverer. Then they would experience a time of prosperity. The leader would die after a period of time, and the pattern would then repeat itself, with the people returning to the god of Baal and other gods. It's a tragic example that's repeated again and again showing how humankind just will not worship the Lord consistently but continues to resort to its way of doing things. In so doing, humans testify loudly that they believe themselves to be much more capable of handling their affairs than

God is. But in a broader sense, this is a picture of believers who have not fully committed themselves to the things of God and their relationships with God are up-and-down experiences with Him. Essentially, the root of it is an unwillingness to completely depend upon God. This process of erosion begins when a person says no to what God says yes to and yes to what God says no to. Where obedience ends, erosion begins, and if this is not reversed, the results will be devastating. Disobedience brings oppression. It brings with it a feeling of being heavily weighed down in mind and body. It conditions you to function below the level of your capability. It demands that you stay on a level that is in agreement with those with whom you are at odds, namely your prodigal. Just like poverty oppresses the human spirit, disobedience oppresses your spiritual well-being. It needs no mention, but it does deserve to be understood that a prodigal relationship can cause oppression on the deepest level, and that of course stems from the nature of the parent–child relationship, even if the child is an adult. Even so, the weight that it brings with it often intensifies the degree of difficulty you may be experiencing without your knowing it. There are underlying causes for it that have to be flushed out if they are ever going to be overcome. When your prodigal is exhibiting behavior that results in feelings of oppression, it can be the result of one of several possibilities: fear, anger, greed, or lust for control, to name a few. In any case, there is always an underlying reason for the behavior. Clinically speaking, any one of these could fill a book, but for the sake of time and space, I would like to explore each one briefly.

Fear, of course, is a natural response to danger, but when misplaced, it becomes the driving force behind any number of behavioral responses, including retaliation, isolation, and fantasizing. With fantasizing leading the pack, when you do not feel that you can handle any given situation, getting even becomes a good way to cover it up and fantasizing appears to be a better way. It's a means of escape from the reality of what you may be facing and what life is really all about. We live in a society today that not only embraces this kind of behavior but actually encourages it. The various programming on TV can attest to that, and millions of people are influenced daily by it. There you will find contestants winning people and relationships instead of prizes. All of this challenges the work required to achieve genuine relationships. What does fear have to do with this? Well, for one, building relationships and overcoming danger requires courage, such as courage to accept rejection when it comes, as well as failure—and they surely will come—which is also a requirement for a wholesome and meaningful relationship. And of course, it takes time to determine if in fact you are suited for a particular person. All of this is totally ignored by those who are competing. That would be bad enough, but in addition millions of people are desirous of the same privilege. Courage, in turn, is the ability to function in spite of those things that may be frightening. If you don't function as such, the tendency is to camouflage the feeling with that of one that is less threatening.

Jesus addresses this issue of fear very succinctly in Matthew 14:27 (NIV). I liken the statement there to a hurricane. The eye of a hurricane is the calm area at the hurricane's center of rotation. It is free of rain and may be free of clouds. On the other hand, the eye wall of a hurricane is an area of intense movement just outside the eye where the strongest winds occur. We can relate this area to where your prodigal is most actively involved in causing havoc. The location of the storm in the text is not only on the Sea of Galilee, which is known to have violent storms during certain times of year. But I also see another storm that comes with gale winds located just outside of courage and fear, which is where the strongest winds blow. If you'll notice, Jesus positions himself in the center of the two. He becomes, as he calls himself, the eye ("I") of the storm between courage and fear. Here lies the point of conflict or storm, if you will. Prodigals are exposed to this kind of activity on a regular basis and often choose to be tossed into a world of fantasy induced by fear, rejecting the need for courage to face genuine reality. Let me say this: we are born with only two fears—the fear of falling and the fear of loud noises. All others are learned. Deep down inside of this storm that has been created in the heart of the disobedient is a learned behavior. I believe anything learned can be unlearned. In order for that to happen, you have to seize control of courage and give it your attention (Matt. 14:27a). As you position yourself in the eye ("I"), you have access to both options. When you are on the outside of the eye, you are on the eye wall. There you only have access to either courage or fear—one or the other. You are going to be on the side of either fear or courage. Courage can only be experienced in the midst of turbulence. You can't be exposed to the eye without being exposed to the eye wall. It's hard to make an intelligent decision on the wall because that's where the winds are strongest. Therefore, you have to seize control of courage. You have to take it. That should tell you something—the pull toward fear is going to be so strong that, even in the eye, getting away from it requires extreme effort. As the eye, Jesus enables you to have equal access to courage or fear. Courage is a choice that must be taken. If you handle this position correctly, you'll gain, apprehend, and secure courage. But if not, you'll succumb to fear. You'll get caught up in the swirling winds of adversity and lose your grip on courage. Courage is available to us all. But since we don't exercise our ability to overcome fear often enough or at best exchange it for something else, we often overlook it as a choice. Because of the presence of Jesus, we can overcome that pull. Remember, He's the eye ("I") in the storm. He's not subject to the condition of the storm; the storm is subject to him.

In Mark 4:39 (NIV), the disciples were terrified of the storm they were up against, and Jesus said to the storm, "Quiet! Be still!" What Jesus was saying in essence, as the eye of the storm, was, *Join me.* He told the storm to get out of the weather and come to Him. He invited the storm to join the peace that comes as result of being in Him. If He is in the storm, there is peace. If He is out of the storm, there is peace. Let's face it—wherever Jesus is, there is peace. Out of the storm, He invites it in, and in the storm, He ushers it out. Therefore, the need is to reflect upon the source of your power and not the cause of your fear. Matthew 14:27 "But Jesus immediately said to them: "Take courage! It is I. Don't be afraid." few requirements come to mind with that statement. Either you are already afraid or you will be. In the case of the disciples, they were already afraid. Astonishingly enough, the source of their fear was also the solution to the fear. Now that's a new concept and one worth exploring. When is the last time you looked to the source of your fear for deliverance from the thing that held you captive? This is exactly what's happening in the case of these disciples, and I dare say it oftentimes happens to us. What could be causing the fear is the lack of understanding and not the object itself. How can we determine that? Understanding comes when you reflect upon the source of your power and not the object of your fear. We give entirely too much attention to the objects of our fears, which are nothing more than a smoke screen. In reality, they are a direct affront to the command of God: "Do not fear." The target in most cases is not you but the faithfulness, goodness, reliability, and presence of God. He can be trusted. So how is the question of finding your deliverance in the object of your fear answered by simply staying in the eye of the storm? Remember, the strongest winds are on the wall, not in the eye.

When Jesus says, "It is I," He wants all attention to be trained on Him. Hebrews 12:2 and 3 (NIV) says, "Let us fix our eyes on Jesus the author and perfecter of our faith … so that you will not grow weary and lose heart." Those who are prodigal have to learn to respond to the Lord obediently in spite of their fears. We see a clear example of this in the case of Peter (Matt. 14:28–32). What I find interesting about Peter is his initial response to his fear. In verse 28, he asks the Lord to bid him to come. Now that's an unusual response to fear, but it's the correct one. The object of his fear was the water and the man on the water, so I would think that he would want to get away from both. A more logical response would have been, "Lord, if it is you, get in the boat." But somehow, Peter understood the very crux of this idea. You don't find peace by running from the storm but by running into it. Peace is in the eye of the storm, not on the periphery—not on the wall, but in the eye. To run is to create more chaos. To get there in some cases, the only thing you may have going for you is the command of God and the promise of His presence. Peter knew the eye ("I") of the storm. He knew that Jesus was in control of the waves and the wind, and if this was Jesus, everything would be all right.

What if your prodigal decided to handle his or her fears this way? What a difference it would make. What kind of changes would come out of that? Think of the creativity and possibilities that would be theirs for the taking if they would just step out on faith in the midst of the turbulence and choose obedience? It just pays to be obedient; it just makes plain old good sense. In the meantime, as you await the transformation of your prodigal this privilege is available to you. It starts in the home and then works its way into society in general. A basic mandate that prodigal children have to be pointed to is that of Ephesians 6:1–3 (NIV): "Children, obey your parents in the Lord, for this is right. Honor your father and mother (which is the first commandment with a promise), so that it may be well with you and that you may live long on the earth."

On a national level, automobile accidents are classified as one of the leading causes of death for those between the ages of sixteen and twenty. I believe a statistic that has not been captured by that report and others is that of the numbers of teens who have died due to disobedience. This would probably show up to be the cause behind the cause and would no doubt prove to be the leading cause of premature death for teens and a host of others. Thrill seeking and risk taking for those in this age group are attempts to offset fear and to compensate for it. Fear, then, is a major cause of oppression. As we have seen, it can be overcome. But then there is also greed. Greed by way of definition can be viewed as the self-serving desire for the pursuit of money, wealth, power, food, or other possessions, especially when this denies the same goods to others. As such, it becomes a form of idolatry, according to Colossians 3:5 (NIV): "Put to death, therefore whatever belongs to your earthly nature." In essence, when idolatry reaches maturity, personal desires become more valuable to the person than God. Another understanding is that greed serves to bring as many things that greedy people consider valuable to those people, making them the center of their own efforts, the ones they aim to please, converting them into their own gods, and creating pride with great concentration on the ego. The pursuit of money and wealth are self-explanatory, but power deserves our consideration.

Power is a measure of a person's ability to control the environment around him or her, including the behavior of other people. Also included in this definition is the idea of selfishness, the act of placing one's own needs or desires above the needs or desires of others. This is where the actions of those who are in opposition with themselves get into trouble. Their desires become more important than others and are sought at the expense of anybody else's. When people have practiced this way of thinking for any length of time, the needs of others are all but nonexistent. There is no need to attempt to understand why people function the way that they do because it defies logic and borders on insanity. The domination of power has completely consumed them, and they will go to any and all lengths to acquire what they desire. So that we don't get confused, the term *authority* is often used for *power*, perceived as legitimate by the social structure. Power, even though we are viewing it from a negative perspective, is accepted as normal in our social structure. The use of power need not involve coercion but can also be viewed as influence. It is through this means that I believe prodigal children and adults prove to exhibit extraordinary manipulation and control over those who care for them the most.

And finally there is the lust for control. As you can see, all of these are based on the same agenda, and that is to control the outcome of their personal desires at the expense of anyone who is willing to pay the price. As I stated earlier, disobedience is devastating, but let me add that it is also disastrous in that it always leaves a trail of carnage made up of well-meaning people who have gotten caught up in the whirlwind of a never-ending cycle of deception and disappointment disguised as a promise to change the next time. By way of encouragement, remember this: at some point, God will remove His protection—namely you—so that those who are prodigal can feel the consequences of his or her disobedience. A clear sign of God's protection being removed is when your private life becomes public. He unveils the true nature of the prodigal. It is certain that they know who they are and what their ultimate motives are, but at this level of disobedience, everyone else also becomes aware of who they are. New sins will be followed by new judgments. We find an example of this in the life of Gideon in Judges 6, where we find the Midianites oppressing the people of God. They returned every year at a certain season to ravish the Israelites afresh. Each year they came with a new approach to oppressing the people. This oppression was caused by the disobedience of the Israelite nation. As a result, God intensified the oppression. I believe that this intensity came about as a result of the severe blow that the Midianites had sustained during the time of Moses (Numbers 31:1–18). Under Moses, the Israelites killed the kings of Midian—all five of them, and their families, including men, women, and children. They even destroyed the cattle, flocks, and goods. The memory of this disaster no doubt inflamed their resentment against the Israelites. This then becomes a sign to not only those who are against you but also those who are closest to and for you. In response to disobedience, God removes your ability to resist any opposition. Each time they say no to what is required of them in the natural scheme of things, the easier it gets to say no to future responsibilities. At some point, the very thing that they are fighting so hard to obtain, control, becomes the very thing that they lose (Rom. 1:21–27).

This accounts for the rapid deterioration of the prodigal person at any given moment. It can show up as one problem after another at a seemingly astonishing pace. I received a call from a police station a few weeks after Conan had been released from jail then a call from him reporting that he had been hospitalized, and finally a summons to appear in court. All of this came when things appeared to be taking a turn for the better. Charles Spurgeon once said, "The Lord does not allow his children to sin successfully." And in Numbers 32:23, God promises that your sin will find you out. Temptation in such cases becomes irresistible. The downward direction that it takes you causes you to lose motivation and weakens your desire to continue to fight or resist. The natural response to challenges is survival, but when that response becomes short-circuited due to rebellion, it overrides what responsible people would do naturally. Therefore, the incentives that formerly directed your decision making are no longer valid, and all problems are viewed as a normal way of life. A quote attributed to Oscar Wilde goes, "I can resist anything but temptation." This humorous comment becomes a serious reality to those who are in a state of continuous rebellion. One might ask, "Doesn't the Holy Spirit enable you to fight off such desires?" The Holy Spirit does empower a believer to resist negative behavior patterns, but only if that believer yields to and submits to His lead. God, the Holy Spirit, does not restrain those who choose to reject His directives. The way this is done is through conviction, which is a little different than guilt. If we look at it from a judicial standpoint, a defendant can be accused of committing a crime due to the suspicion of guilt. But it is not until he has gone through due process and is convicted of the crime that any consequences can be expected. So it is with the Holy Spirit. He not only accuses, He also convicts. He also has a due process that He follows. He warns you before you engage in an activity that will prove to be spiritually illegal, which can include actual crime, but for our purposes I want to focus on the spiritual violations. If the warning is ignored, He then hinders you from following through with the behavior by placing some type of obstacle in front of you to prevent a smooth act of disobedience. If in fact the act can be committed in spite of this, upon completion the soul is flooded with conviction, which is an overriding sense of having done wrong and of the impending judgment looming on the horizon. When this kind of feeling develops, it demands a strategy to find relief. This becomes the underlying motive for future occurrences of unacceptable behavior. Your responsibility as a parent or loved one is to short-circuit this pattern by exhibiting the character of God in the face of whatever comes along. Obedience builds character, and that is the object of our obedience. In other words, you become like those you obey. "Don't you realize that you can choose your own master? You can choose sin (with death) or else obedience (with acquittal). The one to whom you offer yourself—he will take you and be your master, and you will be his slave." (Rom. 6:16 TLB). This I believe is a transferable concept. Just as the four friends of the paralytic in Mark 2 witnessed the forgiveness and healing of their friend as a result of their faith, so it is with obedience; it postpones the wrath of God. Abraham prayed for the people of Sodom and Gomorrah and was taken under consideration based on his request (Gen. 18:16–33). God promised to spare the city for the sake of a righteous representative there who could account for the penalty that would be withheld as a result of their righteousness. Obedience is a transferable concept in that the judgment of God can be tempered and curtailed by the obedience of one. You may recall in 1 Corinthians 7:12–14 the apostle Paul discussing the issue of marriage and divorce. Verse 14 indicates that an unbelieving spouse is sanctified or set apart by the believing spouse even though they are void of righteousness. The righteousness of the believing spouse is transferred to the nonbeliever and the judgment of God is withheld. The supreme example of this is found in the person of the Lord Jesus Himself, in Romans 5:15–17 (NASB):

> But the free gift is not like the transgression. For if by the transgression of the one the many died, much more did the grace of God and the gift by the grace of the one Man, Jesus Christ, abound to the many. The gift is not like that which came through the one who sinned; for on the one

> hand the judgment arose from one transgression resulting in condemnation, but on the other hand the free gift arose from many transgressions resulting in justification. For if by the transgression of the one, death reigned through the one, much more those who receive the abundance of grace and of the gift of righteousness will reign in life through the One, Jesus Christ.

And so it is with you. Your willingness to do exactly what the Lord commands of you can result in the postponement and in some cases the removal of his judgment, affording you additional time to influence the future of those who have become prodigal. You can rest assured that when all seems lost, the Lord is still working on your behalf by minimizing consequences. Of course, there are limitations to what one can do in an attempt to bring about positive influence in the life of another. But I dare say that the idea that another option is being offered brings with it hope in and of itself. For those of you who may still be skeptical, the Bible is filled with example after example of how your behavior can influence the behavior of others. Take for instance 1 Corinthians 15:33, where it is clearly spells out how negative behavior is the dominant factor in unequally matched people. The word used to describe the condition is *corruption*. The thing that is so devastating about corruption is how subtly it works its way into the fiber of one's psyche. Corruption affects everything about people, causing them to go underground, leaving the mainstream world and functioning according to a distorted point of view. Corruption distorts your problem-solving ability. The first thing Adam did when he and Eve sinned was attempt to cover their bodies (Gen. 3). The Israelites resorted to dens and caves as living quarters as opposed to obedience to the Lord (Judges 6). Israel's sin made all their work profitless. All their produce and livestock were stolen after they worked hard to bring it to fruition. Corruption does this; it robs us of what we work hard to gain, and it can all be the result of someone else's influence. When the Israelites obeyed the Lord, they reaped what others had sowed (Josh. 24:13; Ps. 105:44). But once disobedience caused corruption, others began reaping what they had sowed. When disobedience results in this type of corruption, all motivation and desire for improvement are removed. The creativity of life is dissipated, and everything becomes hard because the Lord Himself is no longer your friend but your enemy. There are so many factors that come into play when you disobey God. Nothing goes right, and you find yourself in constant turmoil. This accounts for the prodigal person who continues to create one complication after another with seemingly no effort whatsoever. I recall saying on one occasion in response to our son's continual downward spiral, "What is wrong? Why does this keep happening?" The answer is found here—disobedience is devastating.

But there is hope; disobedience can be overcome. The first thing that needs to happen if you are going to stand effectively against disobedience and thereby influence those who have become prodigal is to call upon the Lord. This has to be done with sincerity. People call on the name of the Lord in combat situations, in courtrooms, in hospitals, and in penitentiaries. When you call upon the Lord, you must be prepared to wait on His response. God sometimes postpones deliverance to ensure sincerity. Things often get worse in response to your request before there are any signs of improvement. Answered prayer is sometimes like a story in progress; you enter in where prayer begins, and the longer you pray, the clearer things become. Sometimes God's answers differ from your request, so it helps to keep in mind that we don't know what to pray for as we should. (Rom. 8:26). Sincerity is important for several reasons. When you call upon Him with sincerity, God reminds you of His love for you in spite of the way things appear. No matter what condition the Israelites found themselves in, when they got serious, God responded to their pleas for help. Love has the ability to override disappointment brought on by disobedience. Love tempers correction with the assurance that what is going on at the moment is for the benefit and good of all involved. Love leaves no room for hopelessness because the very relationship that we have with God was founded upon hope. When we call upon the Lord with sincerity, he reminds us of His power—the power that was used to deliver the Israelites from Egypt and the power that He used to deliver them from the Midianites. The power that God used to deliver you from the power of sin and to bring you into newness of life is the same power that is available to challenge disobedience. Sometimes the cause of rebellion gets lost in its own cycle. I think it is safe to say that, at a certain point, the true cause becomes invisible and is replaced by the consequences of disobedience. When this is the case, most calls for help are designed to remove one from the consequences of one's behavior. As an observer and advocate for change, you will come to realize that you are constantly dealing with the unseen and responding to the effects, not the causes. This is due to the constant eulogizing of one's responsibilities and the resurrecting of irresponsible behavior in their place. Habits are relatively easy to develop but can be extremely difficult to break. However, both require time and effort to do. So the majority of the responses that you see will be based on a source that you will not see. Therefore, you cannot be too hasty in the conclusions that you draw. The issues must be addressed, of course, but with the understanding that the solutions that may be achieved are symptomatic and therefore may not be final. This understanding will minimize frustration in the future. This is where your relationship with the

Lord becomes so important simply because He sees and knows all. Keep in mind that the same Lord who elevated you above your own capabilities and delivered you from great bondage is available to you now. The Lord brought you up. The same Lord is chastening those who are disobedient in order to bring him or her back to reality. Believe it or not, His love does not diminish because of their behavior. It actually grows. Romans 2:4 says this: "Or do you show contempt for the riches of His kindness, tolerance and patience, not realizing that God's kindness leads you toward repentance?" (NIV). The Lord will bring you out. He is capable of empowering those who disobey with the ability to walk away from negative influences. But if in fact there is resistance to this process, the Lord will bring you down. This too is a sign of God's love. All too often, we misunderstand or resist the difficulties of life when in fact, in some cases, those very issues are the instruments that the Lord uses to discipline and strengthen us. Needless to say the disobedient needs strength, which has to be spiritual if it's going to produce the type of results that will be lasting. Spiritual matters are not easily understood when one is operating purely according to the flesh. It goes without saying that prodigal people are running on 107.3 octane all of the time. It is the very thing that keeps them performing in a negative manner nonstop. The influence that is driving this engine must be rendered ineffective and then replaced. The Holy Spirit is the only one who can handle a job of this magnitude, keeping in mind that the major ingredient in the flesh that keeps it empowered in this case is disobedience. Disobedience is a derivative of pride, which is the first and foremost enemy of the spirit-filled life. In order to understand this from a biblical standpoint, we have to revisit the response of Abram to God's promise of making him a great nation. The story is found in Genesis 12. God pronounces to Abram some clear instructions that he is to follow, beginning with, "…Go forth from your country and your relatives..." (Gen. 12:1) The command is clear enough and even has some great benefits that accompany an obedient response. What appears to be an open-and-shut case somehow causes Abram to deliberate and to decide against the explicit instructions as the Creator of the universe has offered them. In verse 4 of chapter 12, we are invited into the very heart of Abram, and through observation, we see a prideful man deciding that his way is better than God's way. This, by the way, is the same attitude of all who decide to do things their own way. "Abram went forth as the Lord had spoken and he took Lot with him." (Gen.12:4) Lot was a relative whom God had made clear was not to accompany Abram. The transition is very subtle and may have been unintentional, but it was nonetheless devastating. By virtue of this behavior, Abram was making a bold statement that he knew better than God what was best for him. If you read through the entire passage, which runs through chapter 19—and I encourage you do so—you will discover that the results of this type of decision making were catastrophic. And more important, it had its beginning in the melting pot of pride.

Several things occurred as a result, and we can learn from this incident and hopefully avoid repetition. First of all, Abram's decision-making process no longer focused on God but was based on fear. When fear becomes your motivation, self-preservation takes first place in your life. We find this to be true in verse 12 of chapter 12 of the book of Genesis. Abram is concerned about his own well-being, not the safety of his wife. He is self-absorbed and blinded by the need to survive.

The next area is that of anger. Anger in some cases works in tandem with fear. Have you ever had a loved one who was scheduled to arrive at a certain location at a specific time but was not there when expected? Maybe it was a child who did not arrive home from school or a spouse who was due home from work.

Of course, this kind of thing happens on occasion and normally does not cause us any great alarm, especially when the absence spans only a brief period of time. But if the period of time should stretch into hours, our attitude changes. What was originally mild concern now turns into anxiety and worry accompanied by fear. If the event extends into the several-hour brackets, the feelings of worry become intermingled with those of anger. Of course, the reason for these feelings is that there is a fluctuation between the concerns that you have for your loved one, hoping no harm has befallen him or her, and your personal feelings of being left in the dark as to where your loved one is. Questions arise in the mind such as, *Why don't they call?* or *Should I have done one thing or another to ensure that this kind of thing would not have happened?* When your loved one arrives safely, there is a great sense of relief that is instantly followed by anger. "Why didn't you call?" you ask immediately. Anger has successfully overshadowed every other emotion (worry, concern, anxiety, fear, terror) that may have been present. So it is with anger—it covers all other feelings and takes on an identity all of its own. When your prodigal appears to be angry for one reason or another, it is usually an attempt to cover an underlying feeling that is not as appropriate to exhibit. There is something acceptable about anger while worry is not. There is something acceptable about rage while fear is not. The causes of anger are many and varied and, in most cases, cannot be identified by any of the parties involved, the perpetrator or those who are the targets of the anger. This is not to say that it is impossible to do so, but I believe a third party is necessary to flesh out the true source of the anger, like a health care professional, pastor, or therapist. It's not that the issue is so complex that it is beyond the scope of the average person; it's just that in most cases, you are too close to the situation and it becomes hard to see beyond what you are experiencing on a regular basis. The emotions of it all become overwhelming and extremely difficult to bear.

But I want to offer to you today some hope as a person who has observed this anger as having another source other than what's being observed is relief in and of itself. You don't have to know the dynamics behind it; you just need to be aware of its presence. You must always keep in mind that anger is designed to achieve something. In some cases, it can be as simple as the accomplishment of one's attitude in spite of the demands and wishes of others. This type usually appears in the form of haughtiness, behaving in a superior, condescending, or arrogant way. Sometimes its goal is to provoke anger in you. This helps with the guilt that is usually accompanied with the prodigal person's lifestyle. At other times, it's designed to ease the pressure of responsible living, the pressure related to things such as getting a job, cleaning an area of the home, or participating in some family event. Disobedience can cause great misery and can be devastating to those who are experiencing it. Be encouraged; this condition is a place where Jesus not only understands but is endeared to those who are experiencing it. Jesus chose to spend some of the most significant moments of His life in misery. In Matthew 26:1–13, and verse 6 in particular, we are told that Jesus was in Bethany. The name *Bethany* means "the house of misery" on account of its lonely situation and the invalids, sick, destitute, disenfranchised, and down-and-out people who congregated there. After Jesus cleansed the temple (Matt. 21:12–17), the chief priest and teachers were indignant. He left them and went to Bethany. Following His triumphant entry (Mark 11:11), He went to Bethany with the twelve. When He made His final remarks followed by His ascension, He went out to the vicinity of Bethany and was taken to heaven. Why did he choose Bethany and not the synagogue or the temple (Luke 24:50, 51)? In both instances we see that the house of misery was an important place to Jesus. "For we do not have a high priest who is unable to sympathize with our weakness, but we have one who has been tempted in every way, just as we are, yet without sin" (Heb. 4:15) Take heart, beloved; you are in good company.

Prayer

Father in heaven, I'm convinced that disobedience has devastated me in several ways. But I'm encouraged to know that you not only understand the misery that it has caused me but have also felt it and chosen to closely associate yourself with those in like circumstances. I thank you for the privilege of knowing that I am not alone in my suffering and for choosing me to be a part of such a great legacy that includes a sufferer who is able to alleviate my suffering, namely You. In Jesus' name, amen.

Memory Verses
Hebrews 4:15, 16

Much like the prophet Jonah, when you resist God's divine process of healing and move away from his will for your life, resentment sets in and you can find yourself traveling in the opposite direction. Remember, it takes an equal amount of time to turn around as it does to continue. If you view resentment as the point of no return and add just a little faith, you'll find your strength renewed.

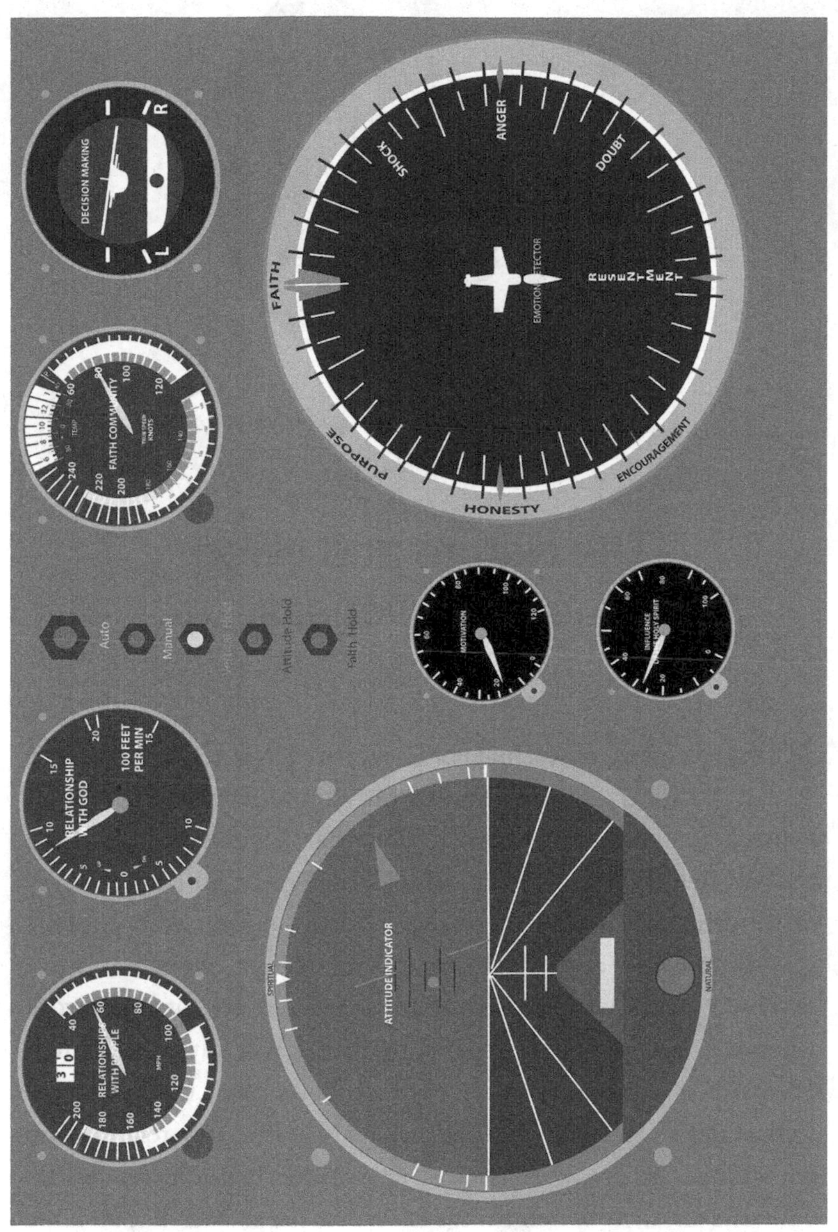
DECISION MAKING
L
R
FAITH COMMUNITY
KNOTS
RELATIONSHIP WITH GOD
100 FEET PER MIN
RELATIONSHIP WITH PEOPLE
MPH
Auto
Manual
Attitude Hold
Faith Hold
MOTIVATION
ATTITUDE INDICATOR
SPIRITUAL
NATURAL
FAITH
SHOCK
ANGER
DOUBT
RESENTMENT
ENCOURAGEMENT
HONESTY
PURPOSE

Chapter 5

The Nature and Need for Forgiveness

Forgiveness is a powerful alternative to revenge. The significance of this statement can never be fully appreciated until you find yourself in the midst of a situation that has all but destroyed the possibility of reconciliation. This has to be an ongoing way of thinking when you are engaged with a person who exhibits very little evidence of making any significant changes from a destructive lifestyle. I believe that forgiveness does its best work when it is undeserved. It does its best work when it's unsolicited. So many things can go wrong within one's way of thinking, as well as one's way of sustaining physical health. Our relationship with Christ is predicated upon it and our ongoing fellowship with one another. When things have become so bad that all hope appears to be gone and resistance is at an all-time high, forgiveness becomes our means of stability. Let's consider why forgiveness is so important and where it actually originated. According to Genesis 3, man was given the responsibility to tend the garden and to have continuous fellowship with God. But man violated those perfect conditions and found himself separated from God. His first response was to cover up his wrongdoing and to hide from God. Of course, this was an impossibility that resulted in being confronted by God and his sin being pointed out. Judgment was passed, and man would never be the same again. Before God executed his final verdict, he provided Adam with a process that would follow him throughout the ages. Adam was clothed by the Lord, and in doing so He instituted forgiveness. This was explained earlier, but the difference is that a system of forgiveness was being established. God was informing Adam that this was the only way to maintain a relationship with Him. As we follow humans' relationship with God from then on, what we find is that in order for an unbroken relationship with God to continue, this process of forgiveness would always include a sacrifice for humans by humans.

The Levitical priesthood became the ongoing method whereby this process could be carried out in a systematic way. Whenever sin was committed, the appropriate sacrifice would then be required. This process continued all the way through the Old Testament. As significant as this process was, it was only to serve as a model of the final sacrifice that was promised in Genesis 3—the person of Christ. The example was set throughout the entire history of the Israelite nation, and every believer would be required to extend it to any and all who stood in need of it. God expects every one of us to keep in mind what He expects of us and how it is based on what He did for us. He has declared in one location the following: "For God made Christ, who never sinned, to be the offering for our sin, so that we could be made right with God through Christ" (2 Cor. 5:21 NLT). Christ was created for the express purpose of providing forgiveness for sin, and under those circumstances we should do no less, which is to be quick to forgive and to maintain continuous relationships with one another. The following will serve as a vivid description of how this can be done in spite of what you may be experiencing.

As you can see, forgiveness is therapeutic and absolutely necessary for life and happiness. A series of characteristics found in forgiveness can be instrumental in personal development as well as environmentally effective in sustaining a good atmosphere where relationships can grow and flourish. It affords you the opportunity to accomplish things that could not otherwise be achieved. One such achievement that is in your grasp is the ability to fortify your relationships. We live in a throwaway society today that takes very little stock in preservation but is more concerned with replacement. Most things that are reparable can almost be classified as relics, antiques, and museum ready in today's economy. We feel that such possessions are to be tucked away and passed on to future generations. This kind of mentality unfortunately affects our relationships with one another as well. When we begin to see wear and tear, the tendency is to get someone new and place those existing relationships in our personalized recycled bins. This type of storage process makes things available but not necessary for our immediate use. You can tell if you are working with or have begun to develop a recycled mentality by the attitude you take toward the behavior of your loved ones or the amount of effort that is added to or being omitted from your attempts to continue to work with them. There needs to be some readjustment in your thinking if progress is going to begin or continue. Instead of focusing on failures and shortcomings, you must draw your attention to strengthening the relationship regardless of the state it is in. Forgiveness affords you the opportunity to do so. It opens the door to an untapped reservoir of resources that are not dependent upon anyone else's behavior or attitude. It becomes more and more obvious that the state of your mental well-being is more important than the confused value systems of those who may be resisting you. It goes without saying that large portions of your waking moments are spent thinking about or responding to one negative experience after another. As a result, your life becomes unbalanced, and you then stand in danger of becoming an enabler, which is taking on the responsibility of another person at almost any expense. Forgiveness offsets this kind of thinking by removing the responsibility from you and placing it squarely upon the shoulders of the rightful owner. It enables you to face the reality of your role while at the same time avoiding being burdened by someone else' responsibility. Once you have trained yourself to make this a regular part of your relationship, you will find that tension is minimized and, in most cases, stress relieved. Granted, problems will persist, but the weight of circumstances surrounding your challenge will no longer dominate your thinking, nor will it be a hindrance to your everyday experiences. Even though there will not be perfection, there will be improvement. As long as forgiveness is being initiated, the relationship will get better. I'm certain that most of us want the best for our children and shudder to think about anything less, so any sign of progress is motivation to keep trying to make a difference. There are no magic formulas to implement that will guarantee ongoing success, but a sense of fulfillment can be experienced when you see the smallest amount of advancement in a positive direction. The main thing to look for is a stronger resolve to continue to fight for the needs of your child. The battle becomes intense along the journey, but as you begin to realize that there is no behavior that can override the ability to forgive, you find the resolve necessary for renewed hopefulness. Yes, there may be times when you feel like giving up, but what offsets those times are the inner workings of the power of forgiveness. As we have seen, forgiveness has the capability to fortify relationships, but it also has the ability to orchestrate a strategy for change. It is important to remain open to the reality of what may be going on around you. There may be a need to challenge some old perspectives that you have held for a lifetime, keeping in mind the magnitude of what you are engaged in. If what you are doing is based on preconceived ideas about the way you feel things should be yet there is little or no progress as a result, that kind of thinking must be discarded. The era in which you were born may determine how you view the circumstances in which you now find yourself. Some of the things you may be called upon to endure today may have been totally taboo during your formative years. But for the sake of the challenges that you are now facing, you may need to adjust that way of thinking and, in some cases, totally discard it.

One of the things you have to develop is the ability to hear things differently. Your child is in a different world altogether and communicates completely differently from the way you may have come to understand communication. When you listen in this manner, you have to interpret what you hear because the meaning may not be seen on the surface. Listening to the unspoken requires great skill and concentration and can only be accomplished through disciplined focus and confident expectation. You have to enter into the world of your child on a level that goes far beyond what may have been suggested by leading sociologists because you have information that sociologists do not, and that is what you have done in your own personal life. You have information that has a direct influence over your child that you may not be aware of. In order to listen to your child in this manner, you have to hear what you are saying and understand where that information is emanating from. Be honest with yourself—what has your child done that you haven't done? There may be some variation of form, but nonetheless you probably did much the same thing. And the degrees of involvement may vary, but in most cases, some of the experience will be identifiable. The experiences that you have had must be revisited in order to understand exactly what I am talking about. I am not a genetic specialist, nor do I understand how it all works, but I do know that my parents influenced who I am and to some extent what I do, and I know that I have influenced what my children do. The reality is that there is a certain portion of what your child does that has come directly from you. So don't be too hard on yourself. Keeping in mind that children are held accountable for their own behavior but with the understanding of why they respond the way that they do and the part that I may have unknowingly played will enable me to persevere when things become difficult. The Bible makes it clear that each person has to give an account for his or her own behavior, but we must remember that the way we as parents respond to that behavior could determine the ultimate direction that behavior may take our children. Healing takes place when the appropriate medication is given or behavior is carried out. The human body is a remarkable machine that operates very efficiently. It gives warning signs when things are not operating the way they are supposed to. This holds true in the area of emotional difficulty as well. Outward misbehavior is indeed an indication of something gone wrong. As parents, we have an inside track based on our own experiences.

One of the greatest principles of the Christian faith is forgiveness. Jesus modeled it for us when He hung on the cross and extended it to the very people who were crucifying Him. This expression of forgiveness was so powerful and unexpected that it brought about the instant conversion of one of the thieves hanging on the cross next to Him. So it is with forgiveness—it should always bring about a change in the attitudes and actions of those to whom it is extended. As believers, we often think of the magnitude of change that conversion brings about exclusively as "being saved." Of course, when a person receives Christ, the change that takes place is extraordinary and cannot be denied, but the elements of that radical change can also be applied to forgiveness. Conversion is the down payment of the life that is to come, ultimately in heaven but also right here on earth. The main issue here is this: you cannot forgive or be forgiven and remain the same. It is safe to say in light of this that the main purpose of forgiveness is to bring about conversion in the life of the recipient. What I mean by *conversion* here, in essence, is to change from one state to another. What makes forgiveness so revolutionary is the fact that God has forgiven us so that we may in turn forgive others. "Whenever you [a]stand praying, forgive, if you have anything against anyone, so that your Father who is in heaven will also forgive you your transgressions. But if you do not forgive, neither will your Father who is in heaven forgive your transgressions. (Mark 11:25–26 NASB).

As believers, we are so accustomed to the term that we sometimes lose sight of its significance and the far-reaching effects that it has on both parties, the forgiver and the forgiven. But as we can see from the above, our own forgiveness hinges upon it. The Lord Jesus was indeed a revolutionary. He went against the system not for the sheer delight of doing so but to provide for us what is absolutely necessary to maintain healthy relationships. Of course, what we as parents want is change, and there is not much that we will not do to get it. I believe forgiveness affords us the opportunity to initiate it. Let's take a closer look at forgiveness and see if we can't discover the potential it offers us to promote change in the lives of those who are bent on doing their own

---

[a] Matt 6:5

thing. There are at least seven words that are used throughout the Bible to describe forgiveness. One of the things that I noticed instantly was that they all have to do with change. For instance, in the Old Testament, forgiveness is identified by the following Hebrew words:

- *Kaphar*: To cover (Deut. 21:1–9; Ps. 78:38; Jer. 18:23)
- *Nasa*: To lift away the sin from the sinner (Ps. 25:18; 85:2; 99:8)
- *Salach*: To send out (Lev. 4:20, 26, 31, 35; 5:10, 13, 16, 18)

The New Testament uses the following Greek words:

- *Apoluo*: To set free (Luke 6:37; 13:12)
- *Charizomai*: To be gracious unto (Eph. 4:32; Col. 2:13, 14; 3:13)
- *Aphiemi*: To send off or away (Matt. 4:11, 20, 22; Rom. 4:7)
- *Aphesis*: A sending away (Heb. 9:22; 10:18)

What we see is that forgiveness has an origin and a destination with the ultimate result of liberation. The need for forgiveness, as we have seen, originated in the garden, and its ultimate destination was you (Rom. 5:12–14). It came as a result of sin, and unfortunately the same need remains today. Forgiveness is designed to accomplish what we cannot—to bring about conversion, to change a person's thinking completely. I would imagine that it would be difficult to comprehend the gist of that kind of thinking without some kind of explanation. After all, conversion is a big concept. Let's begin by taking a look at the thief on the cross. In Luke 23: 33–43, we find this condemned man making an instant change as a result of observing the forgiveness of God. This can be understood as we look at two other tellings of this story (Matt. 27:44; Mark 15:32). In those, we find that both thieves initially felt the same way as the people did about the person of Christ, even in their deplorable state. As a matter of fact, they probably knew each other and could even have been in the same institution and possibly partners in crime. How else could one of them have known that he and his partner were being punished justly? He could speak for himself but not for the other unless he had some knowledge of the other's guilt (Luke 23:41). I believe this thief was converted when he saw Christ's expression of forgiveness towards the very people who were crucifying Him. I would imagine that his parents had given up all hope concerning the possibility of any change taking place in the life of this thief.

Let's examine exactly how this man's life was changed as a result of forgiveness. Please take note that he was a witness of Christ's forgiveness, not a recipient per se. That brings with it tremendous hope for those who may be in the heart of ill repute with little or no escape from its clutches. That means that even those who may not be repentant can benefit from the observation. Your child or children should see you forgiving people publicly. It could make the difference between overcoming and persisting in the same destructive behavior that has been prevalent for so long.

Consider how this man was impacted by the forgiveness of Christ and how it could impact not only the ones we love but also ourselves. The first thing he began to see was the justice of his own punishment. He was getting what he deserved (Luke 23:41). It's not until you begin to realize that you are genuinely wrong that you begin to take the necessary steps toward change. Sociologists call this "bottoming out." After a certain type of behavior has persisted for a long enough period of time, it becomes normal behavior, and it's very difficult to recognize the need for change. Just being exposed to forgiveness heightens your awareness and sensitizes you to the need for some kind of adjustment. Habits are hard to break, and they have a tendency to become normal behavior for those who develop them, including self-destructive habits. That is why there is a need to recognize the behavior of others as different from your own. We have a tendency to believe that everyone thinks the way that we do when we are totally engulfed in our own way of thinking. Getting a glimpse of others is a sure way of positioning oneself for change. This thief on the cross had a choice and no doubt wanted to make it clear that he was not going to succumb to the pressure of the surrounding circumstances as the other thief had decided to do. But when he saw the sinless character of Christ, he was pierced through the heart and instantly saw the need for change. His admission that Christ had done nothing wrong and, as a result, was not angry or bitter about it was more than his resistance could stand. Suffering for unjust behavior would have been justifiable, but innocently submitting to mistreatment on this level and not holding any animosity against the malefactors demanded change. So it is with you as your loved one observes your responses to unacceptable behavior and your willingness to forgive it. It will make an indelible impact. Let me hasten to add that forgiveness and codependency are two different things. Let's consider the following: codependency is the denial, loss, or repression of the real self. It is based on the belief that love, acceptance, security, success, and closeness are dependent upon one's ability to control (or have tremendous impact) on another person's behavior or life. Some common signs of codependency are that people

- Assume responsibility of meeting others' needs to the exclusion of acknowledging their own.
- Feel anxiety, pity, and guilt when other people have a problem.
- Feel angry when their help isn't effective.

- Abandon their routine to respond to or do something for somebody else.
- Feel safest when giving.
- Overcommit themselves.
- Find themselves attracted to needy people.
- Wonder why others don't do the same for them.
- Try to please others instead of themselves.
- Find it easier to feel and express anger about injustices done to others rather than injustices done to them.
- Feel insecure and guilty when somebody gives to them.
- Feel bored, empty, and worthless if they don't have a crisis in their lives, a problem to solve, or someone to help.
- Feel sad because they spend their whole lives giving to other people and nobody gives to them. [14]

On the other hand, forgiveness sees the value in another person and is willing to do whatever is necessary to provide that person with a clear perspective of another alternative. This behavior places the responsibility squarely on the shoulders of the person who is forgiven. One of the fears that surfaces when forgiveness is extended is that of being used or taken for granted by the person being forgiven. Just as the thief on the cross saw the deity and destination of Christ as a result of being forgiven, so it is with your prodigal child. When they come to understand that they have been forgiven, the potential and location of their future will then be brought to bear. They'll begin to sense that there is more to life than what has been driving them to the brink of destruction. They'll see themselves as a valued part of society as well as of the family. As codependency is the result of an

---

[14] "What Is Codependency?" Clinical Solutions LLC. Retrieved from www.clinicalsolutions.org/Codependency.html. (Accessed 11/10/14.www.clinicalsolutions.org/Co_Dependency.html

attempt to meet the needs of someone else at the expense of your own, forgiveness is meeting your own needs by making the other person aware of another alternative, which in turn enables them to see and satisfy their own needs. A person who is codependent feels guilt about the behavior of someone else. In some ways, they take responsibility for another's behavior. Guilt is recognized as a signal for change when forgiveness is extended as a result of someone else's behavior. Codependency attempts to please the one who actually needs to be displeased enough to do something about their condition. The comparison should be clear, and if so, there is no need to fear enablement as long as your focus is on the responsibility of the person in question and not on how you can control what they do.

The thief began to see things with a whole new outlook. Not only was there more to life than he was experiencing, but he was made aware of life after death. Often we hear complaints about those who feel that their time is limited, saying that they have done great harm to themselves and could never make up for it. This kind of thinking may be understandable but unacceptable. God has given us the ability to see beyond the grave. When your perspective of death changes, your perspective of life does also. The reality is that death is always a possibility but it should not be feared. Because of what Christ has done for us, we can move through our responsibilities with confidence. One of the things that the thief makes clear by his response is that, regardless of how bad things may appear to be, there is always hope. One thief was saved, which gives us all hope, but only one so that none of us will assume that salvation is automatic. All too often, we want to see change before we forgive, but as we have seen, it oftentimes works the other way around. Forgiveness should bring change as opposed to change bringing forgiveness.

Forgiveness follows a pattern that is predicated upon the

work of Christ. As we extend and receive it, we become the very expressions of what Christ did over two thousand years ago. Our sin was so great that we could not atone for it, nor could we do anything to remove its consequences. No amount of restitution could satisfy the righteous demands of a holy God. It was so great that our punishment was nothing short of total destruction, even annihilation. But God, through His compassionate grace, has extended to us an opportunity to escape his judgment. Romans 5:15–16 (NLT) puts it this way:

> But there is a great difference between Adam's sin and God's gracious gift. For the sin of this one man, Adam, brought death to many. But even greater is God's wonderful grace and his gift of forgiveness to many through this other man, Jesus Christ. And the result of God's gracious gift is very different from the result of that one man's sin. For Adam's sin led to condemnation, but God's free gift leads to our being made right with God, even though we are guilty of many sins.

Therefore, we should not put any limitations on the forgiving of others. Grace is the kindness of love and of God our Savior toward us based solely upon his concern for us, not our ability to do anything to deserve his favor. As stated in Titus 3:4–7 (NLT),

> But—"When God our Savior revealed his kindness and love, he saved us, not because of the righteous things we had done, but because of his mercy. He washed away our sins, giving us a new birth and new life through the Holy Spirit. He generously poured out the Spirit upon us through Jesus Christ our Savior. Because of his grace he

> declared us righteous and gave us confidence that we will inherit eternal life.

As a principle, therefore, grace is set in contrast with the law under which God demands righteousness from each one of us. But on the other hand, grace gives righteousness to us without any participation on our part whatsoever. Under the law, blessings accompany obedience while grace bestows blessing as a free gift. The law always came with stipulations attached to it, but forgiveness originated from God. Therefore, it is a divine response to an injustice. Knowing the incapability of humans to satisfy God's demands for the wrong being done against Him, God does the most humane thing—that is, He extends grace to the guilty party. It is clearly understood that the receiver does not deserve it, and the giver does not want anything for it. Forgiveness is giving love when there is no reason to love and no guarantee that it will be returned. Forgiveness is to be given when appreciation, tenderness, compassion, and love are nowhere to be found. Forgiveness is repaying evil with kindness and doing all the things that love requires, even when you do not feel the love. Forgiveness is "giving up" all rights and privileges, it's giving notice that a wrong has been done, and it's giving grace—a free gift of your love—with no strings attached. Only when a pure, unexpected, unreasonable, and undeserved expression of forgiveness appears in a relationship does newness enter in and healing begin. This is grace. The posture for forgiveness is available at all times. In Matthew 18:21–35 (NASB), Peter makes this appeal:

> Then Peter came and said to Him, "Lord, how often shall my brother sin against me and I forgive him? Up to seven times?" Jesus said to him, "I do not say to you, up to seven times, but up to seventy times seven. For this reason

[a]the kingdom of heaven may be compared to a king who wished to settle accounts with his slaves. When he had begun to settle *them,* one who owed him ten thousand talents was brought to him. But since he did not have *the means* to repay, his lord commanded him to be sold, along with his wife and children and all that he had, and repayment to be made. So the slave fell *to the ground* and prostrated himself before him, saying, 'Have patience with me and I will repay you everything.' And the lord of that slave felt compassion and released him and forgave him the debt. But that slave went out and found one of his fellow slaves who owed him a hundred denarii; and he seized him and *began* to choke *him,* saying, 'Pay back what you owe.' So his fellow slave fell *to the ground* and *began* to plead with him, saying, 'Have patience with me and I will repay you.'

But he was unwilling and went and threw him in prison until he should pay back what was owed. So when his fellow slaves saw what had happened, they were deeply grieved and came and reported to their lord all that had happened. Then summoning him, his lord said to him, 'You wicked slave, I forgave you all that debt because you pleaded with me. 'Should you not also have had mercy on your fellow slave, in the same way that I had mercy on you?' And his lord, moved with anger, handed him over to the torturers until he should repay all that was owed him.

---

a Matt 13:24

> "My heavenly Father will also do the same to you, if each of you does not forgive his brother from your heart."

Peter knew that in the past, forgiveness was given on a threefold basis—"For three transgressions of Israel ... I will turn away punishment" (Amos 2:6)—but now he feels he should be more generous. So he goes from three to seven, reasoning that this kind of thinking would be more than adequate to elicit a positive response to his question. Since seven was considered the number of completion and perfection, Peter may have thought that anyone who could forgive someone that many times must be a spiritually mature person. With this approach, the offended person would be under no obligation to grant forgiveness except for on the contrary judgment. What Peter had to learn was that forgiveness was not a matter of mathematics but of conduct. God's forgiveness is unlimited. What this parable teaches us is that forgiveness must be, as it is with God, a constant attitude. When God forgives, He forgets. This is the healthiest thing you can do for a rebellious child and anybody else, for that matter. When you understand forgiveness as an attitude and not an act, it has the potential to promote personal healing in addition to the encouragement that others will experience. Love keeps no record of wrongs nor does it ignore them, but rather it exposes them so that they can be faced and ultimately forgotten. When God declared, "I am the one who erases all your sins for my sake; I will not remember your sins" (Is. 43:25 NCV) He was saying in essence that once they have been dealt with, they will be forever forgotten. This parable illustrates this divine trait.

If the talent is taken to be a talent of silver, then according to the Roman calculation "ten thousand talents," this is equivalent to three millions dollars. If the value of the talent were figured according to the Jewish calculation, the ten thousand talents would represent well over three million pounds, or about ten million dollars. But if the talent was actually a talent of gold, then the ten thousand talents would be more than fifty million pounds, or the equivalent of over one hundred and fifty million dollars. Realizing the poverty-stricken condition of this man, the master moved with compassion and forgave his debt, suffering a great personal loss as a result. (By the way, it was customary during that time to require wives and children to be given as payment [2 Kings 4:1; Neh. 5:8].) It should go without saying that the man should have extended the same kind of compassion to others. But according to our text, something completely different happened. One of his fellow servants owed him only three hundred pence, which amounted to twelve dollars—totally out of comparison to what he had been forgiven. God has extended to each one of us one hundred and fifty million dollars' worth of grace in the form of forgiveness, and we have no right whatsoever to withhold a twelve-dollar debt that we are owed. Since it is in our complete control, we must not be like that wicked servant. When it came to giving forgiveness, this servant showed no love or compassion, only hardheartedness and anger. And so is the tendency of the rebellious to become angry when they are expected to do what others have been doing for them all along. There are no equal rights when the personal desire is more important than the needs of others. This is all too often the case in the life of the rebellious. We can see the extent that anger will go to accomplish its ends. We find this servant taking his debtor by the throat and demanding that payment be made immediately. He had totally forgotten the forgiveness and grace that had been shown to him. I believe that a lack of forgiveness on the part of the one offended can result in a distorted view of not only how to maintain a healthy relationship but also the inability to establish one. Without forgiveness, most relationships are doomed to fail simply because we come up short. We all fail to some degree or another. The gauge for forgiveness was established by the example of the Lord Himself. Ephesians 4:32 (NASB) says, "Be kind to one another, tenderhearted, forgiving each other, just as God in Christ also has forgiven you." When it comes to forgiveness, you must be promiscuous about extending it. That is, it must be lacking in standards of selection, indiscriminate. You have to give it up anywhere, anytime, with anybody. And "forget none of His benefits; Who pardons all your iniquities, Who heals all your diseases" (Ps. 103:3 NASB). "If we confess our sins, He is faithful and righteous to forgive us our sins and to cleanse us from all unrighteousness" (1 John 1:9 NASB).

Forgiveness, like love, knows no end, has no boundaries, and is limitless. I guess we do well to offer a method in which to extend forgiveness.

- When extending forgiveness, the person must be given your undivided attention, and you must receive the same.
- You must be open to whatever may surface in the discussion and not be offended by it.
- Show interest in the exchange by leaning forward and maintaining eye contact.
- Most importantly, remain calm and relaxed.

Please keep in mind that forgiving will not immediately soothe your pain; instead, it will introduce a different kind of pain, pain that's filled with hope. You may have to die a little in order to forgive. That is, you die to your own personal desires with all of their rights and privileges. The following steps are taken from the book *As for Me and My House* (Wangerine, 1990) I believe it will be helpful in the forgiveness process.

A. Be realistic:

1. Identify the immediate sin objectively, focusing on what was done rather than how it made you feel.
2. Identify against whom the sin was committed.
3. Identify the consequences of the sin and observe exactly what was damaged, your reputation, your pride, or your car battery. Pain causes tears or blood, which blurs your vision and your perspective can become distorted.

B. Remember your own need for forgiveness:

1. Recall that although you may have done it differently, there have been times that you have sinned.
2. Remember the sins that we see easiest in others are closely associated with our own.
3. Keep in mind that you and your prodigal are not enemies but wanderers in the same wilderness and in need of each other's support.

C. Sacrifice your rights in prayer:

1. Forgiveness places the burden of reconciliation upon the one who suffered the offense.
2. Forgiveness is not a simple speaking of the correct words. It is to be given only when your whole being, your tone, expression, gestures and intent seek the other's healing. This can only be done through much prayer.
3. Keep in mind that praying in faith is focusing on God, not necessarily the problem. God increases our faith as we walk with him regardless of circumstances.

D. Tell your prodigal the sin:

1. Set the stage; be very intentional and not haphazard.
2. Once the sin is confessed forgiveness is to follow immediately.
3. All that you say should be spoken in a spirit of meekness.
4. Follow words with action; the prodigal's father in Luke 15 gave his son what he surely did not deserve; a ring, new shoes and a party.
5. Genuine forgiveness will look for ways to express love.

In Luke 8:40–48, the story is told of Jairus's daughter dying. Jesus pauses to deal with a woman who had a hemorrhage for twelve years and could not be healed by anyone. In the meantime, the girl who was dying died. He stops a funeral procession in the city of Nain to raise the dead son of a widowed mother. Luke 18:35-43 points out that while on his way to Calvary he paused to heal a blind man. While passing through Jericho en route to Bethany, he pauses to spend time with Zaccheus; Jesus was never in a hurry. Nowhere in scripture do you find him telling people to hurry up, come immediately, or get here right away, as mentioned earlier. Even though the crises that people were experiencing were urgent and constituted emergencies on their parts, they did not translate into an emergency on his part. But when it came to forgiveness, he did not hesitate. The prodigal's father is seen running to express his willingness to forgive. Men in the east did not run under normal circumstances. It was only the unusual circumstances that caused them to run, such as we find in 1 Kings 18:46, where Elijah is found outrunning a chariot.

Genesis 45:1–15 reveals the liberating power of forgiveness.

Then Joseph could not control himself before all those who stood by him, and he cried, "Have everyone go out from me." So there was no man with him when Joseph made himself known to his brothers. He wept so loudly that the Egyptians heard *it,* and the household of Pharaoh heard *of it.* Then Joseph said to his brothers, "I am Joseph! Is my father still alive?" But his brothers could not answer him, for they were dismayed at his presence. Then Joseph said to his brothers, "Please come closer to me." And they came closer. And he said, "I am your brother Joseph, whom you sold into Egypt. Now do not be grieved or angry with yourselves, because you sold me here, for God sent me before you to preserve life. For the famine *has been* in the land these two years, and there are still five years in which there will be neither plowing nor harvesting. God sent me before you to preserve for you a remnant in the earth, and to keep you alive by a great deliverance. Now, therefore, it was not you who sent me here, but God; and He has made me a father to Pharaoh and lord of all his household and ruler over all the land of Egypt. Hurry and go up to my father, and say to him, 'Thus says your son Joseph, "God has made me lord of all Egypt; come down to me, do not delay. You shall live in the land of Goshen, and you shall be near me, you and your children and your children's children and your flocks and your herds and all that you have. There I will also provide for you, for there are still five years of famine *to come,* and you and your household and

> all that you have would be impoverished." Behold, your eyes see, and the eyes of my brother Benjamin *see,* that it is my mouth which is speaking to you. Now you must tell my father of all my splendor in Egypt, and all that you have seen; and you must hurry and bring my father down here." Then he fell on his brother Benjamin's neck and wept, and Benjamin wept on his neck. He kissed all his brothers and wept on them, and afterward his brothers talked with him.

When forgiveness reaches its peak, it produces genuine maturity in the life of the offended party. What we find here in the life of Joseph is the ability to see God's hand even in the wrong that had been done to him. This is the mature thinking that liberates. There are several things that occurred in the life of Joseph that enabled him to do this, but one in particular stands out to me: he classified all that happened in his life as having been designed by the will of God even though he was void of any clear understanding of what was happening. He maintained a good attitude. He accepted all that happened to him and did not complain. Most certainly he could have complained to those with whom he was incarcerated. After all, what an inmate is in for and how he intends to get even or to get out or some other way to stay out of jail probably takes up most of his daily conversation.

When the grounds are right, it is not difficult to forgive someone who has wronged, mistreated, or abused you. And so it was with Joseph. His reasons for harboring bitterness would have been justified, but he chose to forgive instead. Forgiveness brings clarity and insight into the situation. What initially seemed quite confusing begins to make sense when forgiveness is extended. He sees God in the midst of it all not only protecting him but also using him to be a channel of blessing to someone else—in fact, an entire nation that was inclusive of a great number of people. His willingness to forgive enabled Joseph to become a whole person, and a well-rounded person for that matter. Where a lack of forgiveness brings bitterness and hardness, we find forgiveness bringing compassion and tenderness. Where the absence of forgiveness brings insecurity and fear, forgiveness brings confidence and godly decision making. Where the withholding of forgiveness brings doubt and distrust, forgiveness brings faith and assurance. This is quite a package being offered by the act of forgiveness. In light of the alternative, forgiveness is a far better response to mistreatment and disappointment. You would think that forgiveness would be a given under most if not all circumstances, but unfortunately it's not.

I believe that there is another dynamic always at work when there is a call to forgive, and that is the spiritual warfare dynamic. One of the subtle tactics of the devil is deception. He's a liar and the father of lies. Satan is a deceiver and a dangerous trickster. His most vicious attacks are directed against the believer. And one of his most effective methods against the children of God is prompting believers to hold onto resentment and deny forgiveness to another. The Bible describes the activity of the devil as schemes of the devil (Eph. 6:11). The Greek word for *schemes* is *Methodia,* from which we get the English word method. Of course, we usually attach a good connotation to it. But when it is used of Satan, the word becomes evil in its meaning and denotes a deceitful scheme. *Scheme,* on the other hand, comes from *Noema,* which denotes thought, that which is thought out, a purpose. As a fisherman uses a lure to draw a fish to a hidden hook and as a hunter conceals a trap for the unwary animal, so it is with Satan; he uses the refusal to forgive to lure and trap the believer. Satan seeks to gain a favorable and strategic place in the life of the believer to do him bodily harm and, more importantly, spiritual harm (2 Thess. 2:9). Unless we acquaint ourselves with his wiles and subtle strategies, we are bound to fall for his attacks. It is precisely the same idea that is conveyed by the injunction, "And do not give the devil an opportunity" (Eph. 4:27 NASB). This warning against yielding ground or giving a foothold to the devil was given in reference to a number of sins (Eph. 4:25–32 NIV), especially the sin of anger and also an unwillingness to forgive. The admonition is a simple one in regards to overcoming the problem of the influence of the devil, and that is to resist him and the promise is that he will flee (James 4:7). To resist is to set oneself against or to withstand. Remember, no matter how difficult things may become or how isolated you may feel, you are not alone. As Peter declares in 1 Peter 5:8–9, making it clear that we are not alone, "Be self-controlled and alert. Your enemy the devil prowls around like a roaring lion looking for someone to devour. Resist him, standing firm in the faith, because you know that your brothers throughout the world are undergoing the same kind of sufferings" (NIV).

Not only are you never alone, but the victory is already won. "I write to you fathers, because you have known him who is from the beginning. I write to you, young men, because you are strong, and the word of God lives in you, and you have overcome the evil one" (1 John 2:14 NIV). In addition, you have to make public what Jesus has done for you.

> Then I heard a voice in heaven say: "Now have come the salvation and the power and the kingdom of our God, and the authority of his Christ. For the accuser of our brothers, who accuses them before our God day and night, has been hurled down. They overcame him by the blood of the

> Lamb and because of the word of their testimony; and they did not love their life even when faced with death. (Rev. 12:10–11 NASB)

Those who do not forgive are being directly influenced by the devil. Just as rebellion is associated with divination (1 Sam. 15:23 NIV), so it is with an unwillingness to forgive; it stems from and breeds further wickedness. As you grapple with the challenges of rebellion, you know that other spiritual dynamics are also at work. It's important not to further compound the problem by striking out in retaliation against the very person you are trying to help by drawing irrational conclusions about what you will and will not accept in the way of their behavior. Of course, some situations will require a firm stand against dangerous behavior, but at the same time there must be a clear delineation between your action and your attitude toward all behavior to determine if, in fact, it's based on your desire to help and not borne out of a spirit of vindication. An unknown author put it this way: "To physically hurt your enemy puts you below your enemy; getting revenge on your enemy makes you even with them; forgiving your enemy puts you on a plane above your enemy." Of course we're not classifying our children as enemies, but the principle is true on any level we may find ourselves. We cannot stoop to the level that our children are on. I must admit the temptation will arise from time to time to lower your standard, but you must not give in to it. One of the things that we are trying to accomplish in our relationships with our children is to get to the point of recognizing that regardless of how they may feel for whatever the reasons may be, they have to respect the opinions and ideas of others; when you travel on the destructive route of rebellion, the first thing that takes flight is concern for others. Life loses its value and must be restored. There may not be a need on their part for restoration, but those of us who can clearly see the need must communicate it to them. As I have attempted to clarify this need, I suspect that in some cases the resistance to this attempt may have intensified the tension between you and those you are trying to help. This is where faith comes into play.

It goes without saying that this is a major project that we have undertaken, to attempt to guide the thinking of adults, in some cases, and those who think they are grown in others. We need assistance in managing this project. This is where I believe faith plays a major role. It becomes our project manager. That being the case, we then must allow it to govern the way we approach things from here on out. If faith is going to serve as your project manager, it will have to be the first thing that you consider when making any decision. What I mean by that is every decision that is made must be balanced on the fulcrum of faith. Any movement that is to be made rises and falls by the support that faith provides. This means that prayer has to be a constant partner to the effective operation of faith. In order for this to happen correctly, you must evaluate yourself properly. Without the support and help of Christ, nothing can or will be done. He is the author and finisher of faith, making him the purpose for our faith. The objectives of Christ must be first in all of our concerns, regardless of the response of those we are trying to help. Of course, they are outlined in His Word, the Bible, but we must be careful to apply those principles in practical ways so that others may see how they work. And a big one is the one under discussion—forgiveness.

In addition to faith becoming your project manager, it also has to be your accountability partner. At any given point, you must be able to determine whether you are operating according to faith or doing things based on your personal desires. When the element of faith is active, there will always be a need for total dependence upon God for results. Things should not be so clear that there is no need to trust God for the future or the ultimate outcome. As we approach faith in a manner such as being accountable to it, the truth of our genuine motives will be disclosed. Not only are we to be accountable to faith, but also we are to look for insight as a result of our belief. Some things cannot be understood by the existing facts but must be mixed with faith in order to produce the conclusions that will benefit our understanding. Faith, like most things that are of any lasting value, takes time to develop. This is especially true of faith; it develops through trial and error. It is forged as a result of constant application to areas that are not completely understood, but results can be seen from that application. What is so remarkable about this process is the fact that the end result is always hope. If the conclusion of the matter is positive, then it automatically gives me confidence for future concerns that may develop. It may appear difficult to understand, but God keeps all of his promises. We are all accustomed to promises. We are also accustomed to seeing them made and seeing them broken.

Who among us can claim that we have never broken a promise? There are many reasons that promises get broken. Sometimes we are negligent, sometimes we forget, sometimes it is due to circumstances beyond our control, and other times we simply lie, knowing that we have no intention of fulfilling what we have promised to complete. A brokenhearted young woman can be found to say, "But you promised to marry me." And the answer comes back, "Yes, but I changed my mind." People do change their minds, and they do break their promises. What about the promises of God? How certain are they? The apostle Paul addressing the church at Rome made this declaration:

> For the promise to Abraham or to his descendants that he would be heir of the world was not through

> the Law, but through the righteousness of faith. For this reason *it is* by faith, in order that *it may be* in accordance with grace, so that the promise will be guaranteed to all the descendants, not only to those who are of the Law, but also to those who are of the faith of Abraham, who is the father of us all ...

God's promise was spelled out in Genesis 12:3 (NASB) with these words: "And in you all the families of the earth will be blessed." The significance of God's promises is based upon this fact: it's impossible for Him to lie. When God makes a promise, you can rest assured that He is going to bring that promise to pass. The first promise that God made to man is found in Genesis 2:15–17 (NASB): "Then the Lord God took the man and put him into the Garden of Eden to cultivate it and keep it. The Lord God commanded the man, saying, 'From any tree of the garden you may eat freely; but from the tree of the knowledge of good and evil you shall not eat, for in the day that you eat from it you will surely die." God promised death as a result of disobedience to His commands to abstain from a particular type of behavior. That wasn't an empty threat; it did come to pass as promised. He then adds in Genesis 3:15, after man's failure, a promise of deliverance from the very condition that man's disobedience had placed him in. A savior was promised, and a savior came in the person of the Lord Jesus Christ. Every promise from then on will find its fulfillment in Christ. "For as many as are the promises of God, in Him they are yes; therefore, also through Him is our Amen to the glory of God through us" (2 Cor. 1:20 NASB).

Since the clarion call is that God keeps all of His promises, how then are His promises being kept when there may be no visible evidence whatsoever of their fulfillment? In addressing this concern, let's take a look at the implications of His promises. Throughout scripture, we find clear evidence of our inability to live up to God's standards. Time and time again, we are told of our desperate need for a deliverer, as we have already seen in the example given in Genesis 2. This is not an easy concept to embrace simply because of what we have become accustomed to throughout life. In childhood, we were rewarded for right behavior and punished for doing what was classified as wrong. If we behaved ourselves properly, we received Christmas gifts, we went to birthday parties, and we were granted a hoard of other things. While there are some promises that come with conditions, when it comes to God, His conditions are designed to broaden the scope of the promise and not to manipulate our behavior. For instance, 1 John 1:9 (NASB) states, "If we confess our sins, He is faithful and righteous to forgive us our sins and to cleanse us from all unrighteousness." Confession is the condition that relieves guilt for whatever the infraction may be, which in turn opens opportunities for discussion that will of course improve relationships. God then broadens the scope of the promise by not only forgiving you as a result of confession but also cleansing you from unrighteousness. Promises that are not dependent upon our righteousness or ability give us trouble because we are just not accustomed to receiving without earning. This is also one of the reasons that grace is so hard for some of us to embrace. The promises of God require patience and trust, not performance or achieving a specific set of goals. This is true whether we understand or not. Even though they are not dependent upon any conditions, some things can get in the way of receiving a promise. The appropriate response is that of dependence. You have to know that God's grace is sufficient and can be depended upon. "Who is among you that fears the Lord, that obeys the voice of His servant, that walks in darkness and has no light?

Let him trust in the name of the LORD and rely on his God" (Is. 50:10 NASB). Even though you may be fearful in these uncertain situations, His fear is working on your behalf, and it is beneficial. "'For My hand made all these things, thus all these things came into being,' declares the LORD. 'But to this one I will look, to him who is humble and contrite of spirit, and who trembles at My word" (Is. 66:2 NASB). It's just a matter of exchanging the fear that you have for the fear of the Lord. Of course, this concept is more readily acceptable when things are not going well, but the truth of the matter is this should be our way of thinking when things are going well too. Isaiah goes on to warn us of the danger of confidence in our own abilities. "Behold, all you who kindle a fire, who encircle yourselves with firebrands, walk in the light of your fire and among the brands you have set ablaze. This you will have from My hand: You will lie down in torment" (Is. 50:11 NASB).

Another area that we must consider is this: the person receiving the promise is not special, just chosen. God uses a random search selection process that takes place without any specific aim. Some time ago, I was audited by the IRS. I inquired as to the reasons for the audit, and of course there were a couple of things that they wanted to question me about as indicated in the correspondence. They then informed me that my name was picked at random. God keeps His promises to *make* you special, not because you *are* special. Abraham, a random choice of God, was not special, just chosen. But he would become special. As a matter of fact, he would be called the friend of God (Is. 41:8). It is God's promise that activates His grace, not the person to whom it is extended. The name *Abram* literally means "Father, God is lofty." But when the Lord established His covenant with Abram, He changed his name (Gen. 17:1–2). …"Your name will be Abraham, for I will make you the father of a multitude of nations" (Gen. 17:5 (NIV)).

The change in his name shifts the application of the promise from the direction Abram was going to include the person that Abraham would become. The new name represented a new identity. He would no longer be identified only as a father of natural offspring but now he would become the father of spiritual offspring. Abraham from thereafter became "father" of the faithful, meaning our faith, which results in righteousness, and our inheritance originated with Abraham (Gal. 3:7, 29). God's promises are designed not only to change circumstances but also to change us. A new name is indicative of a new person. In biblical times, parents took great care in naming children because they knew that children, in most cases, would become who they were called. For example, Jacob's name was changed to Israel because he was to become what that name represented.

> Then God appeared to Jacob again when he came from Paddan-aram, and He blessed him. God said to him, "Your name is Jacob; You shall no longer be called Jacob, but Israel shall be your name." Thus He called him Israel. God also said to him, "I am God Almighty; be fruitful and multiply; a The nation and a company of nations shall come from you, and kings shall come forth from you. land which I gave to Abraham and Isaac, I will give it to you, and I will give the land to your descendants after you." (Gen. 35:9–12 NASB)

When the Lord becomes the dominant factor in your life, the first change that takes place is your name. The direction of your life changes also. Whereas you were once an enemy of God and of the things that He represents, you now become His friend in every sense of the word. As a matter of fact, Jesus calls you exactly that in John 15:15: "I no longer call you slaves, because a master doesn't confide in his slaves. Now you are my friends, since I have told you everything the Father told me" (John 15:15 NLT). Change requires separation. Note what Abraham is leaving; these I believe are the two areas that had the greatest influence on him, and I daresay the same is true of us as well.

The first thing he leaves is his country, which includes his culture and all the influences that it brings with it. Patriotism is not being questioned here, but his citizenship is about to change. He is going to be called upon to change his allegiance, which in and of itself is a far cry from easy. Not only is he going to change his citizenship but also his relatives, which carries with it the influence of his family. His original country was Ur of the Chaldeans. The country of Ur was consecrated to the worship of sin and the Babylonian moon god. These practices would have no place in the new country that Abraham would become a part of. Terah, his father, was connected to the moon god in his worship. Not only did he worship such entities, but ancient rabbinic interpreters portrayed Terah as a manufacturer and worshiper of idols. These factors are no doubt the reason God instructed Abraham to leave his country and his family, at least those who were guilty of such profane practices. So then the background that Abraham represented was not conducive to the fulfillment of the promise that God made to him. In other words, it looked bad. God was in the business of changing people, and in the process, circumstances that seemingly contradicted actually worked in favor of the promise. In order for this to be carried out by the one awaiting the promise the immediate circumstances must be ignored. Unseen forces are at work that may not be visible but are nonetheless real and are designed to keep you off balance. Your prodigal may have no idea of this at all and may feel that he or she is operating independently of any outside influences. But the truth of the matter is that those influences show themselves in very explainable ways, such as distraction, which causes you to get your priorities disorganized; discouragement, which causes you to lose hope; disillusionment, which brings with it unfulfilled expectations; discontentment, which thrives on a lack of appreciation; and discord, which causes divisiveness and favoritism. These are the very things that drive a wayward person deeper into his or her isolation. If you misunderstand them that can result in further separation and broken communication. As you can see, the immediate circumstances can be intimidating, but they have nothing to do with the fulfillment of God's objectives. Since God's promises are sure and steadfast, what then is our responsibility to them? They do require our participation. The progress thereof is determined by obedience, not righteousness. "So Abram went as the Lord had told him" (Gen. 12:4 NIV)). It's a simple sentence, but it elicits a complicated response. Abram trusted the Lord but not with his whole heart. He was told to leave his country and his family, but the scriptures reveal that he took Lot with him. Partial obedience is disobedience. All too often, we are willing to go where the Lord wants us to go and to do what the Lord tells us to do, but we don't do it with our whole hearts. Oftentimes, we take the wrong things with us. We take our agendas, our opinions, anything that is familiar to us, those things we have learned to trust in. You may recall being in an unfamiliar location and looking for something that you could relate to or that you were familiar with. Let me share an excerpt from Bruce Wilkinson's book *The Dream Giver,* specifically from the chapter titled "Ordinary Leaves His Comfort Zone."

> The next morning Ordinary woke up at the usual time. But instead of reporting to his usual job, he packed his suitcase with the usual stuff. Then he added his journal and a bottle of permanent ink.

> Just before he closed the latch, he carefully placed his long white feather inside. Soon Ordinary was walking away from the comfortable center of Familiar, where almost every Nobody lived. He was heading toward the border, where almost no Nobodies ever went. Ordinary had never dared to walk this way before. But like every Nobody, he knew that the farther you walked from the center of Familiar, the less familiar things became. He also knew that most Nobodies who tried to leave the comfort zone of Familiar became so uncomfortable, they turned around and went home.

Abram took Lot with him, no doubt, for reasons that the familiar can explain. It seems so much easier to work with someone you know than to risk meeting someone new and learning from scratch. But when it comes to the will of God, the immediate circumstances must be ignored and total dependence upon God must dominate your decision making, not what you see. Someone else occupied the very land that God had promised Abram. The Canaanites were quite at home where they lived and were not going to readily surrender it to anyone any more than you would your home. But there was an underlying dynamic at work that would enable Abram to continue his pursuit of following the directive given him by God. The fulfillment of the promise was too big for one man to handle. Abram built an altar as a visible reminder of what God had promised him. It may be a good idea at this point to recommend that a visible reminder of God's promise to you be erected as well; whatever it is that you are holding onto as a guarantee of the faithfulness of God needs to be reflected upon. Keep in mind that the relationship that is developing between you and the Lord as you wait is not only a by-product of trusting Him but is also part of the promise. God wants you to benefit from the entire process, not just the fulfillment thereof. You can only experience the excitement that you feel when things change. You have to capitalize on it by embracing the expectation as the fulfillment. Abram built his altar in the place of promise in spite of opposition; remember, the Canaanites were in the land. He then went on to pitch his tent in Bethel, which was the place of protection. In turbulent times, the people went to Bethel to ask God's counsel (Judges 20:18, 31; 21:2). The tent represented the fact that Abram was a pilgrim just passing through. The altar was indicative of his heavenly destination. The same can be true of the visible reminders that you erect; they should provide you with a location that is synonymous to your ultimate destination. God keeps all of His promises in spite of the influence of human nature. The problem is that the promises are not necessarily fulfilled when you want them to be. Life may continue as usual with no visible signs of improvement. This is normal in that things are being done while you wait. Our problem is that we focus on what's expected and not on what's being accomplished regardless of the way things may be. The reality is that we don't like being deprived. In Abram's case, he resorted to Egypt, a place where his needs could be met and that he was familiar with. Egypt had forms of worship similar to that which his father practiced. They practiced idolatry by worshipping other gods (Joshua 24:2). He was so familiar with the culture that he knew what they were going to do when they saw Sarai, his wife. Why? Because he knew how idolaters thought. The moment you make this kind of move, God's promise is no longer clear. You may even begin to question God's goodness as a result. If you don't question him verbally, you will almost certainly do so intellectually and emotionally. Your personal Egypt can be anywhere that addresses your immediate needs apart from God. You don't have to catch a plane to go to your personal Egypt. As a matter of fact, you can travel to Egypt from right where you are seated. Fear is another enemy of receiving God's promise. This kind of thinking sets you up for any of a number of distractions from benefiting from God's making a promise long before it is fulfilled. Proverbs 29:25 (NIV) calls such fear a snare, which includes worrying about what others will do, say, think, and even feel about you. It's the root cause of the following:

- Self-centeredness: Apart from you, no one and nothing matters.
- Distorted perspectives: Things always look worse than they are.
- Unrealistic assumptions: A lie will be more effective than the truth.
- Failure.

Sometimes waiting on God can be frightening. The scriptures tell us that God is readily accessible to those who trust in Him. Psalm 118:5–6 (NLT) puts it this way:

> In my distress I prayed to the LORD,
> and the LORD answered me and set me free.
> The LORD is for me, so I will have no fear.
> What can mere people do to me?

And Isaiah 51:12 (NLT) reiterates it:

> I, yes I, am the one who comforts you.
> So why are you afraid of mere humans,
> who wither like the grass and disappear?

The thing that will help us to overcome fear is this: we recognize the Lord as a strong tower. In Him, we have the ability to be exalted above our circumstances. To be exalted is to be raised inaccessibly high. When you are secure in Christ, people, will not intimidate you. Let's consider what that looks like as we explore the name of God as being a strong tower. As parents, we need to be able to observe what's going on from a higher plane. If we stay on the same level with our children, we will find that their level is confusing, to say the least. I use the term *higher plane* to refer specifically to viewing things from God's perspective and not the perspective of the immediate circumstances. According to Proverbs 18:10, the Lord describes Himself as a strong tower. That tower is representative of another point of view and gives us an instant picture of safety, protection, and security. The tower gives us the privilege to see things from an elevated position, which broadens our scope and activates our defense system. That's why towers were constructed during biblical days. From the higher vantage point, people had the ability to anticipate others' next move. When the enemy was seen approaching a city, those who manned the tower could see them long before they got close to the city and then warn others of impending danger. So it is with our relying upon the Lord in times such as these. It enables us to see things that will pose a problem in the future. We then will be able to curtail the full brunt of any consequences that may be looming in the future. What makes this so important is the tendency we have to focus our attention on what's going on in our current experiences and neglect to consider what is not seen. God is always at work, and nothing He does is wasted. Our responsibility is to be on guard against being hamstrung by someone else's behavior. There is always another way of looking at things no matter how many times you may have tried and failed. Albert Einstein put it this way: "Learn from yesterday, live for today, hope for tomorrow. The important thing is not to stop questioning."[15] There is a great need for wisdom and sound judgment when unbridled resistance is running rampant. The wisdom and sound judgment that is needed will be made available in the elevated position that the Lord places you in. You'll begin to see things that have been overlooked in the past. For instance, Conan was hospitalized at one time for a condition known as rhabdomyolysis, which is a deterioration of muscle tissue that resulted, in Conan's case, from sleeping in one position too long. The condition required a short stay in the hospital, the prognosis was good, and no further treatment was required. But through the discovery of the condition, I was made aware of the extent of his need for clinical help. Up to this point, we did not clearly understand the reality of his addiction simply because it fit within the context of functional. It was only upon arriving at a level of understanding that placed me above my way of thinking that I was able to see the depth of the need and was able to respond accordingly. I believe our relationship was elevated as well. When you run into the tower, you come in on ground level, but then have to go up. Everything is designed to take you higher. From that position your responsibility is also elevated, and the awareness of what is going on around you becomes visible. This heightened awareness brings with it a certain amount of additional weight. Whether it's a supervisor's job or a well-informed parent's role, with increased responsibility there's added emotional involvement. This involvement, however, will bring with it a well-needed sense of control. Parents, don't be alarmed by new outbreaks or recurrences, but view those from God's vantage point and you will begin to discover life as it was intended to be seen—from

---

15 "Albert Einstein Quotes," BrainyQuote, Retrieved from http://www.brainyquote.com/quotes/authors/a/albert_einstein.html (observed on December 2014)

above. When you do otherwise, you automatically resort to what is familiar, which in fact is a step down. When Abram resorted to the familiar, he immediately began a downward journey. The scriptures tell us that he went down to Egypt. When you resort to the world's standard of doing things, it's always a step down. For clarity's sake, this language describes being out of fellowship with God or doing things contrary to His will. You may recall the story of Jonah. His desire was to lead his life entirely according to his feelings. So when he was called upon to reach a specific group of people by introducing them to God's compassion and forgiveness, he rejected the opportunity and ran in the opposite direction instead. The reason he did so was that he did not feel that they were worthy of such treatment for his own personal reasons. Granted, the previous actions of those in Nineveh, to which he was called to reach, were deplorable to say the least. Nineveh was the capital city of the mighty Assyrian empire, located on the east bank of the Tigris River across from the modern city of Mosul (Iraq). Nineveh was the capital of one of the cruelest, vilest, most powerful, and most idolatrous empires in the world. They were known to slaughter people in battle and then dye mountains with the blood from their bodies. They beheaded people and then made monuments out of the heads. People were burned alive and dismembered while they were still alive. One author called Nineveh the city of blood. Jonah could not understand how a just God could allow actions of this magnitude to simply be forgiven. The entire world was flooded because of people's rebellion against God's standards. These people should certainly not escape God's judgment (Gen. 6:13). God completely destroyed Sodom and Gomorrah for their wickedness. But in this case, God had a different plan for the people involved, as well as for Jonah. And so it is with each one of us. God responds differently based on His overall scheme of things. Some children are delivered after brushing shoulders with death time and time again and go on to live productive lives. Others fall victim to the natural consequences of their sin. It is our responsibility to know that God's promises are not dependent upon what we feel should happen but rather that God alone knows what's best for each one of us. Jonah chose to submit to his own desires and felt that his way was the best way. In doing so he lowered his standards, and the downward spiral began. As is always the case, disobedience leads downward. His digression was obvious; he went down to Joppa, and then down into the ship, which led him down into the sea and ultimately down into the belly of the great fish. It didn't stop there. He also descended into deep despair and depression. It does not take much to start the descent—a bad attitude or an unwillingness to submit to clear direction from God. This kind of thinking is distorted and irrational at its best. He thought that God's will was something that he could accept or reject. He thought that he could choose when and where he would share his faith. He felt that he had some say-so in the lives of those he disapproved of. He felt that he had the right to dictate what God's judgment should be on those who were not living according to God's standards. Jonah wanted people to get what they deserved, and he was willing to pay the price necessary to see that it happened. Running from God was the way he attempted to do it. That is not unlike a lot of us; we want people to get what they deserve. If somebody runs through a red light that I am stopped for, the first thought that comes to my mind is, *Where are the police when you need them?* But of course, it's all right for me to speed through a yellow light in an attempt to avoid the red. My first reaction is to look into the rearview mirror and let out a sigh of relief, thinking, *I'm glad there was not a police officer around*. Just as Jonah ran, we have ways to run as well. God is available to forgive those who have violated his standards, and we must be readily available to do the same. It not only gets us back on track, it also covers a multitude of sins, which makes for a smoother ride. Forgiveness is the best way to readjust the course of one's life.

As we have seen, forgiveness is not easy but is absolutely necessary to ensure a wholesome relationship between two or more people. I believe forgiveness has the power to nullify resistance. It is one of the greatest promises God has extended to humankind and must be exercised without delay. It is indeed a powerful alternative to revenge.

Prayer

I stand in need of forgiveness daily, and I have no difficulty accepting it as often as I need it. The receiving is easy enough, but the area I need help in is extending it. Lord, help me to keep ever before me the amount that I owe you in terms of the forgiveness debt. As I compare it to what I may feel others owe me, the scales are completely out of balance, and I can only thank you for your overwhelming love for me, which in turn motivates me to forgive others as often and as quickly as I possibly can.

Memory Verses
Mark 11:22–25

Frustration has a tendency to slow down our rate of travel and draws our attention toward things that we don't have. It's at these moments that we have to press our way forward regardless of the amount of discomfort that doing so might cause. As long as we stay in motion, we have the opportunity to adjust our course of travel. Perseverance is the key.

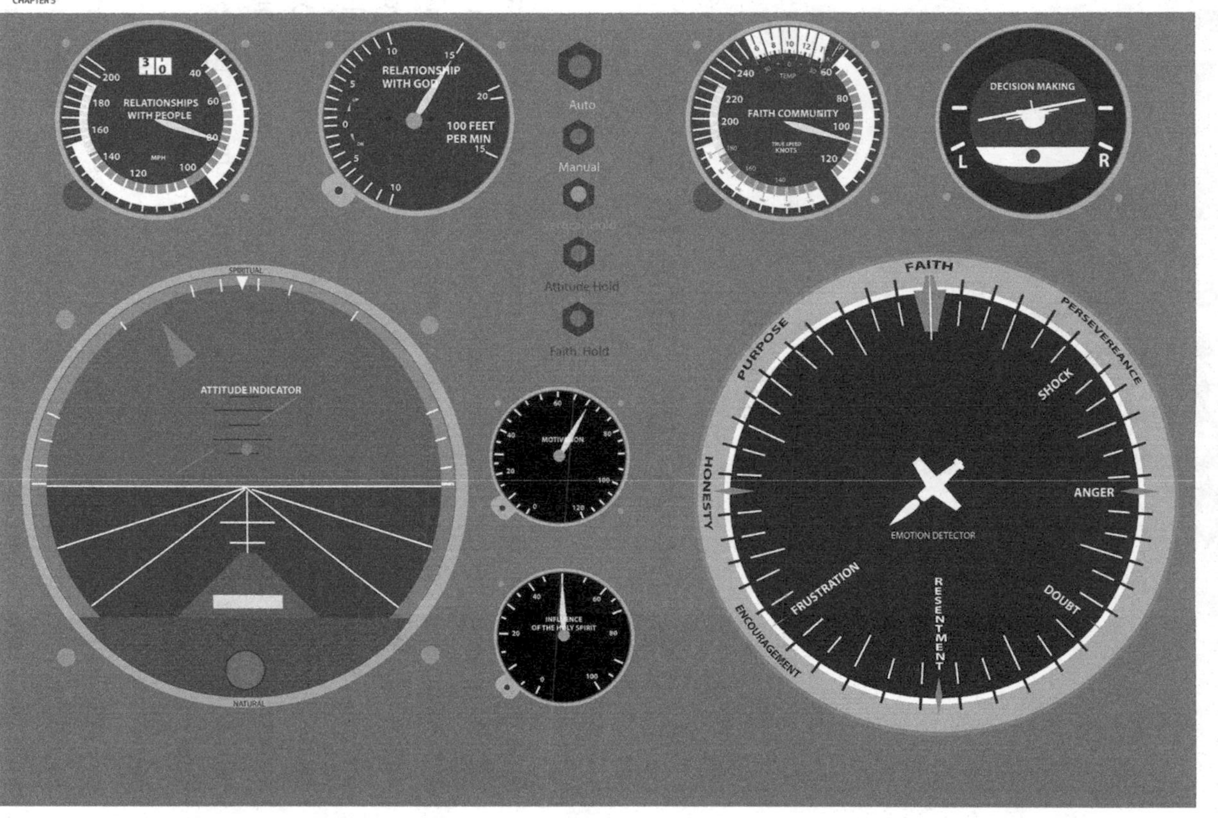
RELATIONSHIPS WITH PEOPLE
MPH
RELATIONSHIP WITH GOD
100 FEET PER MIN
Auto
Manual
Attitude Hold
Faith Hold
FAITH COMMUNITY
TEMP
TRUE SPEED KNOTS
DECISION MAKING
L
R
SPIRITUAL
ATTITUDE INDICATOR
NATURAL
MOTIVATION
INFLUENCE OF THE HOLY SPIRIT
FAITH
PURPOSE
PERSEVEREANCE
SHOCK
HONESTY
ANGER
EMOTION DETECTOR
FRUSTRATION
RESENTMENT
DOUBT
ENCOURAGEMENT

Chapter 6

It's Always Too Soon to Quit

We all need to be motivated to keep going from time to time; in fact, that can easily be classified as an understatement. We all need a healthy dose of perseverance just to make it from day to day. We have to contend with so many things daily that we often lose sight of the provisions that are always at our disposal. Let's see if we can't identify some of those as well as the opportunity to benefit from them. Let's consider first *expectation*. Believe it or not, this is one of our biggest allies. It is one of the few things that remains constant with each one of us. We are all looking for something to happen sooner or later. As we've seen sometimes, the anticipation of a desire can be just as satisfying as the actual fulfillment of that desire. The mind has the uncanny ability to lock onto what it needs to survive, and we need to provide it with adequate material to choose from. Knowledge is one thing and hope is another, but they are both sufficient to give what is necessary to create an atmosphere of anticipation. Survival, though necessary, is limited in its ability to produce the desired result of expectation. Encouragement is always a possibility when you understand that circumstances can change and people can change. It makes no difference how long one has persisted in a particular mode of behavior or a difficult set of circumstances. An internal mechanism has been implanted in each one of us that longs to be expressed, and that longing in most cases is dependent upon one's willingness to change. In order for that to happen, there must be a deliberate action on the part of the person who needs to make a change. In a natural sense, I guess you could say that this true, but we're looking at this from another perspective, one that says perseverance can influence change from the outside in. I'm certain that requires an explanation. When conviction is maintained and standards are upheld, both will prove to have an influence all their own. The first one to be influenced, of course, will be you. Remember, we are governing our behavior by what we expect to happen, not necessarily by what is actually happening. I increase my stability as I am consistent in my behavior; I magnify another's inconsistencies as I remain steadfast in my consistency. Since we are results oriented, we can expect feelings to change. When they do, they will bring with them a new sense of confidence, which will enable you to persist. Remember, we are concerned with the ability to never give up, and this goal must be uppermost in our thinking if we intend to adjust our thinking to that of a revitalized sense of accomplishment. This has to be an ongoing experience if it is going to achieve the end that we are looking to achieve, which includes the need to influence the person who is so desperately in need of our support. As we approach things from this perspective, it will enable us to set a course for a long journey in the same direction, and that direction will prove to be a much-needed stabilizing factor as life continues to be turbulent. Your life has to be a shelter for those on the rough edge of inconsistency so that when they return in pursuit of relief from time to time, you'll be able to provide them with what they may need, not necessarily what they want. In order for that to happen, you have to be capable of giving when, in reality, you should be receiving. An ongoing attitude of expectation will prove to do that for you.

There is a great need for visible signs of improvement as you progress through the challenges of a wayward family member. Character is often a missing ingredient in the life of such a person and can only be imparted by way of example. Talk has long since lost its ability to override the made-up mind of the resistant. There is a great need to see the value or benefit of living responsibly. After a while, people who persist in a destructive lifestyle begin to view all of life through lenses that are distorted, and all the images they see become distorted. The only things they can envision are failure and destruction. This then causes them to believe that not only are they right in the way they think but also that everyone else thinks the same way. Distortion distorts. Distorted thinking also is responsible for most of the conclusions they draw. This then will give somewhat of an explanation to some of the decisions they make that may not make any sense to you at all. They are not based on sound logic. Even though the communication may be clear, the logic is completely distorted. Therefore, the consistency of your attitude becomes important in that it is the only reality that they may be exposed to on a consistent basis. I say all of this just to heighten your awareness of the significance of the element of perseverance. Perseverance is a steady persistence in adhering to a course of action, a belief, or a purpose. Steadiness is sorely lacking in the lives of those who feel that trouble is the only constant that they can depend on, and they feel absolutely justified in bringing as much trouble as they can upon themselves by mistreating others. Causing heartache in the lives of the very people who are trying to help them brings about a distorted sense of peace. They have developed a philosophy that if others feel as bad as they do, then they'll feel better as a result. What makes this even more complicated is that the good feelings that they may experience are quickly replaced by guilt because of the pain that they have caused in others. When that occurs, the destructive behavior is repeated and the cycle continues on. It takes genuine love to adjust to this kind of thinking, but the price is well worth it. Not only do you provide a safe haven for your loved one, which is beneficial to all, but you also establish a solid future for upcoming events by creating an atmosphere that neutralizes or at the absolute least minimizes the impact of future outbreaks. Let me explain—when unusual events occur, such as an arrest or another pregnancy, the natural response from a responsible parent is a feeling of failure and defeat. But since there has been unconditional love expressed throughout and since consistency is attached to that love, there is now a battle of consistencies being waged—that is the challenge to love. That in turn influences their attitude, enabling them to appreciate the availability of love and the steadiness it provides for them. This gives them enough confidence to make promises that have been broken in the past but now appear to have much more meaning because your consistency has met their inconsistency head on, creating a delay in their repetitive failure. This whole process provides greater stability for you and at the same time fends off negative habitual behavior by keeping a picture of the power of positive consistency ever before them. It shows them what that consistency will do even in the face of some of the most powerful addictions known to man.

Now, of course, the truth still remains that even in light of this kind of thinking, encounters of this nature can be very disrupting. So I believe some help in the area of how to handle these disruptions might be appreciated. I'm reminded of the busiest man who ever walked the planet—the Lord Jesus Christ. Even though His schedule was always full, no one ever went lacking, nor was anyone ever overlooked. He did such a thorough job that He was able to make this declaration during the final days of His life, as recorded in John 18:8 (NASB): "'I told you that I am *He;* so if you seek Me, let these go their way,' to fulfill the word which He spoke, Of those whom You have given Me I lost not one.'" You would think that in the light of a claim such as that, there would be no time for anything else. But the Lord has an uncanny way of accomplishing more than most because He views all situations as opportunities regardless of how disrupting they may be. In Mark 6, the following is recorded in verses 30–34 (NASB):

> The apostles gathered together with Jesus; and they reported to Him all that they had done and taught. And He said to them, "Come away by yourselves to a secluded place and rest a while." (For there were many *people* coming and going, and they did not even have time to eat.)[16] They went away in the boat to a secluded place by themselves. *The people* saw them going, and many recognized *them* and ran there together on foot from all the cities, and got there ahead of them. When Jesus went ashore, He saw a large crowd, and He felt compassion for them because they were like sheep without a shepherd; and He began to teach them many things.

The remarkable thing about this passage is the manner in

---

16 Mark 6:32–44: *Matt 14:13–21; Luke 9:10–17; John 6:5–13*; Mark 8:2–9

which the Lord handles a major disruption. Most of us have taken some time off from work or from general responsibilities only to find some interruption barging in on our privacy. If you are anything like me, the experience was irritating to say the least. As we consider the nature of the circumstances we may be facing, the experience becomes even more intense. The example that Jesus provides us with is phenomenal. For one, He and the disciples were en route to a well-deserved vacation. The vacation was initiated by the Lord Himself, which automatically heightens its necessity. If you are working so hard that you don't have time to eat, it's time to take a break. Jesus and the disciples were approached by the very people they were trying to take a break from. As a matter of fact, the people arrived at the destination before the disciples and Jesus did. How would that kind of interruption affect you? You've left the office on Friday for a long weekend with your spouse, and you have already made reservations. As you arrive at the hotel, you find the lobby filled to capacity with coworkers who are in need of your assistance, and they do not hesitate to express their concerns with you. In our case, the scenario could include a phone call from the person you are trying to get a break from with a list of bad news and unrealistic demands. What Jesus does is set forth an example for us that we need to pay particular attention to. His first response is to recognize that the needs of the people are greater than His own, and they do not know how to satisfy theirs. The fact that Jesus and the disciples know that they have a need and have some idea how to satisfy it qualifies them to meet the need of others. Of course, this is an exceptional example in that we are dealing with the Son of God, but the important thing here is that He wants us to follow His example, not compare our inferior ability to His. He goes on to express compassion for those who have these needs and then defines what compassion is by his behavior. Second, he uses the interruption as a teaching opportunity. He teaches them many things that the scriptures declare and that cover the many people who were in need of help. So, in summation, compassion sees the needs of others as greater than one's own. It makes the sacrifice necessary to meet those needs and uses the encounter as an opportunity to give instruction. Undoubtedly, these are very teachable moments, and they must be handled with patience. I believe that this is the response that we should be giving when it comes to the challenges that we are called upon to face regularly. We have to keep these principles in mind because they may be the very things that will enable us to conquer some territory that could otherwise be overlooked. All encounters must be viewed as opportunities in disguise no matter how unsettling they may be. I'm reminded of a saying that I heard some years ago that has still not worked its way out of my subconscious. I don't recall who said it, but it was, "We are all faced with a series of great opportunities brilliantly disguised as unsolvable problems." If I could, I would like to add, "The nature of circumstances is never as clear as it should be because of this very fact." Things are disguised, and we don't see the reality of what is actually going on. There are several reasons this happens. One has to do with the distortion that was mentioned earlier. It has a tendency to cloud issues to the extent of being unrecognizable for their true significance. Instead of identifying areas that need to be addressed and treating those areas as opportunities, there is a drifting away instead because of the lack of clarity and general unwillingness to adapt to anything positive. This includes the rigid structure of the person who has become prodigal so desperately trying to avoid. This type of resistance should not influence your thinking in any way whatsoever because you know that the exercise itself can serve as an opportunity for personal growth as well as the growth of those who may resist. Remember, you are maintaining a posture that is designed to influence the instability of your conscientious objector.

By now you may be saying, *What's in this for me? After all, I do need to be encouraged.* I concur and most gladly so. That something does need to happen in your favor is an understatement, but there is a possibility that something positive could be taking place and has just gone unnoticed due to all of the other distractions that you may be encountering. Let me see if I can explain it this way. I recently read about the temptation of Jesus as it is recorded in the gospel of Mark 1 and made a startling discovery. It reads like this:

> Immediately coming up out of the water, He saw the heavens opening, and the Spirit like a dove descending upon Him; and a voice came out of the heavens: "You are My beloved Son, in You I am well-pleased." Immediately the Spirit impelled Him *to go* out into the wilderness. And He was in the wilderness forty days being tempted by Satan; and He was with the wild beasts, and the angels were ministering to Him. (Mark 1:10–13 NASB)

As I reread the passage, several things became obvious to me, beginning with the nature of the temptation. As Mark describes it, Jesus was not only tempted by the devil but also confronted with wild beasts and the wilderness. These things are representative of spiritual attack, natural calamities, and isolation, all of which are designed to weaken one's resolve. This temptation was constant for forty days and nights, and according to Matthew 4, Jesus had abstained from eating as well. These circumstances were most extreme. It's hard to be spiritual when you are hungry, threatened, and lonely, but the Lord Jesus was able to do so. Something became clear to me that I had never noticed before, and it proved not only to be significant but to revolutionize my life. At the end of verse 13, Mark indicates that the angels were ministering to Him. This ministry did not take place at the end of the temptation or challenge, but encouragement was going on in the midst of it. That means that He was able to withstand the pressure because He was under the constant watch and care of God. It is for this reason that I believe we can do the same. I'll go as far to say that regardless of how frightening circumstances may be or the degree of difficulty you may be experiencing, God is not only with you but currently ministering to you. If your circumstances are desperate and it appears that all hope is gone, pause for a moment and consider what is going on around you; you will discover that God is actively at work in your life and His angels are forever doing His bidding. Psalm 34 clarifies this in verse 7 (NIV): "The angel of the LORD encamps around those who fear him, and he delivers them." You can rest assured that God is in the process of providing for you what is necessary to bring you through what is most difficult but possible. Temptations are not easy or pleasurable to face, but you can find pleasure in knowing that the Lord is actively involved in every broken promise, every disappointed expectation, every legal notification, every missed opportunity, and every painful experience that has to be repeated. We need all of the help we can get to persevere through the uncertainty of what may happen next. That's not to say that we are preoccupied with what may happen next, but it is to say that we are not going to allow it to dominate our decision making or be paralyzed by the unpredictability of the future. Things can become disheartening at times and bring about a loss of motivation to continue. But we cannot become weary in our pursuit of doing what's right and what's best for our prodigal loved one. Weariness is a natural reaction to repetitive activity with no noticeable progress, improvement, or relief. It is not the same as becoming tired or exhausted from a hard day's work or overexerted from heavy labor. No, weariness reaches beyond the physical realm and works its way into the very core of our motivation or desire to continue on. It zaps you of all wonderment. It eliminates hopefulness. It argues against progress. It retreats in the face of disappointment. It insists on being the dominant thought in your emotional makeup. It never allows you to recuperate long enough to think differently and recognize that there is always another alternative. It actually requires more energy than some forms of physical exercise. The type of weariness I'm referring to is mental and emotional brought about from prolonged stress due to the loss of hope. As devastating as this can be, there is an antidote for it, and that is expectation. As long as we know that the end result will be beneficial or profitable, we can continue on. Excessive sleep will not eliminate emotional weariness or fatigue. *The solution lies in what you are willing to believe about the future.* Please make note of the idea that belief plays a major role in the ability to eliminate weariness. I am convinced that a sense of relief can be experienced as a result of expecting it as much as the actual removal of it. If being weary were an end in itself, things wouldn't be too bad, but unfortunately it doesn't stop there. Weariness unchecked often leads to a loss of heart, meaning a loss of desire to not only go on but also the ability to believe that you can. It becomes extremely important to look forward to what could happen if we keep our attitudes in the right place and what will happen if we trust God to bring about the necessary changes in us, resulting in a renewal of energy and a heightened desire to continue on.

Another remedy for this deadly nemesis is to stay on the lookout for opportunities to assist others in their plights. Excessive consideration about one's own well-being always weakens one's willingness to keep going in spite of the way things may be at present. But like anything else that has any lasting value, it takes time for it to come to fruition. The best way to see the progress of a newly planted seedling is to forget about it until the time has come for it to bear fruit. Your job is to provide for it, to water and feed it and to cultivate the soil in which it has been planted. You are learning some lessons that cannot be acquired anywhere else on the planet, and you have to take advantage of it. Look deeply into the areas of life that cause you the most pain and begin to draw your attention toward them. Most of the major events that take place in your life are designed for others. Very rarely do you learn something the moment you need it. Of course, you are the immediate benefactor, but the results go much further and deeper than you can ever imagine. *All of life's circumstances can be defined as pressure points that give us an indication of where we are in spiritual experiences.* You must always keep in mind the idea that you are never alone in your challenges, as undoubtedly you have come to understand at this point. Since this is a reality, then the natural questions arise, On whom can I depend, who is with me on whom I can rely upon for help, and how can they help? Not only is there someone with you, but they are also working on your behalf to ensure that things will turn out according to His will. *But how does that benefit me now?* you may say. Let me see if I can explain it this way. I can remember times when I've narrowly escaped a car accident or some other near catastrophe. When the dust in my mind settled, I inadvertently considered what could have happened but didn't, and somehow this made my current experience sweeter. After my adrenaline level had returned to normal, I would breathe a sigh of relief and thank God for what He had done, after which the aftershock would set in, making me aware of what could have happened and did not. I'm certain that if you look hard enough, you will discover that the same has happened to you on occasion where your loved one is concerned. The ability to persevere is going to be due in part to how you respond to the various disturbances that keep occurring in your life. You can experience success over most if not all of the conflicts you will encounter because, as a parent or guardian, you have the direct support of the Lord Himself working on your behalf. If I know that the creator, manufacturer, and supplier is working on my behalf, I can rest assured that when I need a specific product, it will be provided. If that is the case, then your response should be to react to disruptions by focusing on the Lord and not on the issues at hand. We often think of God in a positive sense when conflict arises. We look for Him to do something that will have a favorable outcome for us. But this may not always be the case. Sometimes we have to include the negatives to appreciate the full value of the positive when it does come, thereby compounding the blessing. What could have been often generates a great sense of appreciation of what actually is. When we are moved deeply with a sense of God's goodness and the narrowness of an escape, we often conclude—if not verbally at least emotionally—"Had it not been for . . . ." We have all had our "had it not been" experiences. When we reflect upon the providential protection of the Lord and we question how this protection came about, we often use a literary device called litotes to express what we are feeling. Litotes is an understatement used for effect in which a positive is expressed by stating the negative, giving the positive more impact. For example, "If the Lord had not been my help, my soul would have soon dwelt in the abode of silence" (Ps. 94:17 NASB); "If your law had not been my delight, then I would have perished in my affliction" (Ps. 119:92 NASB); "And do not lead us into temptation, but deliver us from evil" (Matt. 6:13 NASB). We use this approach all of the time. (Think of a meal. The positive says, "That was a good meal." Litotes says, "That meal wasn't bad.") We as a people have taken the use of litotes to another level. in cases such as responding to a singing or an instrumental group. Instead of saying, "They were good," we say, "They were bad" or "They were terrible." Other ethnic groups get confused when we talk like that. This kind of language can be used when we have been positively affected by something as well as negatively. Of course, just as in the case of certain words in the English language, only the context can clarify the correct usage. A song, a meal, a person, or an experience can move us to draw these conclusions. Regardless of what they were, they often leave us with an opportunity to reflect. It's at these times that we develop our own litotes. The statement contains the emotion, making the emotion even greater. When a joke is told and the teller remains stoic, the joke has a greater impact than if the teller had laughed at his own joke. The containment makes it funnier. When we contain ourselves, we heighten the intensity of our understanding of what has or will happen now that we know that God has already done something. As we wait for Him to do something, it deepens our appreciation for what God is doing, and the value of God being with us is increased. It enables us then to persevere a bit longer because we can now view circumstances from a new perspective. This perspective helps us to realize that God knows the past that *didn't* happen (Matt. 11:20–24). So then, when you are reflecting upon what could have happened, you are reflecting upon what God did not allow to happen. What is happening has been selected for you. Things that were once unbearable now take on new meaning simply because they have been scrutinized by the Lord, have met His approval, and therefore are designed for our benefit and not our harm (Jer. 29:11). I know that life can really become difficult at times where a prodigal person is concerned. Sometimes it just didn't make sense. With all of the effort and love that is being poured into them, their seemingly opposite and negative reaction can be just too hard to bear—that is, until You begin to realize that the Lord was not only aware of what was going on but was actively involved in everything that was taking place. This brings you to the conclusion that nothing that comes into your life would be more than you could handle. The only thing that could not be handled would never happen to you. (1 Cor. 10:13). Now exhaustion was just that, not hopelessness. In my experience I felt that I could bear whatever came my way because the manufacturer and supplier had given His approval. When you opt to think like this, it is normally accompanied with great emotion for an obvious reason, as was the case with me. The thought that God had acted on my behalf without my knowledge generated as much joy as what God had actually allowed to happen with my knowledge. What could have happened but didn't brought joy, and what did happen brought me joy. I was then able to experience joy from both ends. Now when you begin to experience those kinds of feelings, you can keep going. What we have to be on guard against is the sudden ambush, or the sneak attack. Since we have this understanding, it becomes the enemy's goal to make us forget it. Our enemy does not give us advance warning of his attacks; therefore, we have to stay alert and be on the lookout (1 Peter 5:8). The image is that of a pride of lions attacking and devouring its prey. Lions are powerful animals that usually hunt in coordinated groups and stalk their chosen prey. However, they are not particularly known for their stamina. Thus, although lionesses can reach speeds of fifty-nine kilometers per hour (forty miles per hour), they can only do so for short bursts, so they have to be close to their prey before starting the attack. They take advantage of factors that reduce visibility; many kills take place near some form of cover, they hide behind bushes, or they hunt at night. They sneak up on the victim until they reach a distance of about a hundred feet or less. Typically, several female lions work together and encircle the herd from different points. Once they have closed in on a herd, they usually target the closest and weakest prey. The attack is short and powerful; they attempt to catch the victim with a fast rush and final leap. The prey is usually killed by strangulation. The prey may also be killed by the lion enclosing the animal's mouth and nostrils in its jaws, which would also result in asphyxia.[17] This is a clear picture of what our enemy is out to do to us. He wants to strangle us. He wants to cut off our oxygen supply. In Psalm 124:1, 4–5 (NIV), David says, "If the Lord had not been on our side when men attacked us … the flood would have engulfed us, the torrent would have swept over us, the raging waters would have swept us away." Cutting off the oxygen supply of the believer is a direct attempt on the part of the enemy to cut off our relationship with God and thereby render us ineffective. What's under attack in these verses is your soul. The word *soul* means similar things in the Hebrew and the Greek. *Soul* as it is defined in Hebrew is *Nephesh*, "a breathing creature." In the Greek, it is *Psuche,* which means "breath." Both suggest that the survival of the soul is dependent upon inhaling oxygen. But it is more than that. This term may also indicate the entire inner nature of a person, including their personality, which is all that pertains to the person (Deut. 26:16). So when David describes the stream and the raging waters, he's referring to the enemy's attempt to suffocate any signs of life in you whatsoever. What you have here is the idea of being drowned by the issues of life, being bombarded by one issue after another. Most of us can attest to that situation.

The soul is intricately tied into God. When He created man, He breathed in him the breath of life and he became a living soul. And if you are born again, that soul is now regenerated by God because you are in-dwelt by the Spirit of God. So the spirit is life that God breathed in us, and the breath that we breathe is His. The devil's aim is to cut off your oxygen supply that is the very source of your life. The attempts of the enemy to suffocate

---

17 http:// En,wikpedia.org/wiki/portal

us are actually attempts to silence God. It is much bigger than just you. There are always goings-on behind the scenes that must be taken into consideration. You are so valuable to God that He monitors very closely the issues of life that you are confronted with to ensure that they do not hinder your ability to breathe. There are times when you may feel that you are out of breath, but hold on—your spiritual lungs are being stretched, and in due season you will get a second wind. *It's always too soon to quit.* As a matter of fact, quitting just isn't an option. When you recognize what you have been delivered from and understand what could have been your experience, you can't help but conclude that the Lord indeed deserves to be blessed—by you. Excitement replaces anxiety, and apprehension gives way to thanksgiving and praise. As you become accustomed to the faithfulness of God, you begin to appreciate His character and can relax in His will. Knowing God on this level builds your faith. You are no longer a prisoner to what may happen in the future because you know who holds the future. Not only do you know who holds the future, but you also know that He is holding you. You can breathe a sigh of relief knowing that the end has already been secured and your best interest was taken into consideration before that decision was made. Your faith will be preserved, the enemy will not overwhelm you, and you will not be restricted from the ravages of fear. What entraps us all too often is the fear of what could happen. This kind of thinking can result in poor decision making, which can prove harmful to you and the person who has become prodigal. All of the events that occur are designed to frighten and discourage you. Once that happens, the life of God is snuffed out in your life due to a lack of oxygen. Consider this: Proverbs 29:25 (NASB) reminds us that "The fear of man brings a snare"—a trap that is for capturing prey. In 1 Timothy 3:7, it is made clear that we escape such snares by maintaining a good reputation; 2 Timothy 2:26 reminds us that we escape by repentance. Isaiah 24:18 (NIV) puts it this way: "Whoever flees at the sound of terror will fall into a pit; whoever climbs out of the pit will be caught in a snare." We escape by resisting fear, not running from what frightens us. Adopting this attitude will enable you to persevere for the duration and to give you all the help that you will ever need. The Lord made heaven and earth and all that dwells therein. He regulates their behavior so that everything is in submission to Him. Remember, He knows the past that didn't happen. It makes no difference how unusual or devastating things may be; He is the designer and manufacturer and the engineer of such. Second, when it comes to perseverance, we have to remember *God's faithfulness*. If we don't capitalize on our experience with God in previous circumstances, we have totally forgotten what God has done for us in the past. Very rarely will you find your experiences, good or bad, standing in isolation. No matter what is happening in your life today, its influence is not limited to just today; it has a counterpart in the past or in future. The writer of the book of Hebrews helps us to understand this concept by beginning chapter 10, verse 34 (NASB), with the word *Remember*. The society that we live in is so inundated with the future that we don't enjoy our current experiences. Don't get too comfortable with that new computer that you have because you know an upgrade is right around the corner. It's no small matter to be called upon to remember. The writer takes us all the way back to the cross: "after you received the light." For those of you who are really saved, something happened when you got saved—a war broke out. "You endured a great conflict of suffering." This is par for the course. All of this was designed to make you aware of the new authority that you were under and the keeping power of the new captain of your soul. He does not say, "Remember the good old days." But he directs our attention toward our ability to make it through extreme difficulties in anticipation of better things. All too often we find this term in the midst of what appears to be new, admonishing us to consider what has already been done (1 Chron. 16:12; Ecc. 12:1). This places the emphasis on the need for continuing endurance. This is expanded on in Hebrews 10:36.

The first-century Christians suffered publicly and were exposed to insult and persecution. They were called upon to endure such hardship because of their certainty of the faithfulness of God. God had been faithful in the past, and they anticipated that He would continue to be so. In track and field, runners in particular are assured victory by focusing on the finish line, not those who may be behind them, beside them, or even in front of them. If they are running their race, these other things will not distract them. But in the race of life, it's not only all right to look back, but according to our text, it is recommended. It's not a contradiction of Philippians 3:13 (NASB), where Paul says, " ...but one thing I do; forgetting what lies behind." There, he boasts about his pedigree—circumcised the eighth day, of the tribe of Benjamin, a Hebrew of Hebrews, and concerning the law, a Pharisee. This kind of thinking hindered his progress in Christ because it placed the emphasis on human effort and not dependence upon God. But when it came to remembering the light, he shared what he had become and not what he had been, thereby glorifying God (Acts 22). An effective way to fortify people against future trials is to remind them of the courage they displayed in past ones. God uses loss to strengthen His people for the purpose of helping others. They knew what it meant to stand their ground in the face of extreme suffering. The term "stand your ground" is usually translated "persevere." They would do well now to recall their steadfastness in the past. In whatever they might now be facing, they would be helped if they would remember those earlier days after they received the light. Unfortunately, what we do when we experience repeated problems is say things like, "If it isn't one thing, it's another," or "I knew it was too good to be true." And how about, "It's always something." We need to view those interruptions as ordained of God and signs of His faithfulness for the purpose of perseverance.

Perseverance enables you to replace negative emotions with positive ones. Sometimes negative emotions just get the best of us, and we find ourselves giving in to them. And along with them come negative responses that very rarely, if ever, turn out positively. Do you accept your losses joyfully? Perseverance has to push through that negativism. In the process, there are times when you feel it's too much, and outbursts of anger would just be so much easier to facilitate. In most cases, that is the time to keep going. Let's face it—serving the Lord is hard but not as hard as doing your own thing. "The way of the treacherous is hard" (Prov. 13:15 NASB). Once you do things your way, things instantly become harder. Perseverance and patience are under trial, and difficulty brings out a hidden beauty that you were not aware of. I call this replacement therapy. If you persevere, God will literally replace negative emotions with positive ones. Also, we find in Isaiah 61:3b (NCV) these comments: "I will give them a crown to replace their ashes, and the oil of gladness to replace their sorrow, and clothes of praise to replace their spirit of sadness." Natural responses have to be replaced by the power of God. In order for God's joy to be fully operable, it also has to go through extreme pressure. You then have to regard affliction, sufferings, and the discomfort that they cause as instruments in the hand of God to fashion in you His will for your life. The kind of struggles the first-century Christians were undergoing made little difference because their confidence in Christ was firm.

They were publicly exposed to insult, which was particularly demeaning. The phrase; "Sometimes you were publicly exposed to insult and persecution..." Hebrews 10:33 NIV) comes from the Greek word *theatrizomenoi*; we get our word *theater* from it. It's one thing to have people laugh with you; it's something altogether different to have someone to put you on stage, invite guests, and laugh at you. All kinds of feelings surface—anger, fear, and shame. But God replaced them with a totally unnatural response. They joyfully accepted the mistreatment. That's a little different from acceptance. Their response was supernatural. God doesn't necessarily remove the circumstances, but through perseverance other alternatives emerge. When and if perseverance stops, alternatives also stop, never to come again. Mark it well—when you stop persevering, you will never realize your full potential, nor will that insight ever be revealed. The passage of 2 Kings 4:2–7 bears this out with a description of how the oil stopped flowing when the containers to hold it ran out. We are so single minded in our approach to issues such as this that we miss viable alternatives. Just like you can't think two thoughts at the same time, you can't generally feel two contrasting emotions at a time. You can't be joyful and angry and bitter at the same time. That's why the apostle says, "Rejoice in the Lord always." It is a matter of choice. I know that may be hard to believe, but it is true. You determine your feelings, not your circumstances. The joy of the Lord is your strength. As the first-century Christians persevered through this public ordeal in Hebrews 10:33, they were able to choose joy over what might come naturally and find strength when the next challenge came, the confiscation of property (v. 34), all because they persevered. Perseverance produces the consequence of confidence. Perseverance exposes alternatives when you wait (Heb. 10:32–39).

> "The word persevere means to "patiently endure." It involves overcoming difficulties and

> withstanding pressures. The writer reminds his readers that they have demonstrated this quality, an expression of their confidence in Christ. They stood their ground despite suffering. They remained faithful despite insult, persecution, and even the loss of property. And they took a stand beside those in prison. The challenge now is to hold on, confident, till Jesus comes."[18]

Perseverance is reinforced by the promise of reward (Heb. 10:35–36). If you know you are going to get something out of this, you will stick to it. In some ways, confidence is a reward in and of itself. But the text says I'm essence that his reward will be rewarded. Confidence will increase confidence. It is a genuine double blessing. It will be rewarded as well as provide you with reward. So the question arises, Why would you want to throw something like that away? In the face of such an obvious blessing, it would appear that this would be a no-brainer. But the truth of the matter is that not only do we throw away our confidence, we also throw away people. We throw away people by refusing to repent; we get hurt and refuse to forgive. We abandon our effectiveness by engaging ourselves in illicit activity. Single acts of indiscretion are destroying people all over the place. We are not accustomed to holding onto anything too long. Needless to say, these are all the result of the society that we live in. "Blessed is the man who perseveres under trial, because having stood the test, that person will receive the crown of life that the Lord has promised to those who love him" (James 1:12 NIV).

Simply put, we live in a throwaway society where nothing is designed to last very long. This includes our patience and

---

[18] Lawrence O. Richards, *The Bible Reader's Companion* (Wheaton, IL: Victor Books, 1991), p. 864.

ability to endure when things become difficult. Temptation was undoubtedly knocking at the door of those first-century saints, and they were on the verge of giving up. Why else would they be admonished not to do so unless it was being considered? The temptation to quit is not the problem, but the unwillingness to choose the correct alternative is, as we have seen, which comes only through perseverance leading us to a biblical response. Those described in the book of Hebrews were faced with severe persecution and had to be encouraged to hold on. Perseverance was what they needed to reflect upon. As the light of the Son is cast upon your life, as it were, the reflection that He is looking to see is that of perseverance. What clouds perseverance is a faulty response to persecution no matter what form it comes in. It can take on the appearance of impatience, disappointment, anxiety, frustration, anger, pride, and the like. The light of the Son should burn off these impurities. In order for that to happen, the facet of your life that needs to be exposed to the Son is your ability to persevere. Turn your attention toward the Son and begin to see some of the rewards that are associated with persevering.

- You are rewarded with strength and stamina.
- You are rewarded with insight and wisdom.
- You are rewarded with respect.
- You increase your influence in the lives of others.
- You will develop a good self-image.
- You become liberated in your thinking.
- And ultimately, of course, you are rewarded with an eternity with Christ.

Albert Einstein is quoted as saying, "It's not that I'm so smart; it's just that I stay with problems longer. I think and think for months and years. Ninety-nine times, the conclusion is false. The hundredth time I am right. Many of life's failures are people who did not realize how close they were to success when they gave up." And Michael Jordan said, "I've missed more than nine thousand shots in my career. I've lost more than three hundred games. Twenty-six times I've been trusted to take the game winning shot and missed. I've failed over and over and over again in my life … and that is why I succeed." To add to that, home run hitters in baseball strike out much more than most other players because they keep on swinging. Your greatest asset in some cases is to just stay with it longer than anybody else! Now where God's will is concerned, it's not a competitive endeavor but a faith-building process that cannot otherwise be achieved apart from your sticking it out to the end. *Remember, it's always too soon to quit. Use your giving-up point as your breakthrough signal, resulting in the realization of God's will!* God's will for you personally is the place where your greatest potential is unveiled. When you get to the point where you have all but given up, a neon sign should flash in your mind—"God's will," "God's will," "God's will." Perseverance relies heavily upon a lifestyle of faith. Faith is the nerve center of perseverance. In the human body, there is a group of closely connected nerve cells that perform a specific function in the body. *Faith,* as the nerve center of the body of Christ, has closely connected nerve cells that perform a specific function in the life of the believer. One of the functions of faith is perseverance. The nerve center, which is faith, sends signals to various parts of the body to perform a specific task. When there is trauma to the physical body, the nerve center dispatches the appropriate cells to address the issue. If there is bleeding, cells known as platelets will be sent to the site to start the clotting process to prevent a person from bleeding to death. In the case of the body of Christ, when there is spiritual trauma, the nerve center of faith generates perseverance cells, alerting the person not to give up. Perseverance is dependent upon faith to move it where it needs to go. Evidence that the platelets are operating correctly is that the bleeding stops. Evidence that perseverance is operating correctly is that you become unwilling to give up or to quit (Col. 1:21–23). In the face of doubt, perseverance brings assurance; in the face of disappointment, perseverance brings hope; in the face of disillusionment, perseverance brings satisfaction. What alerts faith to activate the perseverance cells?

- Doubt
- Disappointment
- Disillusionment, the feeling that something is not what it was anticipated to be

Faith is responding to the Word of God, the Bible alone without any supporting props. The Word as declared concerning the life of Jonah says, "No sign is to be given to it but the sign of Jonah the prophet" (Matt. 12:39 NASB). In the story of the rich man and Lazarus (Luke 16:19–31), Jesus denies the request for the spectacular and insists that the hearer must respond to the word given to him (John 20:29 NASB). The Word demands self-surrender and commitment. Hence, the very nature of the Word and of faith becomes an obstacle to the proud and the powerful. Faith is the medium by which the power of God is made visible, which for our purposes is perseverance.

It moves mountains, heals the sick, and is the means of entrance into the kingdom. It may be mingled with doubt, as with the father who sought healing for his son ("I do believe; help my unbelief!" [Mark 9:24 NASB]), or as with John the Baptist in prison, who, even with his doubts, was confirmed by Jesus as the greatest of the offspring of woman (Matt. 11:2–15). Peter's (and the other disciples') perception was faulty, but Jesus affirms Peter's confession as the foundation stone of the church. The Bible portrays the early faith of the disciples in all its limitations and weaknesses, yet it is still faith in that it is their positive response to Jesus' word and work. Again, faith is the nerve center of the body of Christ. He is the author and finisher of our faith. Our response to that faith in the face of difficulty is perseverance. All of the above examples demonstrate the idea that failure did not deter those who live by faith, nor did it stop them from persevering. Those who walk by faith do not shrink back. Fail they may, but they do not quit. They place everything under the umbrella of faith and keep moving forward. I'm convinced that you can do it too. It's always too soon to quit. Consider this:

> When he had come back to Capernaum several days afterward, it was heard that he was at home. And many were gathered together, so there was no longer room, not even near the door. And he was speaking the word to them. And they came, bringing to him a paralytic, carried by four men. Being unable to get to him because of the crowd, they removed the roof above Him; and when they had dug an opening, the let down the pallet on which the paralytic was lying. And Jesus seeing their faith said to the paralytic, "Son your sins are forgiven." (Mark 2:1–5 NASB) Perseverance payed off and resulted in great dividends.

Prayer

Father in heaven, there are times when I feel like giving up. But then I remember that you are not only the Creator of all things but also the regulator of the very things that you create. Therefore, when experiences appear to be unbearable, I reflect upon your concern and control over the occurrences of my life, and my energy is renewed, my stamina is restored, and insight is increased. It is through this revelation that I am able to thank you for my experience. I pray that you will continue to guide my determination as I focus upon you and on what is expected of me by persevering in spite of the circumstances in my life.

Memory Verses
Hebrews 10:35–36

Even though despair may be a very real experience, it should only be viewed as a sign of spiritual exhaustion, which often occurs when you are nearing your destination. You have traveled quite a distance, and your journey has taken some time. Although discomfort may be present, balance and a sense of normalcy have returned to your life, and confidence keeps crowding out despair.

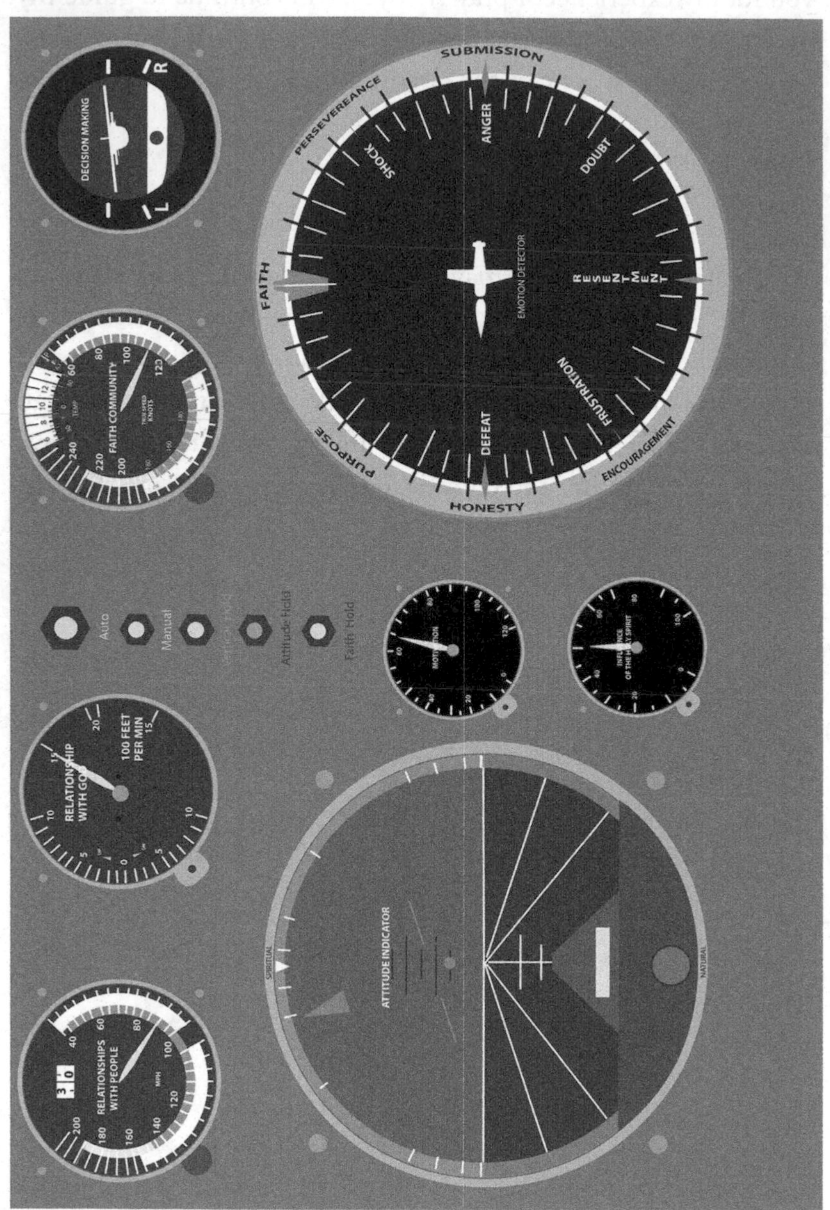
DECISION MAKING
L
R
FAITH COMMUNITY
KNOTS
RELATIONSHIP WITH GOD
100 FEET PER MIN
RELATIONSHIPS WITH PEOPLE
MPH
Auto
Manual
Attitude Hold
Faith Hold
MOTIVATION
INFLUENCE OF THE HOLY SPIRIT
ATTITUDE INDICATOR
SPIRITUAL
NATURAL
SUBMISSION
PERSEVEREANCE
FAITH
PURPOSE
HONESTY
ENCOURAGEMENT
SHOCK
ANGER
DOUBT
RESENTMENT
FRUSTRATION
DEFEAT
EMOTION DETECTOR

Chapter 7

Songs in the Night

In Job 35:10, we find it declared that God gives songs in the night. One of the things that plagues the broken heart is sleepless nights, when memories run rampant and fears are magnified. It is then that you come to realize the devastation of loneliness and the need for supernatural comfort from on high. In the public arena, you may find strength simply by association. The routine of daily activity has a tendency to cover the pain of sorrow and grief, but it's not so in the darkness of a bedroom, where shadows become images and images become reminders of a life no longer there. It is at these times that we have to remember that God provides us with songs in the night. Of course, I have associated night with the normal twenty-four-hour period in which the sun sets and is replaced by darkness known as night. But there is also a deeper definition attached to nightfall, and it fits metaphorically into the category of the darkness that overshadows the soul. The sun can be at its peak, yet the effects of a scarred soul can be as bleak as a rainy midnight. It is here that I believe that the Lord administers healing of the soul. Sometimes this is taking place unbeknownst to the person being healed.

It is in silence that the voice of God can be heard the loudest and the melody of His music frees the soul that has been captured by the pangs of loneliness and despair. It is not an easy thing to attain, but it can be done. The soul is trapped within the framework of the human body and is confined to the limitations that have been placed on it through the sin of Adam and the ongoing influences of this world. The interference that occurs during the course of any given day prevents us from seeing the depths of God's desire to strengthen our relationship with Him. A cadence of the heart produces a rhythm that can only be heard in the midst of tragedy. I don't believe that God manufactures it, but I do believe that He takes advantage of it because we tend not to do it voluntarily. It is in the location where there are no props or outside stimuli to confuse the issue, only the solitude of a life that is longing for the relief that only God can bring. It is where genuine music is manufactured—not the type that may find itself in the quarters of entertainment but the sort that penetrates the level where the soul resides. This cannot be found in the midst of well-being but rather in the realm of inadequacy. It is not the companion of confidence but of uncertainty. It is where heart and soul meet and the intellect is left to fend for itself.

The question arises, then, how do I acquire this song? It cannot be achieved by personal desire, giftedness, or effort because it is supernaturally endowed. It is a song that can be sung only when all else has been removed, where no obstacle can interfere with its objective, and where the longing in a heart that has been broken is satisfied. It is vital for the purpose of meeting the need of the soul and the renewing of the spirit. It is not in our power to declare the Lord's goodness in song when all else is adverse in our lives, but it is possible to look at adversity with a new perspective when the needs of the heart are exposed. This is the only entrance into the soul. There are no shortcuts, nor is there any rote formula that enables you to gain access. The only way in is through the doorway of adversity. This, I might add, is a sacred location that many have traveled through, but few have understood the vast potential for change that rests on the threshold of a tenderized heart conditioned by pain. Far too many people have run from the opportunity with little awareness of the benefits that they are leaving behind. God is looking for those whose hearts have been broken for several reasons. One, a broken heart brings you directly in contact with the need to understand people on a human level—or should I say a feeling level. What I mean by that is this: in life, we often relate to people on the basis of our personal feelings, whether we like, care for, or approve of them. If they pass our scrutiny, we allow them to enter into a closer relationship with us, not the closest but close enough to realize that we are no longer just a part of the human race but are now individuals. Even so, any feelings that are involved are generally superficial. If anything should happen to those we know on this level, it will have little or no effect on us. This of course is due to the need that we have to protect our feelings from those who could ultimately do us harm, albeit unintentionally. We do not like to feel bad. This is why the negative feelings that may occur as a result of an irate driver cutting in front of us or endangering us by some other irresponsible driving decision do not last very long. We surmise that it is not worth brooding over because a total stranger caused it. We are very selective in whom we will allow to make us feel anything, negative or positive. As we saw in an earlier chapter, feelings are a major motivator in the behavior of children in their developmental stages and will be responsible for a large portion of their decision making throughout their entire lives.

A broken heart changes the playing field and brings you into the feeling world of others with less apprehension. The field changes but not the rules. The scope is broadened in that there are more opportunities for expression because of the sensitivity associated with a tenderized heart. It's a heart that is literally on guard for those who may qualify for further involvement with you beyond casual encounters. Those encounters are filled with unspoken signals that are communicated on a level that is synonymous to that of an unspoken prayer request. You know the need, but you are not comfortable enough to verbalize it to others. But there is a willingness to let others know that there is a need.

A broken heart neutralizes that kind of thinking in that it invites others into the realm of actuality and is not comfortable with portraying an image of congeniality. Life takes on meaning because it now means something to have genuine encounters with people. There is a heightened desire to know people and to help people regardless of race, religion, or political affiliation. This cannot happen within the realm of comfort. When you begin to show care for people, it influences them to become more of who they are and not what others expect them to be. Obviously, people are not going to be completely open immediately, but they will be more than willing to take things further. *Friendship* is such a common word these days. It almost sounds as familiar as "good morning." Yet regardless of its commonality, actual good mornings are still sought and valued. So it is with friendships; they are still sought after but so vaguely understood. Occasionally, you can encounter a person and immediately know that he or she is suited for further contact based on the nature and outcome of the encounter. I recently had that experience with an old elementary school friend whom I had not seen in over forty years. He was in town and decided to give me a call when told where I worked. The contact was made, a conversation ensued, and the thirty minutes or so proved be the most delightful I had experienced in quite some time with a person who, for all intents and purposes, had become a stranger due to time and separation. One of the things that I attribute the success of this encounter to was the condition of my heart as well as his. Two people who have been broken are now becoming whole through the encounter. This cannot happen within the realm of conceit, dishonesty, or delusion. Different things impact people differently. The birth of my son opened my heart, the life of my son conditioned my heart, and the death of my son tenderized my heart. A tenderized heart is one that is pliable. It can now be shaped into the surrounding mold of life's experiences with confidence and poise.

Reshaping a heart is indeed a difficult thing to do—impossible if not heavily influenced by the Lord's active involvement at every turn. Reshaping can only be done in the crucible of life's circumstances that result in the broken heart. It is at these times that our relationship with the Lord is renewed and reshaped as well. Part of what takes place during these times is the preparation for what is going to take place in the future. As life unfolds, new revelations occur daily at each stage of development. Most of this goes on without any fanfare or recognition. This attitude has been created by a series of events that have been occurring for the duration of your life. Some valuable things have taken place that have gone unnoticed. Even so, they have had a subconscious impact on the way you act and think. It is within this workshop that creativity is formed and significant contributions to humankind are made.

The very pattern and outcome of your life are determined by the nature of your heart, so there is no wonder that the Lord puts so much into its conditioning. Once the realization of what part the heart plays in one's existence becomes clear, the rest of life lines up behind that realization. The heart is the core of who you are and what you will become, and it deserves the utmost of care. Solomon puts it this way in Proverbs 4:23: "Above all else guard your heart for it is the wellspring of life."(NIV) Everything that your heart is exposed to should be scrutinized very carefully. One of the things that needs to be understood about the heart is the means by which God chooses to comfort it. He challenges our faulty belief system in that we are no longer able to hide behind the façade of what I call rightism, which is the right response for whatever the circumstances call for. There is an honesty and openness that comes when there is a need for genuine healing in the midst of unbearable pain. The obvious answers no longer fit, and the expected responses are no longer appropriate. Each word spoken has meaning; each action has purpose; and all fears, though identifiable, no longer have the same influence over you that they once held. Healing comes according to your willingness to tap into the resources that rise to the surface as you endure the discomfort of the process. There is nothing easy about it, but its meaning has such depth that it lures you on to experience what is coming next and how you can process it effectively. It's within this context that songs develop in the night during the moments of darkness, loneliness, and separation. They are the rays of hope that emerge in the difficult times, overriding one's inability to envision the hand of God to be actively involved in the process. It is He who determines if in fact you are going to gain all that He expects of you at this time. He has put great confidence in you by requiring you to respond to the removal of what has been so dear to you. It is not without purpose; it brings with it a capability that you could not have known existed otherwise. I believe the Lord actually auditions you to determine whether you have what it takes to say to others what you are experiencing from God. Have you ever noticed that some people who undergo extreme hardship are never any better for it? As a matter of fact, some even emerge bitter as a result. In other cases, some just go on without making any significant contribution to those around them at all.

The only way that you can successfully achieve the status of spokesperson for those who are in like circumstances and those who sympathize with such is to make sure that your song is heavily influenced by an attitude of thankfulness. What are you to be thankful for? After all, these circumstances are not welcomed and sought after for the benefit of pleasure, resulting in a sense of appreciation. They are difficult and painful. What I have come to understand is that thankfulness and a hoard of other possible responses are decisions. How else could the Lord require us to be thankful in all things as well as for all things (1 Thess. 5:18; Eph. 5:20)? I believe Isaiah 12 will be of some help to us at this point. Here we find a description of a person who has emerged from the darkness of night onto a platform of praise, resulting in a song.

> In that day you will sing:
> "I will praise you, O LORD!
> You were angry with me, but not anymore.
> Now you comfort me.
> See, God has come to save me.
> I will trust in him and not be afraid.
> The LORD GOD is my strength and my song;
> he has given me victory."
> With joy you will drink deeply
> from the fountain of salvation!
> In that wonderful day you will sing:
> "Thank the LORD! Praise his name!
> Tell the nations what he has done.
> Let them know how mighty he is!

> Sing to the LORD, for he has done wonderful things.
> Make known his praise around the world.
> Let all the people of Jerusalem shout his praise with joy!
> For great is the Holy One of Israel who lives among you."
> (NLT)

In context, Isaiah is referring to the day that Jesus reigns on earth during a period called the millennium, which is set forth in chapter 11 of the book of Isaiah. In that location, you will find a description of what things will look like during that time. Lions are described as lying down with lambs, and children played with venomous vipers with no ill effects. In a more immediate sense, I believe God created a private millennium in the lives of those who are going through the darkest of night in preparation for the things that others will need to say to them. This attitude is developed as you make a conscious decision to thank God for said circumstances rather than focusing entirely on the grief associated with your loss or complaining about its existence. As you think about it, you will find that you have some positive things to say about what God has done in the midst of what is going on. Each case is different and requires consideration of your overall relationship with Christ. Remember, thankfulness is a decision not dependent upon circumstances or your current condition.

Very rarely does the Lord teach you things the moment you need them. In most cases, great preparation has gone into equipping you for this moment. You must apply some effort in setting aside your concern for a moment to give the Lord a chance to activate the training He has provided you with. You have had some positive experiences with the Lord; in technological terms, you just have to search your hard drive to determine in which folder your mind placed them. When you do, it becomes your responsibility to start talking about them. If the only time you can say something positive about the Lord is when things are going well, that is an indication that your relationship with Him does not have real depth. Everything that has occurred in your life has meaning and purpose, and nothing has been wasted. It only becomes refuse when you ignore or forget it. The question you have to answer is this: What has God brought me through? God's school of preparation is always in session, and you have worked through some levels of course work. At the level you find yourself now, you are qualified to talk with conviction and confidence. In other words, you are a graduate student, and you set the tone for those who are yet to come. This melody is produced as you approach your circumstances with an attitude of thanksgiving. The main thing set forth during this millennial period is peace. You have to lay down your arms of resistance in order to personalize the value of being in a hostile environment. That's what made the civil rights movement of the sixties so effective. In God's economy, if the lion in you is ever going to forgo retaliating against those who are your natural enemies, such as anger, bitterness, resentment, and depression, and function in tandem with them, you are going to have to lay down your arms. The Shepherd still prepares tables in the presence of our enemies (Ps. 23:5).

When this is accomplished, you will find your negatives being replaced by positives. You have to be at peace with yourself if you are going to influence others for peace. We have as an example Jesus Himself. He turned away His anger from us even though we were deserving of punishment. He laid down His authority and right to issue out judgment by choosing rather to undergo the very same kinds of things that you may now be experiencing so that His relationship with God the Father might move to another level. Anger can be replaced by comfort. Comfort is an important attribute for you to have a handle on because those who are comfortable with who they are and what they may be experiencing acquire authority. This in turn enables you to not only speak in like manner but to require the same of others. Your effectiveness while moving through the darkest moments in your life is going to be determined by the way you handle internal struggles. Again, we have a public appearance, and sheer pride will enable us to keep it up. Image management is important to some. But once comfort has become a part of your existence, it is no longer an outward appearance but an inward change that responds naturally to whatever comes its way. God wants us to be comfortable with where we are in Him. Thanksgiving generates this attitude, but comfort sustains it.

In the crucible of your condition, it will be determined just what it means to be saved. If God is your salvation, you shouldn't be afraid. Life can be frightening when you are faced with a giant the size of death, but even he has been overcome. Let me hasten to add that the nature of death is frightening with all of the unknowns that are attached to it, and it is undeniably world shaking. It comes with the intensity of a full-scale war directed at every bit of security that you may have ever had. It shakes the very foundation of who you are and what you will ever be. There is no way of minimizing this. But at the same time, it brings with it a sense of confidence, knowing that if you can endure this, you can do anything. When I use the term *salvation,* I am speaking in terms of those who have experienced God's deliverance—that is, the deliverance from the power and practice of sin. There is always the option to handle things in a way that anesthetizes the effects of what you may be feeling at any given time. There is no difference with death. It brings with it the potential for phenomenal growth as well as for the systematic dismantling of everything that you viewed as substantial for your well-being, piece by piece. Overcoming fear is a major step in moving toward the former. When we are afraid it affects our decision-making ability. We become irrational in our thinking. A good example of this can be seen in Exodus 14, where we find the Israelites trapped at the Red Sea with no possibility of escape. Moses, understanding the nature of the situation, did not respond to the immediate danger by making an effort to escape from the approaching enemy, but rather he addressed the true enemy of the people by commanding them to maintain their physical positions while immediately instructing them to remove their emotional apprehension, which was to fear not. In the light of what they were facing, this was the most rational position they could take. Before you can do anything, fear must be brought under control. Fear, just like thanksgiving, is a decision.

Negative fear epitomizes weakness and must not only be overcome but also ultimately replaced with the ability to trust God when all around you seems so dim. What emerges when this kind of attitude is accomplished is courage. It takes courage to call on the name of the Lord when darkness falls. Let me hasten to add that courage operates in spite of fear; again, it's a matter of choice, and I feel it's worthy of mentioning again with a few more details. After all, fear is a recurring theme in life. Jesus knows how to handle fear, as evidenced by his response on the Sea of Galilee during a storm (Matt. 14:22–33). It was there we derived a formula for addressing this issue of fear. He instructs us to do three things: to take courage, to identify ourselves as He did when He said, "It is I," and to not fear. Please refer to page 63 for further details, but suffice it to say that Jesus declares himself to be the eye ("I") of the storm, which is located between courage and fear. Jesus identifies Himself as the source of our peace in the midst of this emotional storm. It is here that the song of the heart can reverberate with the melody of the soul, and the desire to move forward then becomes possible. The name of the

Lord is significant in that it is representative of different aspects of his character. Who is this "I" identified in the storm? The names associated with God are based on the area of need to be addressed. When things are dim and uncertain, you need to have clarity of vision. *El Roi* is a term meaning "the God who sees." The Hebrew for *see* (*ra'ah*) is the word from which *roi* (El Roi) is derived. May we be so bold as to give El Roi the freedom to search our innermost thoughts and ways so that we might truly "participate in the divine nature, and escape the corruption in the world caused by evil desires."

Because El Roi watches over you, He is able to perform what He promises. If we truly appropriate this truth, there is nothing that can happen to us that we cannot be at absolute peace about. He sees where you have come from and where you are going. He sees what you need as well as what you don't need. He sees what He wants to make of you and how He's going to achieve it He saw something in Gideon that far exceeded his fear. He saw a "valiant warrior" when all that Gideon could see were the surrounding circumstances and the overwhelming odds that were against him and his people (Judges 6). The darkness of night is not a bad place to be if in that place you hear God and there begin to understand His tender mercies and unconditional love for you. He has a plan for you, and no one or nothing can stop it. You are valuable to God, and He trusts you. No matter what the experience, God is looking for you to prevail. In order to do so, there are three requirements: total obedience, complete surrender, and absolute faith.

There is an upside to down, but one must observe it very carefully to better understand what it looks like. Your spiritual equilibrium must be balanced to see it clearly. That is accomplished, first of all, through obedience. Many things need to be considered when death occurs, most of which are obvious, but some of the more important things can go unnoticed if not evaluated properly. Take, for instance, adherence to God's directives as they are outlined in the Bible. There are going to be times when you do not want to do things God's way, say things that God wants you to say, or respond the way God wants you to respond. The reasons could be a lack of information in terms of outcome or just plain old discomfort, depression, and in some cases rebellion. But obedience says that God has foresight that is just not available to you. When agreement is hard to come by, activate acceptance instead, and what was formerly not understood will take on new meaning with clarity. You will begin to see things that just were not visible to you due to an unbalanced equilibrium. There is always a hidden factor that must be conformed to if you are going to see things from God's perspective and ultimately obey them.

Submission is not a positive-sounding term, but when it has to do with your will versus God's will, its value increases. Submission is positive because it pushes through the natural human tendency to resist and reveals the true value that you place on the results that submission brings. A lack of submission speaks more about your value system than it does your attitude. The wisdom of God surpasses knowledge and is always just beyond our comprehension if we try to figure it out. Some things will just not be completely understood and are best suited for submission and not clarity. But you can know this for sure: when the Lord's reputation is at stake, He decreases the chances of your succeeding without Him (Judges 7:2). God has selected you for a very important assignment, and the degree of difficulty is in direct proportion to the ultimate blessing that will follow; the greater the difficulty is, the greater the blessing will be. That is not to be read and fully understood until the mission is completed. I spoke to a naval officer recently and inquired about top naval operations, what they were called, and how they worked. He explained to me that some highly sensitive naval missions are carried out under the direction of what are known as closed orders. In some cases, missions are carried out without even the commanding officer of the ship knowing the full nature of the mission until certain things are accomplished. The way it works looks something like this: the commanding officer is given some specific ordinance, and once the ship has arrived, further directions are given. It is at this point that orders and further clarity of the mission are given. In the Christian world, we call it progressive revelation. Needless to say, these types of missions are highly classified and fall into the category of being top secret. As for the nature of what you are facing, some things will never be completely understood, nor do they need to be. The orders are closed, so to speak. But be assured of this—all that you need has been provided. What is not understood is not necessary at this point. Deuteronomy 29:29 (NLT) says it best: "The LORD our God has secrets known to no one. We are not accountable for them, but we and our children are accountable forever for what he has revealed to us, so that we may obey all the terms of these instructions."

Obedience to the amount of information that you have is key; God will take care of all of the unknowns. It's just no way to describe the need to trust the Lord to work on those things that you have no control over whatsoever. Of course, those are the things about which we ask, "Why?" The sooner you come to the realization that no matter how much information you desire it will never be enough, the better off you will be. The kind of song that God is trying to develop in your heart is indeed below the surface and must be drawn out. Isaiah 12:2–3 (NASB) adds another clue to this song.

> Behold, God is my salvation,
> I will trust and not be afraid;

> For the LORD GOD is my strength and song,
> And He has become my salvation.
> Therefore you will joyously draw water
> from the springs of salvation.

This is best done in the confines of destitution. At first glance, that might sound unfortunate, but it is not. God designs people on the basis of their songs, the ones that are in their hearts, the ones that can only be understood and appreciated through the veil of darkness that is caused by death. "Drawing water from the springs of salvation" is imagery that is developed from the experiences of a hot Middle Eastern country. On the last day of the celebration known as the Feast of Tabernacles, the Jewish nation used to bring water in a golden pitcher from the fountain of Siloam and pour it, mingled with wine, on the altar with great rejoicing. This event prefigured the words of Jesus: "on the last day of the feast" (John 7:2, 37–39 NASB). The pouring out of the water indicated repentance. The description of a well as opposed to a stream is significant. Streams may run dry, but fountains were indicative of an ever-flowing source (John 4:14; 7:38). What we have then is a picture of unlimited satisfaction, unlimited resources, unlimited insight, and unlimited effectiveness. The answer to the *why* question is that it comes from within, out of the heart, where of course the issues of life flow continuously. That is why certain people cannot sing certain songs. There has been no excavation work done within that heart, there has been no drilling below the surface, and all you get is what you see. The delivery of the contents of your song is heavily influenced by the contents of your personal testimony. All that has gone into your life thus far should result in celebration. In the midnight of life's most difficult experiences, God turns stanzas into expressions of worship. God is looking for those who have allowed His process to run its course and now have a reason for praise.

An illustration of this can be found in the gospel of Luke 1:57–79. Gabriel, an angel, visited Zechariah and told him that his prayers had been answered and his wife was going to have a son. The significance of this event was due to the advanced age of Zechariah's wife, Elizabeth, and her inability to bear children. The angel pronounced that Zechariah would have a son in spite of his old age and his wife's barrenness. Things got dark when Zechariah questioned the angel as to how this could be possible. This lack of faith and trust in the word that came from the angel resulted in his being unable to speak until the child was born as a sign of its validity. When John the Baptist was born, who was the son of promise, Zechariah sang his song, found in verses 67–79 of chapter 1. In the darkness of his inability to speak, a melody was forged, a heart was tempered, and a song emerged. All of life has a melody to it. We are all walking in the rhythm of a cadence that has been ordained for each one of us. It is similar to the beat of each person's heart. An EKG that is normal for one may be abnormal for another. What may appear highly unusual for you may be normal for someone else. Melody and rhythm are created by the way you respond to the experiences of life. Each situation is a beat, a cord, or a movement leading toward a specific conclusion, which is ultimately to glorify God.

God is always on the lookout for people who are willing to capitalize on the expressions that are constantly being developed in their hearts. During the course of any given day, several things are constantly going on within people's thinking as well as their attitudes, motivated by occurrences that are prompted by emotional upheaval, psychological distress, and extreme difficulty. Of course, I don't want to turn this into a blues workshop, but the truth of the matter is that this is where reality meets life and life takes on new meaning with depth that had not previously been understood. Without it, there is very little significance to one's experiences. We now have the ability to overcome apprehension that previously may have been a hindrance to accomplishment and success. At this level, people no longer have the same kind of influence over you that they once held. Your needs are now being met by the internal awareness of your capability. You have tapped into a resource that has always been there but was inaccessible due to the unavailability of the proper understanding of how life really works. Thomas Merton, the author of *No Man Is an Island* and *The Seven-Story Mountain,* wrote that all you really need is in your life already. He called it the "hidden wholeness." This is in complete agreement with 2 Peter 1:3, seeing that His divine power has granted to us everything pertaining to life and godliness through the true knowledge of Him who called us by His own glory and excellence.

Higher institutions of learning rarely produce this kind of understanding. We are all to some degree dependent upon the opinions of others and in need of their approval. Nobody else can sing your song. There is no need to be concerned with copyrights when it comes to your song. It takes God a lifetime to develop it in you, an eternity for you to fully understand it, and a willingness to share it with others to completely appreciate it. After all, God's main objective is to meet the needs of others through you. As I hope we have come to realize, God has to do a whole lot in and to you before He can do anything through you. Life, as you are now called to face, can be the difference between enduring your experience and enjoying it.

The transferring of your spiritual encounter with God as it is happening to you and to those who are observing you can do the latter. God invites others to gain from your experience. This is where your song takes on new meaning and others gain similar insight into the evidence of God's desire to minister through you to all who will make themselves available to him. What then can be expected? In essence, paraphrasing Isaiah 12:1-6 They will cry aloud in repentance, they will cry aloud in remorse, they will cry out in desperation and ultimately in appreciation for what God has done. As they search for answers and a greater understanding of God and they come to the realization of what it means to worship Him fully, they will shout for joy. In turn, they will themselves want others to know, and the cycle will be complete. Regardless of the song and the issues of life that are used to shape it, the end result will be glory to God and praise and honor given to him by his people.

God is looking for people who will not only sing their song through their lifestyles but will also become supporters of those who are singing their songs. This of course places you into the realm of being used by God to further the cause of Christ and the nature of your experience. One of the things that happened to me after the death of my son was the development of a desire to be with people who had gone through like experiences. For instance, I wanted to be in the coroner's office with parents who were there to identify their children. My heart longed to be available to give support just by being able to say that I understood what they were going through and that in time the pain would subside. They needed to know that God was auditioning them. They needed to know that they were there because of a song they had to sing. God is building a heavenly choir here on earth that will echo His praises throughout all eternity. Choirs here on earth are made up of a select group of people who can sing; so it is with this choir. I don't believe all believers will be in this heavenly choir. I don't believe that this choir will be made up of those who are current choir members. I believe there will be a section of people in this choir that will be made up of those who have experienced the death of a child. I believe that God the Father Himself will direct this choir because He too will understand the nature of the experience that its members have undergone, for He too lost a child, His Son, His only begotten Son. The nature of death originated with a choir as Satan, the minister of music, decided that he wanted what belonged to God. Offering praise to Him was not enough; he wanted to be the recipient of that praise. God in turn expelled him from heaven, and he began a lifelong pursuit of steering people away from giving God the honor that was due Him and redirecting that honor to himself or themselves. Sin then became an issue that has plagued us ever since. To prevent you from wanting to do the same when you enter the heavenly choir, God has given you what personally belongs to you, and no one can take it from you, nor do you desire to have anyone else's. It is only fitting that it should end with the choir. God gave His only Son so that He could provide a way to undo what Satan has done. Satan's response to God's desire to correct the problem has been to stop the arrival of Jesus, God's son. His strategy was and still is to kill and destroy children before they reach adulthood. Whether it's killing children to prevent the Savior from coming or killing children to prevent them from talking about a Savior that has already come. God the Father is so sensitive to each one of us that he tests everything that he requires us to experience (Heb. 4:15). He then issues the appropriate circumstances to those whom he designates to take on the responsibility. When you begin to realize that your experience is in part a selection process, your entire view of life and your circumstances changes.

When God gave his only begotten Son for the forgiveness of sin, He voluntarily positioned Himself to be a part of this choir. He feels what you feel, and He empathizes with you. As He stands before you in glory with arms raised, your response will be one of quiet awe as you reflect upon the unimaginable. As you think about the visibility of your faith, the purpose of your pain and the unexplainable, unspeakable joy will permeate your very soul as a result of your being selected to sing in this choir. The only expression that remains will be that of praise. This end result is designed to motivate you to fight for those who so desperately need your help. The volume of neither the song nor the voice from which the music is coming determines the weapons of this warfare. Victory will be complete when God the Father raises His arms to direct the choir. The veil that has covered your understanding will then be lifted, and the impact of your faithfulness will be realized.

Not only is God looking for people who, through this process, have developed something to say, but he is also looking for people who are willing to fight for the causes of others in like circumstances. The people of God need somebody to fight for them now. Hold your head up high, throw your shoulders back, and walk through this tragedy with confidence for you have been chosen by God to audition for this choir. Since the battle originated with the heavenly choir, it's going to be won in like manner. Maybe you can recall Jehoshaphat's response to the threat posed by the Amonites and Moabites. We read in 2 Chronicles 20:21–23 (NASB),

> When he had consulted with the people, he appointed those who sang to the LORD and those who appraised Him in holy attire, as they went out before the army and said, "Give thanks to the LORD, for His lovingkindness is everlasting." When they began singing and praising, the LORD set ambushes against the sons of Ammon, Moab and Mount Seir, who had come against Judah; so they were routed. For the sons of Ammon and

> Moab rose up against the inhabitants of Mount Seir destroying them completely; and when they had finished with the inhabitants of Seir, they helped to destroy one another.

The fight could not begin until God cranked up the music ministry. Have you ever noticed that some people work better to the sound of music? Maybe you are one of those people who perform better when there is quiet music in the background or even loud music that stimulates you to pursue your craft with passion. In either case, something about the music connects you with that task at hand and enables you to accomplish it better or with increased confidence. I believe this attitude originated with the Lord Himself as we see him here completing a task to the accompaniment of music. When the angels in heaven rebelled against God, it was the director of music who led the revolt. Undoubtedly, the music influenced the decision making of those who followed Him. Whether it is the emotional stimulation that takes place when music is played or sung or the sense of abandonment of consequences that some music creates, the idea is the same—the outcome will be influenced by the music.

What makes a song that's being developed in the night so intense is the fact that the real battle is for your soul. Warfare on this level goes much deeper than what appears on the surface. In other words, it is not only the emotions that are associated with death that cause you difficulty but also the moment in time that the death occurred. I believe the timing is influenced by a well-orchestrated spiritual plan that has been constructed by the prince of darkness. He does his best work at night. He takes advantage of every opportunity to influence your thinking and to corrupt your mind with poisonous thoughts and negative reminders. I am totally convinced that you can never really be prepared for the call that comes informing you that your loved one has died. Whether they were in a coma for several months or they were involved in an automobile accident, the shock is the same. It is in this environment and at this moment that indelible imprints are being forged in your mind that will remain forever. The intensity may vary from person to person, but the lack of preparedness is the same. So the devil takes advantage of it and creates images that will continue to affect you during the healing process. He knows that the pain will subside, and so he does all he can to prolong the process. There is a great need for comfort when the intensity of one's emotions is this great. Comfort in this context has a two-fold purpose—help for you and help for those you will come in contact with in the future. So the enemy wants to stop any future support that you may offer for others. This battle is going to be fought and won in the darkness of night. Even though it's a battle that is already won, it's one that requires action on the part of the victor. Keep in mind that the weapons that you have access to are more than sufficient to handle the battle that you are up against. A song is being developed that will prove to be the forerunner of greater things to come. Your role is to maintain a good attitude and to behave appropriately. Submit to the master plan of a God whose ways and thoughts are above yours. When the pain of a dark night engulfs you, which is part of the developmental process, you have to trust in a God you cannot see and submit to a plan that surpasses your understanding. This is going to require faith. Even though each person's experience is different, all experiences have some similarities, and they can only be understood through agreeing with the possibilities that they represent. In doing so you must allow the Bible to guide your actions and to determine your behavior, not your emotions. This may be easier said than done, but nonetheless it must be done. During those hours of darkness—and they may far exceed twenty-four—the Bible must become your navigational system and be followed to the letter. It will provide you with the light that is necessary to safely guide you along your journey. You need not be afraid of the dark, for it is the place where light does its best work.

Prayer

Father in heaven, even though the darkness is overwhelming and frightening at times, my comfort is in knowing that you are with me and you understand how I feel. Emotions play a major role in my comprehension of these very difficult moments in my life, but they are constantly being balanced by your Word. Help me to use the quietness of darkness to hear your voice clearly as you forge my song in my heart and help me to interpret its meaning carefully with the intentions of following your lead explicitly.

Memory Verses
Isaiah 12:2; Job 35:9, 10

No matter which direction your emotions may vacillate, faith will always bring you back to true north. The closer you get to balancing your life, the clearer your purpose in life becomes and your circumstances take on new meaning. God literally adds rhythm and melody to your life. You then realize that, through it all, you have become a stronger person, equipped to help others navigate the stages of grief and disillusionment.

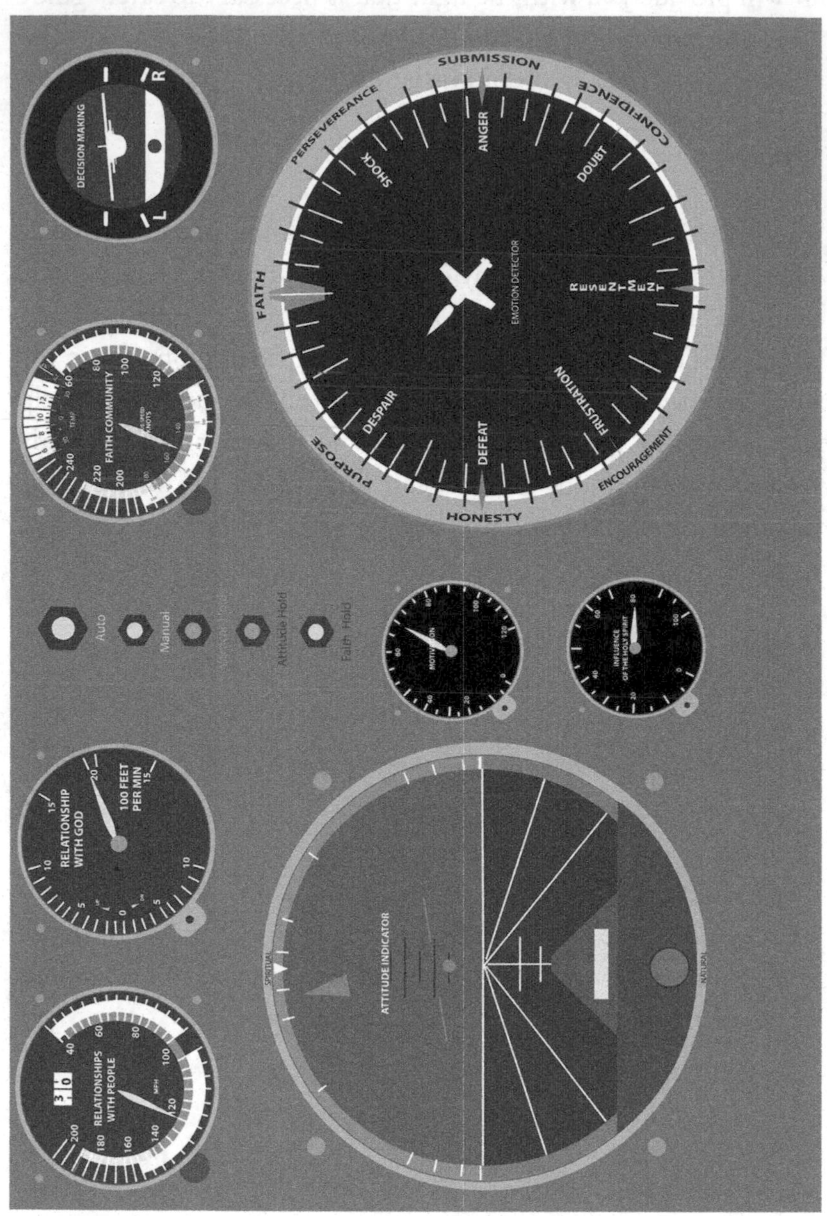
DECISION MAKING
L
R
FAITH COMMUNITY
EMOTION DETECTOR
SUBMISSION
CONFIDENCE
ENCOURAGEMENT
HONESTY
PURPOSE
FAITH
PERSEVEREANCE
ANGER
DOUBT
RESENTMENT
FRUSTRATION
DEFEAT
DESPAIR
SHOCK
Auto
Manual
Attitude Hold
Faith Hold
MOTIVATION
INFLUENCE OF THE HOLY SPIRIT
RELATIONSHIP WITH GOD
100 FEET PER MIN
ATTITUDE INDICATOR
RELATIONSHIPS WITH PEOPLE

Chapter 8

Life after Death

Life should be enjoyed, and nothing takes away that possibility like the loss of a loved one. I believe it can be done if one develops and maintains the right attitude. Denis Waitley and Boyd Matheson, in their leadership booklet titled "Attitude" from the *Successories* library series, tells the story of a human resource executive who went out in the field to determine how laborers felt about their work. She went to a building site in France.

She approached the first worker and asked, "What are you doing?"

"What are you—blind?" the worker snapped back. "I'm cutting these boulders with primitive tools and putting them together the way the boss tells me. I'm sweating under this blazing sun. It is back-breaking work, and it is boring me to death."

The HR staffer quickly backed off and retreated to a second worker. She asked the same question: "What are you doing?"

"I'm shaping these boulders into usable forms, which are then assembled according to the architect's plans. It's hard work and sometimes it gets repetitive, but I earn five francs a week, and that supports my family. It's a job—could be worse."

Somewhat encouraged, she went to a third worker. "And what are you doing?"

"Why can't you see?" beamed the worker as he lifted his arms to the sky. "I'm building a cathedral!"

Attitude is in the eye of the beholder. Life for the believer is to be enjoyed, not endured. We are called to "Rejoice always. I will say it again: Rejoice" (Phil. 4:4 NIV). Your ability to enjoy what you do as well as what you are experiencing is dependent upon your attitude. If you are going to enjoy life in the face of a prodigal who who never comes home, you have to approach life from God's point of view and not from what may come naturally. When the call came that my son had died, in many ways my life ended too—that is, life as I had known it for the past thirty years. The thoughts that flooded my soul included thoughts of total defeat such as, *I will not be able to go on. There is no reason for living. I will never be happy again. This cannot be happening to me.* I was even grateful for my age because I felt like I didn't have that long to live anyway. The date was October 1, 2007, when I was fifty-eight years old. It doesn't take long to see the fallacy in this kind of thinking, but it seemed all too real at the time. I was totally engulfed in what came naturally, and that was hopelessness. In order for one's natural perspective to change, it has to be replaced by one that is greater. One of the first signs of change that developed was desire. I became concerned with others who were experiencing the same kind of things as I was. I became concerned about parents who had lost children. I recall the dread associated with going to the medical examiner's office to identify the body of my son. I was gripped with fear and filled with emotion. Today, the trauma has all but subsided, and I know it is a result of how things were dealt with during the process as outlined in this book and my personal relationship with Jesus Christ. I don't know that I can overemphasize the value of the things that have been written, not because I wrote them but because of what these principles enabled me to do. The loss of a child is unbearable, to say the least. It cannot be downplayed no matter how you turn it. But this change was followed by a renewed perspective. I did have reason for living; I could be happy again. A new sense of confidence emerged, and I began to believe that my experience could serve as an example for others to find the same confidence. Perspective is important: to enjoy the Christian life, you have to see every situation as an opportunity to advance the human cause. All of creation fits into the context of God's overall plan. Death is a part of that plan and must be understood as such. Philippians 1:21–26 gives us an example of what this looks like. Paul was chained to the palace guard; the Praetorian Guards, as they were called, were the crack elite troops of the Roman Empire. These were the Green Berets, Navy Seals, and Marine Corps recon troops combined. They were personally chosen by Caesar to serve as his personal bodyguards. As a further incentive to perform at their best, they were the highest-paid workers in the entire Roman Empire, even among doctors, lawyers, and engineers. When they retired after twelve years, they were made leaders in Rome. These were well-trained military personnel who were not easily influenced by prisoners. The purpose of God was to add one more item to their list of accomplishments, and that was a personal relationship with Him. There was not a more strategic group that Paul could have been exposed to if he was going to reach the Roman Empire for Christ. God was the engineer who orchestrated Paul's imprisonment. Nero paid the bill and chained a future leader of Rome to Paul.

In two years at four-hour shifts, he could have witnessed to these guards at least 4,380 times. These guards had an inside route to the emperor, and as a result, even some of Nero's family members became believers. History records that Nero had his wife, mother, and children killed because they became Christians. Undoubtedly, we can call this a "chain" reaction to the attitude of a man who understood that his misfortune had a purpose and, if viewed properly, could impact the lives of others in a very positive way. God has placed you where you are for a reason. Those with whom you come in contact need your help. Things may be uncomfortable now, but a renewed attitude will enable you to go with the flow. Prior to salvation, Paul viewed prison as a place to confine people, a place where punishment was executed. But after salvation, it became a new possibility; it now meant a captive audience, not limited mobility. The perspective you need to live by if you are going to live once again is that of Romans 8:28 (NIV): "And we know that in all things God works for the good of those who love him." God has a purpose for the results that your prodigal may have caused. When you take on a perspective such as this, you are well on your way to enjoying the Christian life. Joy comes when you surpass the limits of your immediate circumstances. You cannot enjoy doing the same thing at the same level in the same manner for long. You cannot enjoy the Christian life and be inactive at the same time. We err when we think joy is accomplished by doing nothing; rather, it is going above and beyond what we are capable of doing naturally. In doing so you will discover new opportunities generated by ability that you did not know you possessed. Discovery generates joy. Paul's freedom had been taken, as had his friends, his ministry, and his privacy, but one thing they could not take from him and one thing your prodigal cannot take from you is your purpose in life. Paul echoes this attitude throughout his writings. In Acts 20:24, he states that his life was not worth anything apart from fulfilling his purpose in life. What is your purpose for living? Is it power, pleasure or possessions? If you are going to find joy in your current state, it must be Christ. Paul's letter to the Philippians was full of joy and rejoicing because, in spite of his circumstances, his life had purpose and meaning regardless of how uncomfortable it might be. After all, very few things that are worth anything come without some discomfort. He had joy in spite of trouble as long as Christ's cause was advanced. He had joy in spite of detractors as long as Christ's name was proclaimed. He had joy in spite of his impending death as long as Christ was exalted. He had joy in spite of not fulfilling his personal desires as long as his fellow believers were assisted. This is a picture of a man who enjoyed life. To have joy in the midst of trials requires a mind that is fixed on something trials cannot touch, and that is God's perspective. Remember, you don't belong to yourself but to God. He's in control. In order to think like this, you have to let God reshape your personality. If you are going to enjoy the Christian life, not only must you see things as God does, but you also have to realize that you are no longer a prisoner of your personality (2 Corin. 5:17). Paul was no longer destination oriented but process oriented. He mentioned earlier that he had a desire to depart and be with Christ (Phil. 1:23), which would have been far better for him, enjoyable even, but for the sake of others he decided it would be better to stay. The process became more important to him than where he would rather be. He opted not to fight it but to embrace it. He allowed it to run its course without any resistance. Your personality may want to smile its way through it or grit your teeth through it or think your way through it or just casually accept it. But in any event, if you are uncomfortable where you are, you want to go somewhere else. The tendency is to think that a change in environment will bring a change in how you feel. If you are having difficulty on your job, your enjoyment will be found when you leave the job either temporarily or permanently. Nevertheless, you spend your day watching the clock. If you are having difficulty in the home, you look for enjoyment outside of the home. If you are having difficulty with your church, you then become certain that joy is going to be found in another church. Even Paul felt uncomfortable in prison and longed to go somewhere else. But he didn't respond to what came naturally to him; he chose rather to look more carefully at the process of being where he was as opposed to doing what he felt would be better for him. That caused him to place the needs of others above his own, and that is where he found joy. What you have experienced with Christ must be expressed to others—encouragement, comfort, fellowship, affection, and compassion. These traits don't come naturally, but when you practice them, your personality changes. We are all selfish by nature, and there is a tendency in us to think only of our needs, our conflicts, and our progress, forgetting those of others. To offset this, you must challenge your way of thinking. We have been conditioned to think a certain way, and we feel that this is the only way to think. So we give it very little thought, keeping us imprisoned. We have to allow Christ to redesign the way we think. In fact, we are told in Philippians 3:12–16 to think the way that He does. We all have a pattern out of which we derive our thoughts. Those of us who were fortunate enough to have a lot of positive influence from our family backgrounds and upbringing may have greater resources to draw from. Others of us may need to work a little harder. But all of us need to allow Christ to redesign how we think. We start this process by being open to new ideas. Paul did it by admitting that he had not arrived and that he needed to grow (Phil. 3:12–13). If Paul needed to grow, how much more do you and I have to? He knew his thinking had to change. Changed thinking requires personal evaluation.

When you think that you are better than someone else, your thinking becomes distorted. Distorted thinking always has to be challenged. Oftentimes, we get satisfaction from comparing ourselves with others. If Paul had done that, he would have been tempted to be proud of his accomplishments; surely nobody had done as much as he had. In order for our thinking to be changed, we have to compare our thinking with that of the person of Christ. As we evaluate ourselves, we have to be careful not to make ourselves better than we are, nor are we to make ourselves less than we are. A key phrase in the scriptures that I have come to appreciate is "one thing."

You may recall the rich ruler in Mark 10:21, whom Jesus told, "One thing you lack." "One thing is needed," he said to Martha in Luke 10:42. And the Psalmist said, "One thing I ask of the Lord, this is what I seek that I may dwell in the house of the Lord all the days of my life." (Psalm 27:4) All too often, we find ourselves getting involved in too many activities in an attempt to dull the pain of a missing prodigal. Very few professional athletes succeed in participating in multiple sports. The winners are those who concentrate and specialize in doing one thing well. Paul says, "But one thing I do" (Phil. 3:13 NIV). Concentration and focus are the key to enjoying the Christian life.

Rivers are enjoyed when they flow within the banks of their confinement. If a river is allowed to overflow its banks, the area surrounding it becomes a swamp.

Learn to view your circumstances as a part of God's providence. Some of us are classified as thermometers and others are thermostats. Thermometers don't change anything around them—they register what is going on around them, that is, the temperature. It's either going up or down. A thermostat, on the other hand, regulates the surroundings and changes them when they need to be changed. Thermometers lack the power to change things; instead, they allow circumstances and conditions to change them. Paul rejoiced in the Lord greatly in spite of the nature of his circumstances, and in doing so he was acting as a thermostat; he accepted all things and he could do all things (Phil. 4:11–13). The call to each one of us is obvious. We are to be content realizing that contentment is not complacency. It is not an escape attempt; it's confidence in the midst of the battle. Paul says that he has learned to be content. It didn't come immediately upon salvation; it came through experience. Paul had several. He learned contentment by being shipwrecked, being beaten with rods, by being stoned, by being lost at sea (2 Corin. 11:25). He learned through these experiences that God could be trusted. The word *contentment* actually means "being contained." It is a description of a person whose resources are within them, and they do not have to depend upon those things that are without (thermostat). You can be content because of God's provisions. He is always working in advance to arrange circumstances and situations for the fulfilling of His overall plan and purpose for you.

As we come to the end of our journey, we need to keep in mind that life is not a series of accidents; it is a series of appointments. "I will counsel you and watch over you" (Ps. 32:8 NIV). The story of Joseph serves as an example. I would encourage you to read his story and observe how the conclusion thereof leaves us with this thought. "You intended to harm me, but God meant it for good" (Gen. 50:20 NIV). Your story will end on the same note if you allow the power of God through the indwelling of His Spirit to control and dominate your life. Nature depends upon hidden resources to give them power to survive. Trees get their power from their root systems, which is the most important part of the tree, not what you see. Trees may lose their leaves and be barren for a while, but if the roots run deep enough, leaves will reappear, and depending upon the type of tree it is, fruit or flowers will emerge. So it is with you; there is a blossom that awaits you. It may not be visible to the naked eye, but if your roots run deep enough, a harvest is on the way.

Prayer

Father in heaven, discomfort is taking on new meaning for me because of the realization that you are with me every step of the way. It's hard to understand at times, but it's comforting to know that I am never alone nor am I forgotten. I am no longer driven by understanding but rather by the assurance of your promises.

Memory Verse
Genesis 50:20

Arriving at your destination is always exciting no matter how turbulent the trip has been. Once you return to a life of faith, all of life balances out, no matter how many times the process is repeated. Like a compass keeps one from getting lost, so it is with faith. It is true north that will always get you home.

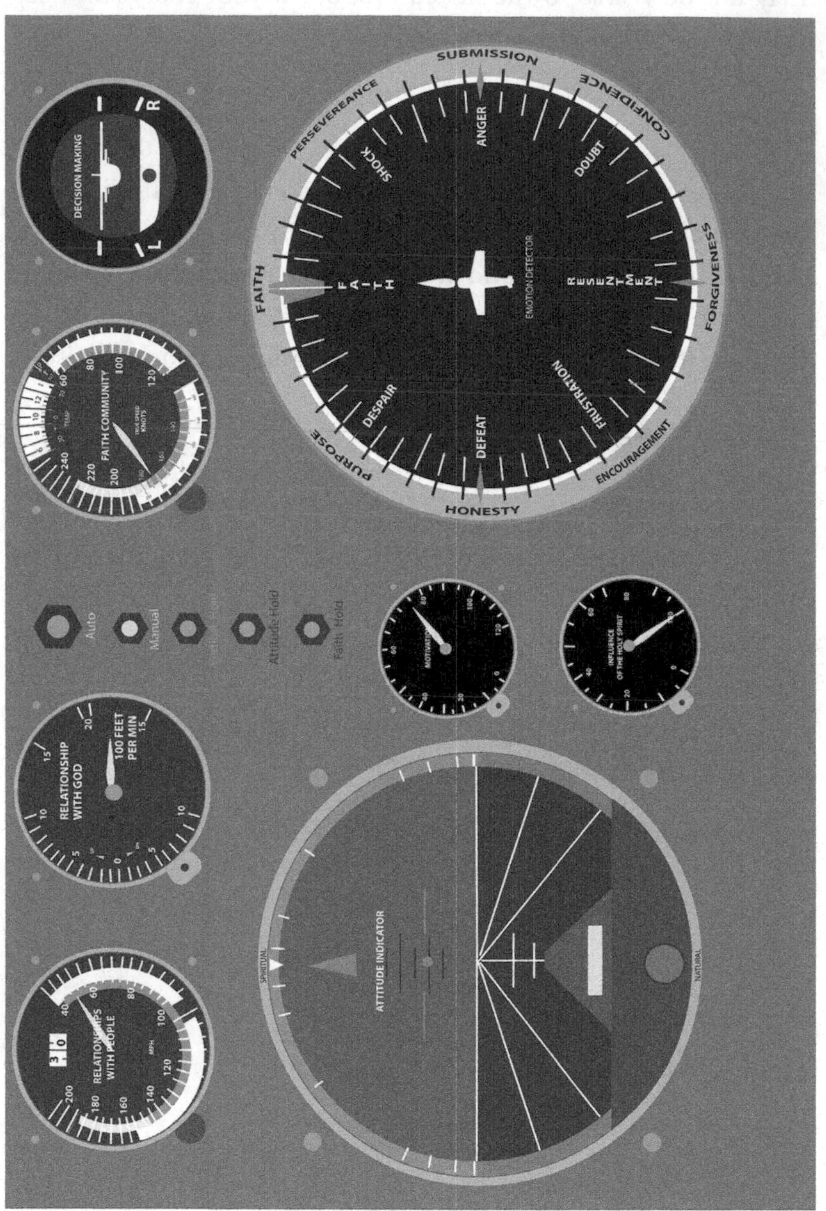

DECISION MAKING
L
R
FAITH COMMUNITY
TRUE SPEED KNOTS
RELATIONSHIP WITH GOD
100 FEET PER MIN
RELATIONSHIPS WITH PEOPLE
MPH
Auto
Manual
Attitude Hold
Faith Hold
SUBMISSION
CONFIDENCE
FORGIVENESS
ENCOURAGEMENT
HONESTY
PURPOSE
FAITH
PERSEVEREANCE
ANGER
DOUBT
SHOCK
FAITH
EMOTION DETECTOR
RESENTMENT
FRUSTRATION
DEFEAT
DESPAIR
MOTIVATION
INFLUENCE OF THE HOLY SPIRIT
ATTITUDE INDICATOR
SPIRITUAL
NATURAL

Epilogue

Live Your Life to Please God

The older I get, the more I realize that a large portion of my life has been lived attempting to please others. It began with my parents and then moved to my peers and followed me all the way to the workplace. As Christians, we try to please those with whom we serve. We inherently want to please people. We want to please those we follow, those whom we lead, and those with whom we serve. Pleasing and being pleased are important to the human experience. Being pleased is also important to God. Living your life by faith pleases God. What does a life that pleases God look like? A life that pleases God is evidenced by prosperity, prayer, purpose, forgiveness, honesty, and peace.

Prosperity: Psalm 35:27–28 (NASB) clarifies that the Lord takes pleasure in the prosperity of his people, not only materially but also spiritually. In the first portion of this Psalm, David is asking God to fight for him, but at the end he leaves the battlefield and enters the courtroom, where he testifies of God's vindication of him. To vindicate someone is to declare them just in what they may have done. He then goes on to add that as a result the Lord is to be magnified. So the idea is to magnify the Lord for how He has allowed you to prosper, either spiritually or materially. God expects each one of us to prosper in both areas not exclusively for our benefit but for the sake of others and ultimately for His name's sake. Therefore, you do not have the option to be prosperous; it's mandatory. You cannot stay where you are, nor can you be satisfied with what you have accomplished because the resources that God has are endless and so should your pursuit of them be. God is pleased when you trust Him enough to magnify His name for the ways in which He has prospered you. God is pleased when you talk to Him.

Prayer: Proverbs 15:8 informs us that God is delighted when we choose to talk to Him. When we agree with Him at this level, it assures us that everything is working properly. We pray because of the Spirit of God that dwells within. Just like a car will not start without properly adjusted and clean spark plugs, genuine prayer will not start without the prompting of the Holy Spirit. Spark plugs transfer heat from the combustion chamber to the engine's cooling system. So it is with the Holy Spirit. He serves as a heat exchanger, transferring the power of God through you and then back to God. Unfortunately, some of our praying has been stalled because the Holy Spirit is grieved; we've become sluggish and ineffective in our praying. Prayer is more of a relationship than it is a request. We've downsized its power by limiting it to making requests. God is pleased when we pray.

Purpose. Psalm 37:23–24 points out that the Lord is pleased with the path that you are on because He put you there. Not only does God delight in the way of a good person in general, but He also does so with His written word (Is. 30:21). He does not always show the way from a distance, but He leads you step by step. The psalmist has elevated the Lord above his own satisfaction in being vindicated. He does not take a position of superiority; rather, he expresses satisfaction for what God has done and has to tell others about his experience. God wants others to know what He has done for you, and that is clearly seen as you live your life on purpose. You bring God pleasure when you live like you have been forgiven.

Pardon: We have done a lot of talking about the shortcomings of our prodigal children, but what about you? You have been forgiven also. Micah 7:18–20 (NASB) reminds us that our sins were forgiven because of what Christ has done for us. We learn five things about God in his forgiveness in these three verses, and they should be a part of our response to it.

- He does not stay angry forever.
- He likes to show mercy.
- He is compassionate.
- He deals with sin decisively.
- He keeps his word.

God takes pleasure in your recognition of your personal need for all of these. God has forgiven you for every failure you may have experienced and has expressed complete acceptance of you in spite of them. God is pleased when his standard becomes your practice.

Honesty: He is delighted in your personal convictions because they are evidence of your honesty and integrity. Proverbs 11:1 (NASB) helps in this regard by pointing us to weights and measures. To increase their profits, many merchants used two sets of stone weights when weighing merchandise. Lighter stones were placed on the scales when selling (so the lesser quantity was sold for the stated price), and heavier ones were used when buying (so that more was obtained for the same price). Honesty is the best policy because of the grave consequences that come from being dishonest. Make truth telling, trustworthiness, and honesty your practice, and you will please God. Finally, when your life is pleasing to God, he blesses you with peace.

Peace: The type of peace described in Proverbs 16:7 is of the type that diffuses the enemy's opposition. This is not internal peace but external; we need both. An example of that can be seen in Genesis 26:18–29, where we find Isaac in conflict with the herdsman of Gerar. Each well that Isaac dug, they protested that the water belonged to them, and so he surrendered them to the herdsmen. The text doesn't indicate what was said, but the response of the herdsmen gives us a clue. Isaac called on the name of the Lord, and the herdsmen's attitude changed; they wanted to make peace with Isaac. That's the type of peace being described—*Yahweh*, self-existing one. That is the name that God revealed Himself as when he was encountered by Moses (Ex. 3:14 NASB). God responds to identity questions posed by Moses by saying, "I AM WHO I AM. Thus you shall say to the sons of Israel I AM has sent you." God identified Himself by using a verb and not a personal pronoun. Those of you who know anything about the English language know that verbs don't describe, they act. I AM is an indication that God is ready to take action. The peace that God affords you is the privilege to know that whatever you need the Lord to be or whatever you need the Lord to do, He will become and do to assure you of His peace. This kind of peace is not dependent upon requests, negotiation, or diplomacy but upon the great I AM. The apostle Paul in 2 Timothy 4:6b says that "And the time of my departure has come" (NASB).

> Departure means to loosen again; to undo. It is applied to the act of unloosing or casting off the fastenings of a ship, preparatory to a departure. The proper idea in the use of the word would be, that he had been bound to the present world, like a ship to its moorings, and that death would be a release. He would now spread his sails on the broad ocean of eternity. The true idea of death is

> that of loosening the bands that confine us to the present world; of setting us free, and permitting the soul to go forth, as with expanded sails, on its eternal voyage. With such a view of death, why should a Christian fear to die?[19]

It's interesting how the Bible depicts death versus how we view it. It's viewed as a trip or a journey to a distant location. Traveling has always been viewed as something positive. What comes to mind is exotic islands and extravagant hotels. In more cases than not, those who travel attempt to get the most out of the trip by sightseeing along the way. Life for the Christian in many ways is a sightseeing tour en route to a permanent destination. Most trips require preparations, and so it is with the Christian journey. If you have implemented the principles that I have attempted to share in this book, you will have taken some major strides in ensuring that those who may become prodigal have made the proper preparations for the journey that lies ahead. But even more than that, you will have prepared yourself for whatever the future holds.

Prayer

Lord, life's journey indeed can take some winding turns, including some turbulent detours, but my confidence is in knowing that your desire for me is to prosper through them all because of your overwhelming care and concern for me, evidenced by your forgiveness and ever-present peace. Even though I do not know what the future holds, my confidence is in knowing that whatever the need, you as the great I AM will be able to provide.

---

[19] *PC Study Bible*, Biblesoft. Commentary: Barnes Notes. Computer software.

Memory Verse
Exodus 3:14

According to the settings on your faith coordinator gauge, you are now prepared to make a safe landing. We have been given the okay to land from the flight tower. Follow the directions of the flight attendants. Remain seated, keep your seat belt fastened, and wait until the plane has come to a complete stop. Thank you for choosing us to help you navigate the grief and disillusionment of losing a loved one. As you make your way to the baggage claim area, remember that pleasing God by faith always results in a safe and secure landing.

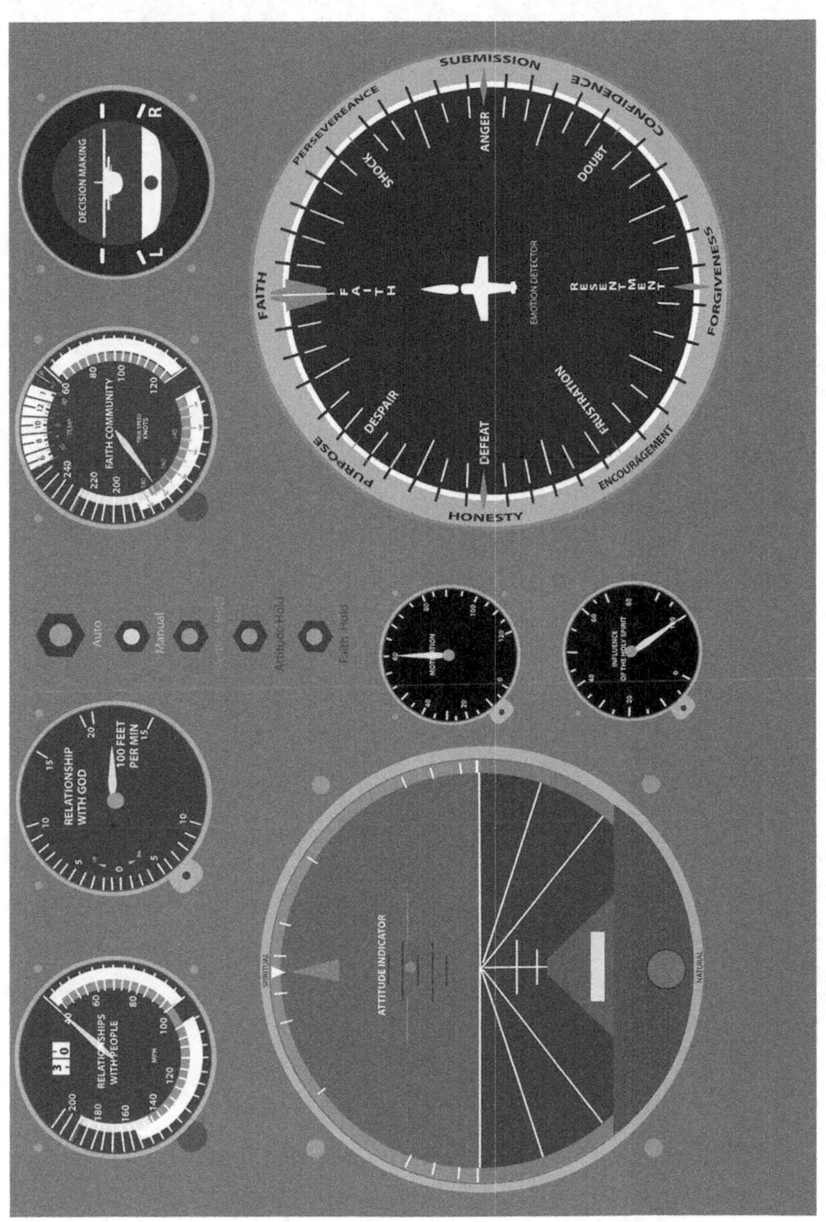
DECISION MAKING
L
R
FAITH COMMUNITY
TRUE SPEED KNOTS
RELATIONSHIP WITH GOD
100 FEET PER MIN
RELATIONSHIPS WITH PEOPLE
MPH
Auto
Manual
Attitude Hold
Faith Hold
SUBMISSION
CONFIDENCE
FORGIVENESS
ENCOURAGEMENT
HONESTY
PURPOSE
FAITH
PERSEVEREANCE
ANGER
DOUBT
SHOCK
DESPAIR
DEFEAT
FRUSTRATION
RESENTMENT
EMOTION DETECTOR
MOTIVATION
INFLUENCE OF THE HOLY SPIRIT
ATTITUDE INDICATOR
SPIRITUAL
NATURAL

Conan Citings

Chapter 1 (Page 14)
Conan's life was changed when he refused to adjust to his new family environment.

Chapter 2 (Page 30)
Conan did whatever he could to fulfill his need to be loved, even at the expense of others.

Chapter 3 (Page 47)
The obstacle that Conan ran into was the penal system, which distorted his perspective of faith.

Chapter 4 (Page 64)
Just like Jonah, Conan could not sin successfully.

Cover Flap
A picture of Conan on the table in the background of my photo.

All images have the number 30 in them, which represents Conan's age at death.

Discussion Questions for Group or Personal Study

1. Have you ever been lost? What emotions did you experience as a result? In what order did they come, and in what order did they leave?

2. All new experiences bring with them a measure of anxiety. Define the differences between negative and positive anxiety. In what ways have you suffered or benefited from both?

3. Can you recall a time when you grew as a person? Which personal relationships affected by it and how?

4. When the routine of life wears on you, do you voluntarily make changes or are you dependent upon random occurrences to make that decision for you? What can you do to have more input into that decision-making process?

5. How often do you reflect on something that you don't want to forget? What actions do those thoughts motivate you to take? If none, what can you do to change that outcome?

6. When you are disappointed, who suffers most—you or those who disappointed you? Describe in what ways the suffering is experienced. What steps can you take to eliminate this outcome?

7. In what ways do you adjust to make the relationships in your life work? What part does forgiveness play in the process? Be specific.

8. Think about the last time you felt like giving up. How were you able to get back on track? Identify who or what helped you to do so.

9. Your experiences in life have shaped you into the person you have become. You are unique. Are you now satisfied with who you are, or would you prefer to be somebody else? If yes, who and why? Be honest.

10. Consider the people you are concerned about pleasing. Does your life improve because of this concern, or could you do things a bit differently with a greater measure of success?

11. After having read the book, make a list of specific changes you personally intend to make as a result. Be sure to establish a time line to motivate the accomplishment of your goal.

12. In what ways has this book influenced your views on blended families? Have your views changed, or do they remain the same? Explain your answer.

13. What can you do as a married couple to strengthen your relationship and improve your parenting skills?

14. One of the clear takeaways from this book is a song in the night. In what ways have you taken advantage of it? Share with someone else what it is.

About the Author

Christopher A. Bell Sr. is the full-time assistant pastor at Christian Stronghold Church, a growing inner-city church in West Philadelphia. He has served in that capacity for over twenty years. His position has exposed him to countless grief-stricken families, and he has conducted numerous funeral services. He is a graduate of Geneva College and holds dual degrees in urban ministry management. He is a national speaker and biblical counselor. He lives in Middletown Pennsylvania with his wife, Renee. Their mission is to encourage others to pursue the likeness of Christ and to empower them through instruction, mentoring, and coaching designed to equip them to embrace a life empowered by God's Word and His purpose. The following passage serves as his personal motivation for writing this work:

> Now I rejoice in what was suffered for you, and I fill up in my flesh what is still lacking in regard to Christ's afflictions, for the sake of his body, which is the church. I have become its servant by the commission God gave me to present to you the word of God in its fullness—the mystery that has been kept hidden for ages and generations, but is now disclosed to the saints. To them God has chosen to make known among the Gentiles

the glorious riches of this mystery, which is Christ in you, the hope of glory. We proclaim him, admonishing and teaching everyone with all wisdom, so that we may present everyone perfect in Christ. To this end I labor, struggling with all his energy, which so powerfully works in me. (Col 1:24-29 NIV)